Encounters with God
in Augustine's *Confessions*

Encounters with God in Augustine's *Confessions*

Books VII–IX

Carl G. Vaught

State University of New York Press

Published by
State University of New York Press, Albany

For information, address the State University of New York Press,
90 State Street, Suite 700, Albany, NY 12207

Production by Michael Haggett
Marketing by Susan M. Petrie

Library of Congress Cataloging-in-Publication Data

Vaught, Carl G., 1939–
    Encounters with God in Augustine's Confessions : books VII–IX / Carl G. Vaught.
        p. cm.
    Includes bibliographical references and index.
    ISBN 0-7914-6107-6 (alk. paper)
    1. Augustine, Saint, Bishop of Hippo. Confessiones. Liber 7-9.   2. Augustine,
Saint, Bishop of Hippo.   3. Spirituality—History—Early church, ca. 30-600.
4. Christian saints—Algeria—Hippo (Extinct city)—Biography—History and
criticism.   I. Title.

BR65.A62V37 2004
270'.2'092—dc22   2004043451

10 9 8 7 6 5 4 3 2 1

For Jennifer and Cheryl

Contents

Preface

When Augustine writes the *Confessions*, there are no confessionals. Rather, he speaks to God directly, praising his creator and confessing his sins without depending on an earthly mediator. The Catholic penitent approaches the confessional with fear and trembling, while the faithful Protestant refuses to approach it at all. By contrast, Augustine lives before this distinction emerges and stands in between the alternatives it generates, taking confession seriously, but addressing the same source of power that the Protestant reformer encounters directly. Like the Catholic he is, the great rhetorician incarnates the relation between God and the soul by constructing a verbal confessional; but like the Protestant he anticipates, he explodes what he constructs by responding to a passage from Paul's Epistle to the Romans and by describing the transformation that occurs when he listens to the voice of God in silence (8.12.29).[1] To be sure, Augustine's account of his conversion has often been regarded as the most remarkable rhetorical construction in the text, either fabricating an event that never occurred, or embellishing an episode that could have been described much less dramatically.[2] However, Augustine himself understands the episode as a divine interjection that transforms his fragmented heart into a center of certainty and serenity (8.12.29).

An equally important but less controversial point is that Augustine's *Confessions* unfolds on three levels: the author praises the greatness of God, confesses his sins by writing an autobiography, and defends his faith by describing the conditions that make memory, temporal experience, and existential transformation possible. In each case, the dynamism of his discourse takes us beyond the surface of the text into the presence and absence of the one to whom he speaks. The richness of the language Augustine uses permits him to stand before God as a unique individual, but it also enables him to reach out to his audience so we can overhear what he reveals about the texture of his life. Since God already knows what Augustine wants to say, the ones who benefit from the *Confessions* are the writer himself and those who listen to what he says. The author comes to himself by depicting what unfolds within his private confessional, but he also leads his readers into the place between God and the soul where we can make confessions of our own. If this should occur, our attention will shift from Augustine to ourselves; and the language of God and the soul will become a living issue rather than a historical curiosity.

If we try to respond to Augustine's reflective and rhetorical intentions, we will soon discover that the *Confessions* is a difficult book. For many readers, there are too many prayers, too much self-flagellation, and too much philosophy. What other book begins by praising the greatness of God (1.1.1) and ends with an account of the nature of memory (10.8.12–10.27.38), the problem of time (11.14.17–11.31.41), and the hermeneutics of creation (12.1.1–13.13.53)? Where else can we find an autobiography about the sins of infancy and about an adolescent act of mischief that becomes an obsession (1.7.11, 2.4.9–2.10.18)? Who besides Augustine pictures sexuality as a boiling caldron that seethes and bubbles all around him (3.1.1)? In Book VII, he describes a mystical experience in which he sees the invisibility of God with a trembling glance (7.17.23). In Book VIII, he depicts his conversion to Christianity when he puts on a new garment called "Jesus, the Christ" (8.7.16–8.12.30). And in Book IX, he recounts a mystical experience with his mother, dominated by conversation and by auditory metaphors rather than by visual images, and culminating in a shared experience of ecstasy unparalleled in the mystical tradition (9.10.24–26). The *Confessions* expresses a range of feelings that is difficult to describe, but it also displays a powerful capacity for reflective discourse. Unlike most philosophers, Augustine can feel deeply and speak profoundly in the same sentence. Indeed, his most famous book poses difficulties for interpretation because it weaves together what most professional philosophers try to separate.

How shall we respond to a book as rich and complex as this? What approach should we take? What questions should we ask? What answers should we expect? What purposes should undergird our inquiry? Without trying to answer these questions prematurely, at least this much should be clear from the outset: we cannot plunge into the *Confessions* without calling ourselves into question. Augustine speaks as a psychologist, a rhetorician, a philosopher, and a theologian; but he speaks most fundamentally from the heart. If we are unwilling to probe the depths of our souls, we will never understand Augustine; for he makes insistent demands that we trace out the path he has traveled in our own spiritual and intellectual development.

In the past two decades, I have tried to come to terms with these demands; but I have only begun to find the place from which Augustine is speaking in the past few years. If one philosopher pays tribute to another by taking him seriously enough to criticize, it is even truer that the highest honor we can pay a great thinker is to try to rise to the level of his thinking. The time has come to rescue Augustine from critics who deny his originality[3] and to develop a philosophical framework rich enough to express a distinctively Augustinian approach to the language of God and the soul.[4] Only if we do this is there room for us to stand beside Augustine, and only if we open ourselves to the fundamental questions he raises can we participate in a dialogue with him that transcends both hubris and humility.

No one undertakes a project of this kind alone, and I want to thank my students and colleagues who have participated in it and have helped make it possible. First, I express my gratitude to the students at Penn State and at Baylor who have attended my lectures and seminars about the *Confessions*, some of whom have been my research assistants. Roger Ward at Penn State and Chris Calloway and Travis Foster at Baylor have been three of these students; I am indebted to all of them for their assistance. I am also grateful to three other research assistants in the philosophy department at Baylor: Natalie Tapken for preparing the notes for the book, many of which include contents that have a bearing on the text; Kristi Culpepper for making a number of corrections on the edited manuscript; and Christi Williams for proofreading the penultimate version of the manuscript and for preparing the index. I am also grateful to the thirteen philosophers who came to Penn State for a week in 1992 to study the *Confessions* with me. We thought and talked until we were exhausted; but in the process, the text opened up in ways that none of us could have anticipated. Some of the papers from this conference and from my graduate seminars appear in a two-part issue of *Contemporary Philosophy*, vol. 15, published in 1993. Recently, Baylor University sponsored a Pruitt Memorial Symposium devoted to the topic, "Celebrating Augustine's *Confessions*: Reading the *Confessions* for the New Millennium." Professor Anne-Marie Bowery and I were the codirectors of this conference. Finally, I am grateful to President Robert Sloan, Provost Donald Schmeltekopf, and my colleagues in the Philosophy Department at Baylor for providing me with a supportive and exciting academic environment in which to bring this project to completion. However, I am grateful most of all to Robert Baird, the Department Chair, who read the penultimate version of the manuscript. He not only made valuable suggestions about what I have written, but also encouraged me to turn the project loose after more than a decade of work.

I have presented parts of chapter 2 at a number of institutions and philosophical meetings: the Graduate Christian Forum at Cornell, the

Convocation Lecture Series at Bethel College, the Distinguished Lecture Series at Baylor, the Philosophy Department Colloquium at the University of Essex, the Faculty of Divinity in the University of Edinburgh, the "D" Society at Cambridge, the School of Philosophy at the Catholic University of America, the Philosophy Department Colloquium at Penn State, the Baptist Association of Philosophy Teachers at Furman University, and the Interdisciplinary Program at Valparaiso University. I want to thank those who attended these lectures for comments and criticisms that have helped me sharpen some of the issues in this final version of the book. I have also published parts of chapter 2 as a paper entitled "Theft and Conversion: Two Augustinian Confessions," in *The Recovery of Philosophy in America: Essays in Honor of John Edwin Smith*.[5] I want to thank SUNY Press for permission to reprint parts of this paper and to express my appreciation to John Smith for helpful comments about it.

I am grateful to Colin Starnes and James O'Donnell for their encouragement. I met Colin at his farmhouse near Halifax in the summer of 1992 soon after his book about Augustine's conversion appeared; and I participated in a session of James's NEH Seminar at Bryn Mawr the following summer, where teachers from a variety of disciplines discussed a wide range of problems and raised questions about his three volume text and commentary about the *Confessions*. I value the work of these classical philologists because it is the most encouraging sign that Augustinian scholarship is beginning to move beyond the place where Pierre Courcelle left it in 1950. I am pleased to add my philosophical voice to their attempts to reorient the discussion of Augustine's most influential book.

Finally, I want to express my gratitude to Professor Richard Swinburne, who helped me find an academic home at Oxford where the first draft of this book was written. I also want to thank Professor Rowan Williams at Christ Church for allowing me to participate in his course about Augustine; Christopher Kirwan at Exeter College for discussing some philosophical problems about the *Confessions* with me; and Robert Edwards, a medievalist and colleague at Penn State, for making detailed comments on an earlier version of the manuscript. My wife, Jane, recognized long before I did the similarity between Augustine's rhetorical approach to philosophy and my own. I am delighted that her photograph of me, reading the prayers in the *Confessions* aloud on the outer banks of North Carolina at sunset, appears on the back cover of the book. I am also proud of our daughters, Jennifer and Cheryl—young women when my work on Augustine began, but now women with careers of their own. In the light of all they have done for us, this book is for them.

Introduction

This book is a detailed analysis of Books VII–IX of Augustine's *Confessions*, and it comes to focus on three pivotal encounters between God and the Soul. The first is his philosophical conversion, the second is his conversion to Christianity, and the third is the mystical experience he shares with his mother a few days before her death in Ostia. At a time when philosophy and theology are moving in so many directions, I have chosen to deal with these experiences, not only because they are fundamental stages of Augustine's existential and reflective transformation, but also because they are archetypical expressions of the human spirit. This is true when Augustine calls our attention to these experiences in the *Confessions*;[1] and it is still the case today, however reluctant many of us may be to fasten our attention on these issues.

My own version of Augustine's enterprise is that God, the soul, and language are the most important problems a philosopher can consider, that religion is the region where all the enigmas of the world converge,[2] and that solitude is the place where the ultimate issues of life intersect.[3] Yet we must never assume that the problem of God and the soul and the subtle uses of language it requires are either resting places or private problems with which we must struggle alone. When we confront these issues, we face enigmas to be pondered rather than problems to be solved; but having struggled with them in private, we should also address the public context in which our life and thought are embedded.

What draws me to Augustine's *Confessions* is that I see myself on almost every page. As the Renaissance poet, Petrarch, is the first to notice, the *Confessions* is not only Augustine's story, but also the story of Adam and Eve, and hence the story of us all.[4] It is a microscopic expression of a macroscopic theme: in a single life the relation between God and the soul unfolds as sustained encounters between an individual and the ground of its existence,[5] where the experiences that emerge from these encounters demand the richest linguistic responses of which we are capable. As

1

Augustine says himself, "What can anyone say when he speaks of thee? But woe to them that keep silent—since even those who say most are dumb" (1.4.4).

Augustine's account of his three encounters with God presupposes a metanarrative of creation, fall, conversion, and fulfillment in the light of which he believes that the lives of all his readers can be understood. However, this does not mean that each of us moves through every stage Augustine traverses, that all of us do so in the same way, or that the particularity of our unique situations can simply be subsumed within a universal pattern. Augustine is convinced that the pattern is there, and one of his most important tasks is to call our attention to it. However, the author of the *Confessions* not only addresses us as tokens of a type, but also as unique individuals. In doing so, he stands in between the global human situation and the particular modifications it exhibits. The *Confessions* thrusts us into the hyphenated place between the universal and the particular, the past and the future, the community and the individual, and God and the soul, challenging us to listen, not only to what God says to Augustine, but also to what God says to us.

The problem of God and the soul and the language appropriate to it are intertwined in a variety of ways. First, the interaction between God and the soul unfolds within a temporal, spatial, and eternal framework, mobilizing the language of the restless heart as a way of bringing space, time, and eternity together into a metaphorical and analogical unity. The relation between time and eternity is expressed most adequately in metaphorical discourse, while the relation between eternity and space requires analogical uses of language for its appropriate articulation. In both cases, figurative discourse is the key for binding God and the soul together. Second, this pivotal relation involves both unity and separation and expresses itself in creation *ex nihilo*, in the fateful transition from finitude to fallenness, and in the quest for fulfillment that attempts to reestablish peace with God. All these stages of the cosmic drama require figurative discourse for their adequate expression, but they also involve a performative use of language that reflects the dynamism of God, the discord of our fragmented spirits, and the vibrant interaction that can develop between the soul and the ground of its existence. Performative discourse is the language of creation, the language of the restless heart, and the language that permits God and the soul to confront one another in the space that opens up between them. Finally, the two strands of our inquiry come together because the primary mode of interaction between God and the soul has a linguistic dimension and involves speaking and hearing as its fundamental expression. However important seeing may be, speaking and hearing generate the context in which the ultimate issues of life can be addressed. If these issues are to be dealt with adequately, the language of God and the soul must not only be figurative and performative, but must also be sufficiently intelligible to bring stability to the human situation.

Figurative language points to the mystery of God and to the separation between God and the soul; performative utterances point to the power of God and to the space between the creator and the creature in which they can disclose themselves; and intelligible discourse points to the Word of God, to the self-transcendent structure of consciousness, and to the hope that both God and the soul will have something to say when they meet. In this book, this hope is grounded in Augustine's existential and ecstatic language about God and the soul and in the conviction that its figurative, performative, and intelligible dimensions will enable it to leap across the centuries to speak decisively in the postmodern world.

Augustine stands like a colossus for more than a thousand years, casting his shadow over the development of the Middle Ages. As one of the translators of the Confessions reminds us, "every person living in the Western world would be a different person if Augustine had not been or had been different."[6] The story of Augustine's life reveals the secret of its impact: though he is one of the most original philosophers and theologians in the Western tradition, he is also a person in whom powerful feelings, strength of will, and greatness of intellect converge. Augustine is one of the greatest psychologists since Plato, the greatest rhetorician since Cicero, and the greatest Christian thinker before the birth of Thomas Aquinas. In all three domains, the greatness of his soul expresses the complexity of his life, the power of his spirit, and the profundity of his thinking.

The most important fact about Augustine is that he combines philosophy and passion in equal proportions. Yet his passion pours into his philosophy, not to confuse or distort it, but to give it impetus. Augustine not only gives us his thought, but also gives us himself. "He does not skim the truth off the [surface of] experience and give us that"; rather, "he gives it [to us] in the [concrete] context in which he learned it."[7] Augustine's head and heart interpenetrate and sustain one another, and his experience and his thinking are equally important because they express inseparable sides of the same person. Though he presents himself as a rhetorician, a psychologist, and a philosopher with unquenchable passions, what he wants most is truth about God. Augustine seeks the ground of truth as the light in which all other truth exists; and to find it, he not only undertakes a philosophical journey, but also speaks to God from the center of his being.

Despite its intrinsic interest and its lasting significance, Augustine's account of his development is perplexing. It begins with infancy and childhood, but has nothing to say about either stage that could not have been said about any other person. This permits Courcelle and others to move quickly through this part of the text, focusing instead on matters of historical interest peculiar to Augustine.[8] Yet even from an historical point of view, the *Confessions* is not his complete life story. Augustine finishes writing the book when he is forty-six and the narrative portion of the text concludes with the death of his mother thirteen years earlier. This leaves the reader with a truncated account of his life, and it leaves commentators philological and historical room to speculate about the disparity between the stages of Augustine's conversion and his recollection of the events more than a decade afterward.

If we are to understand the existential books of the *Confessions,* we must move beyond the postmodern rejection of a metaphysics of presence to an affirmation of a metaphysics of the presence and absence. Augustine never asserts that God is fully present to consciousness, but suggests instead that by learning to live in the present, and by developing a metaphysics appropriate to it, we can come to grips with both the presence and absence of the one to whom he speaks. Sixteen centuries before the postmodern conversation begins, Augustine knows that the soul is not a transcendental signifier and that God is not a transcendental signified that brings lifeless stability to the human situation. Rather, the relation between God and the soul involves dynamic interaction; and the language appropriate to it permits neither term to be reduced to a frozen persona in a metaphysical or ontotheological charade. Because he knows this, Augustine shifts our attention away from the logocentrism of traditional metaphysical discourse to the dynamism of his experience with God and to the language of the heart that expresses its significance.

On more than one occasion, Augustine says that he is not telling the story of his life to inform God about it, but to speak to other men and women in God's presence (5.1.1, 8.1.1, 10.1.1–10.4.6). Though he could scarcely have foreseen the impact that his book would make on future generations, in addressing "that small part of the human race who may come upon these writings," he makes it clear that he wants to bring his readers into the vertical relationship between God and the soul from which he speaks (2.3.5). Augustine's deepest wish for the *Confessions* is that those who read it may understand "what depths there are from which we are to cry unto thee" (2.3.5).

In this book, my way of responding to Augustine's intentions is to retell the story of his encounters with God, to interpret them in terms of the philosophical framework that I am about to introduce, and to indicate how Augustine's development finally brings him to the place where faith can undertake the task of seeking understanding. As this book unfolds, I will not only present my interpretation of Augustine's three encounters with God, but will also attempt to immerse the reader in Augustine's narrative. Otherwise, the existential dimension of Augustine's experiences will be compromised, and Books VII–IX of the *Confessions* will be reduced to concrete occasions for merely abstract reflection.

THE FRAMEWORK OF THE ENTERPRISE

Augustine's *Confessions* develops within a three-dimensional framework: the first is temporal, the second spatial, and the third eternal. These dimensions generate three axes along which it moves, and each axis exhibits two orientations that point in opposite directions. The temporal aspect of Augustine's life moves forward and backward; the spatial side of his existence points outward and inward; the eternal horizon in which he lives stretches upward and downward; and when these axes converge, they establish a place where his life and thought unfold, both for himself and for his readers.[9]

The two orientations of Augustine's temporal development are important because they allow him to embrace the future and to recover the past. His life is a sequence of episodes that develops toward a culmination, but he also plunges beneath the flow of his experience in a courageous effort to remember the most significant stages of his psychological, spiritual, and philosophical development. He does this, not because he loves the past or because he is proud of his achievements, but because he wants to remember the sins that separate him from God, and by reliving them, to allow himself to be gathered up from the fragments into which he has fallen. (2.1.1). Augustine's recollection of the past and his expectation of the future are ways of finding God, where what he remembers and what he anticipates give him access to what would otherwise remain beyond his grasp.

The spatial side of Augustine's life also develops in two directions, not only moving outward toward the cosmos, but also moving inward toward the soul. The story of his life begins with his parents, nurses, friends, and education and culminates in a philosophical and theological framework that makes his experiential and reflective development intelligible. This development permits him to transform the narrow spatial context with which he begins into a way of thinking that gives him access to a larger world. Yet the most crucial episodes of his life occur within the depths of his soul,[10] where it is not so much what happens to him, but how he responds to his circumstances that matters.[11] The internal space in which Augustine comes face to face with himself, the marks his interactions with others make on him, and the ways in which these encounters point toward God are the most important elements of his spatial development.[9]

The eternal axis along which Augustine moves makes the interplay between the soul and the ground of its existence possible, pointing upward toward God and pointing downward to his fruitless attempts to flee from his presence. In the first case, Augustine seeks to bring himself into a positive relation with the source of power that creates and sustains him. In the second, he tries to flee from God in a downward movement that implicates both his will and his intellect. The upward movement begins as an intellectual ascent and culminates in a response to a divine command that he surrender his will to a source of power that transforms his life. By contrast, the flight from God is an intellectual attempt to escape the searching light of truth and a desperate effort to insist on his own willfulness in opposition to the will of God.

This upward and downward development reflects a double movement in Augustine's soul. In the first case, he transcends himself to find God (7.10.16, 7.17.23), opens himself to the expression of God's grace (8.12.29), and attempts to understand the gift he has received (10.1.1). In the second, he flees from the center of his being, falls toward the earth, squanders his possessions in a far country, and attempts to escape the voice of God by embracing the nothingness from which he comes. The upward development expresses Augustine's faith that seeks to understand its ground, while the downward spiral reflects his abiding identification with the plight of the Prodigal Son (1.18.28). The *Confessions* is a battleground between these two directions, and it is only as he attempts to overcome the conflict between them that he finds God in the heights and in the depths of his soul.

An adequate attempt to understand the *Confessions* must move within temporal, spatial, and eternal dimensions simultaneously. The temporal side of the discussion gives us access to Augustine's historical development and to the narrative devices he uses to express it. The spatial aspect of the inquiry allows us to take up the relation between Augustine and his surrounding context and points to the problem of the individual and the community. And the eternal horizon of our enterprise enables us to deal with Augustine's encounters with God and with the pivotal moments when he finds him. Finally, in the place where time, space, and eternity intersect, Augustine sees the light of truth with his intellect, responds to the voice of God with his will, and expresses the unity of God with his being, where his being, his will, and his intellect interpenetrate to become a transformed image of the ground of his existence.

The temporal, spatial, and eternal dimensions of the *Confessions* are not only schematic and categorial, but also exhibit a descriptive richness that allows us to approach the text in concrete terms. The temporal aspect of Augustine's life expresses itself in the narrative stages of the book, in its plot and cast of characters, and in the concept of human development that underlies it. The spatial side of his experience points to the problem of the private self and the larger world, to the relation between the individual and the community, and to his attempts to understand the connection between them. Finally, the eternal axis along which he moves leads to the formula that becomes the motto of his life: as he tells us on more than one occasion, "Unless you believe, you shall not understand."[12] This formula allows Augustine to express the spatial and temporal sides of his development from an eternal point of view, to speak to God from the center of his being, and to bridge the otherwise unbridgeable chasm between God and the soul.

Augustine's attempts to bridge the chasm between God and the soul pose an existential crisis that demands a resolution.[13] This crisis mentality is appropriate to Augustine, for he understands his life as a series of conflicts that he must resolve to become who he is. The crises that define Augustine's development are important, not simply as episodes, but because they allow him to understand and to embrace the meaning of his life. It is here that the stages of his life and the crises to which they point have a bearing on the vertical dimension of his experience.

The resolution of the crises that Augustine undergoes brings him fulfillment in time and space by bringing him into relation with the eternal axis along which he discovers the meaning of his life. Indeed, each stage of his development points beyond history by implicating the meaning of his being. As an infant, Augustine begins to sense that he is what he has been given (1.6.7). This generates hope and expresses itself religiously when he embraces a life of faith.[14] In childhood, he learns that he is what he wills to be and that he is what he can imagine

(1.8.13–1.9.14).[15] Later, he discovers that he is what he can learn (1.18.28–29)[16]; and when he faces a prolonged identity crisis that begins in adolescence and extends into youthful maturity, he finds that he must choose what he is to become (2.1.1–9.6.14).[17] Because all these stages point not only to the development of life within a social context, but also to what each stage means, they mobilize Augustine's awareness of the vertical dimension of existence. This leads him from time, to space, to eternity, pointing to the need for all these dimensions in any adequate approach to the problem of God and the soul.

Though psychological considerations help us understand the temporal, spatial, and eternal dimensions of Augustine's journey, it is not sufficient to deal with them in psychological terms alone. If we are to gain a richer understanding of the framework they generate, the rhetorical facet of each axis must also be taken into account. The temporal aspect of Augustine's rhetorical strategy is exemplified most forcibly in his willingness to emphasize the elements of dissonance in his story in contrast with the continuities that it exemplifies.

It is appropriate to follow Neoplatonic commentators in looking for coherence in Augustine's development,[18] but his rhetoric also underscores the importance of temporal discontinuity as he moves from state to stage. Floggings by his teachers (1.9.14), stealing pears with adolescent friends (2.4.9), the sudden death of his closest companion (4.4.8), sexual addiction (8.5.10–12, 8.7.17), and a series of professional disappointments bring his temporal development to a standstill. The powerful rhetorician's depiction of these episodes not only allow him to point to the negative elements that interrupt his progress, but also permit his readers to pause in their linear progression through the text. In doing so, we are permitted to brood over incidents that Augustine depicts and to confront the episodes that bring him face to face with radical discontinuity.

The spatial dimension of Augustine's rhetoric is expressed most clearly in his use of gardens to generate open spaces that give him access to God. Gardens punctuate the metaphor of a journey with "spatial" moments that often display a dimension of eternal significance. For example, the place where Augustine is converted to Christianity is analogous to the garden of Gethsemane[19]; and the garden at the center of the house where Augustine and Monica participate in a shared mystical experience is analogous to the Paradise they long to enter.[20] In both cases, Augustine stands apart from the temporal flow of his story to participate in a spatial context that gives him access to eternity.

UNITY AND SEPARATION IN AUGUSTINE'S THINKING

Though the relation between God and the soul is Augustine's central theme, his attempts to deal with this issue reveal a tension in his thinking that pervades every stage of his reflective development. This tension surfaces most clearly as an interplay between Neoplatonic and Christian strands in his thought. Neoplatonists maintain that a continuous series of levels connects God and the soul, while orthodox Christians insist that an act of creation *ex nihilo* holds them apart. Augustine exploits the Neoplatonic dimension of continuity by inverting the downward path of emanation and by participating in the soul's ascent to God;[21] but he also emphasizes the Christian dimension of separation by insisting that God and the soul are not simply different in degree, but different in kind.

The interplay between Neoplatonism and Christianity in Augustine's thinking presupposes two models for understanding the relation between God and the soul. When he leans in a Neoplatonic direction, he embraces a part-whole account of this relation by defending the view that the soul is part of God. In a characteristic passage he says, "I would not be, I would in no wise be unless you were in me. Or rather, I would not be unless I were in you, "from whom, by whom, and in whom are all things" (1.2.2). However, Augustine also embraces an alternative account of the proper relation between the creator and its creatures. According to this interpretation, the soul stands in contrast with God and bears an imagistic relation to its source, where this relation must be distinguished from the part-whole analysis of the Neoplatonic tradition. It is true that Plotinus often relies on a distinction between an image and an original instead of the more simplistic contrast between a part and a whole,[22] but the imagistic relation the doctrine of emanation involves differs from the corresponding relation creation *ex nihilo* presupposes. At appropriate stages in the following chapters, we will attempt to understand this difference.

A more straightforward way of raising the question about the relation between Neoplatonism and Christianity in the *Confessions* is to ask whether Augustine is a Neoplatonist or a Christian, and whether it is possible for him to be both, as Courcelle and many others have maintained.[23] My answer is that though Neoplatonism is the dominant influence in his early writings and though Neoplatonic concepts provide much of the vocabulary of his mature theology, Augustine is a Christian who subordinates Neoplatonism to his own purposes rather than a Neoplatonist who disguises himself as a Christian theologian. One of the clearest ways to express this point is to say that creation *ex nihilo* is incompatible with emanation as an explanation for the existence of the cosmos. In the first case, God and the world stand over against one another in radical contrast; in the second, they flow into one another as elements of an ontological continuum.[24]

Augustine uses both ways of speaking to express his fundamental insights about the relation between God and the soul; but when he states his cosmological views with the greatest precision, a metaphysical chasm separates God from the world in such a radical way that a Neoplatonic continuum can never mediate it. According to Augustine, God creates the world from nothing; according to Plotinus, the One creates the world out of itself. The nothingness with which Augustine struggles is absolute and is much more elusive than the lower limit of a Neoplatonic continuum. Augustine not only joins the Neoplatonist in equating evil with the privation of goodness, but also insists that evil is a distorted tendency of the soul to seek complete annihilation as it attempts to flee from God. Thus, the Augustinian contrast between being and nothingness differs fundamentally from the Plotinian distinction between the One and the privation of which the concept of matter is the clearest expression.[25]

When Augustine rejects the emanation theory by insisting that God creates the world *ex nihilo*, and when he elaborates the significance of this distinction for Christian theology, he baptizes Plotinus just as successfully as Aquinas baptizes Aristotle. Indeed, the first baptism is superior to the second because Augustine grafts the richness of Platonic discourse onto the Christian doctrine of creation rather than imposing Aristotelian categories upon the dynamism of creation *ex nihilo* that they inevitably obscure. Augustine suggests that after God creates the world, the world participates in God by reflecting his infinite richness. This dimension of participation presupposes a continuum between God and the world along which Augustine moves; but it also presupposes the act of creation that brings the continuum into existence in the first instance.

As *Vere Esse*, God is the upper limit of a continuum that finite beings can approach but never reach; and as creator *ex nihilo*, he is infinitely beyond them as the source that brings them into existence. Yet it is important to emphasize the fact that discontinuity comes before continuity in Augustine's thinking and that it is the foundation on which the ontological continuum between God and the world is established. To repeat: an ontological continuum permits Augustine to appropriate the linguistic flexibility of Platonism, moving back and forth between the metaphorical unity and analogical separation between God and the soul.

However, the successful baptism of Plotinus hinges on the fact that creation *ex nihilo* comes first and is the metaphysical foundation on which the relation between God and the soul depends.

When Augustine occupies the middle ground between God and the soul, the place from which he speaks displays several important characteristics. First, it is a region in which the soul is an image of God and where this imagistic relation connects and disconnects them. The original is prior to the image and expresses itself in creation *ex nihilo*, but the image that emerges from it is a being with its own integrity and reflects the richness of the source that generates it. Second, the image of God is not only a thinking being, but also a center of power that expresses itself in the freedom of the will. In the *Confessions*, the will is a dimension of the soul that is distinct from both thinking and feeling; and it is the moving principle that allows it to transcend itself by embracing a positive relationship with God. Third, though the will is a center of power that can exercise its freedom, it sometimes degenerates, leading from a positive orientation toward God to a radical separation from him that raises the problem of sin and redemption. Along the vertical axis that defines the relation between God and the soul, the will sometimes turns away from its source and plunges into an abyss that threatens to destroy it. Fourth, though the redemption that liberates the soul from this predicament is mediated by the intellect, it also depends on a transformation of the will. Knowing God is a necessary condition for finding the transformation Augustine seeks, but deciding to follow him requires an act of the will that reorients the soul. Finally, Augustine's alienation from his origins can be overcome only when God speaks; for though an intellectual vision opens him to a source of intelligibility that transcends him, it is equally clear that the transformation of his will requires a divine interjection. Indeed, it is only when this transformation occurs that the intellect and the will are bound together as a re-created image of the source that generates them.

It is customary to claim that we are images of God because we are rational creatures; for unless this were so, we could never raise the question of our relation to the origin that transcends us. Augustine commits himself to the view that the intellect sets us apart from the rest of creation and makes it possible for us to understand what is at stake in the relation between God and the soul. However, Augustine's position is much more sophisticated than this: to be an image of God is not only to think, but also to reflect God's infinite richness. The difference between God and the soul is not primarily a distinction between finite and infinite centers of reason, but a contrast between God as an infinite ground and a creature that is both finite and infinite.[26] We could never be related to God if we were merely finite beings separated from him by an infinite chasm. The soul is both a finite and an infinite reflection of its creative ground, and the restless heart displays both finite and infinite dimensions that allow it to move beyond its natural limitations toward the source that creates and sustains it. It is the interplay between these finite and infinite dimensions that allows us to move up and down the ontological continuum generated by creation *ex nihilo,* using metaphorical language to bind God and the soul together, and analogical language to hold them apart.

By describing the stages of his spiritual development, Augustine not only appeals to our intellect, but also puts our souls in motion. His technical term for the motion of the soul is *voluntas*—a volitional faculty that cannot be reduced to feeling or cognition and that expresses the self-transcendence of the person that can bring it into a positive relation with God. Without pointing to this aspect of our nature, we would be unable to distinguish one individual from another. Individuals differ, not only because they exhibit different characteristics, but also because they express distinctive wills. The structure of our finitude and the power of our wills distinguish us from one another; and taken together, they enable us to reach beyond ourselves toward the ground that sustains us.

Augustine not only describes the soul as an intersection of intellect and will, but also as a center of willfulness. Willfulness emerges when we deny our limitations and when the infinite dimension of our souls attempts to become divine. When this occurs, we make the fatal transition from a center of power that is both finite and infinite into an infinite center of self-accentuation. Willfulness stands over against God as a negative imitation of omnipotence and attempts to cancel its finitude by mastering both itself and the world. Yet when the will becomes willful and attempts to control its own destiny, it falls into an abyss from which it is unable to emerge without divine intervention.

Augustine develops two definitions of willfulness that he uses throughout the *Confessions*: first, it is an infinite attachment to a finite good rather than an appropriate attachment to what is infinite; second, it is a negative act we perform for its own sake. In the first case, sin is curiosity or sensuality; in the second, it is pride that separates us from God. All three kinds of sin generate a problem from which the soul is unable to extricate itself, and they have negative personal and social consequences because they shatter our relation to ourselves and the relationships that bind us to others. The attempt to enjoy what we ought to use as a way of making access to God produces what a later Augustinian monk describes as "the bondage of the will," where bondage of this kind separates us from God, paralyzes the soul, and destroys the community in which we exist.[27]

Augustine often describes the bondage of the will in sexual terms. In a crucial passage at the center of the book, he tells us that will becomes lust, lust becomes habit, and habit becomes necessity (8.5.10). When we are caught in the chains of necessity, sexuality becomes an addiction that not only enslaves the individual, but also has disastrous consequences for the community. Augustine sometimes focuses on the sins of the flesh as if the flesh and sexual activity were the same. However, we must remember that he has a more profound understanding of the body than this. He does not regard sexuality as inherently negative, but only as the most obvious way in which willfulness can manifest its destructive consequences. Augustine struggles with sexual addiction so persistently because it points beyond itself to a more serious problem: the addiction that binds him reflects a degeneration from will to willfulness, symbolizes the stain that defines the human predicament, points to the idolatry of exclusively finite attachments, and produces a disorientation of the will that destroys the community in which it is embedded.

A profound experience of absolute nonbeing undergirds Augustine's account of this process of degeneration. When he moves beyond the Neoplatonic account of evil as privation and as a way of turning away from God, he commits himself to a radical way of understanding nothingness that must be distinguished from its relativized and domesticated counterpart. Nonbeing depends on Being as the primary concept, but it also becomes absolute when the freedom of the will breaks beyond the ontological continuum on which it is located and affirms its infinite dimension for its own sake. Having begun to undertake it, Augustine finally turns away from a systematic discussion of the problem of evil because nonbeing and the willfulness that seeks to embrace it cannot be understood by placing them within a larger context. The most obvious indication of this is his account of the pear-stealing episode (2.8.16–2.10.19)—an act that he performs for its own sake that stands outside a rational framework. The kind of nonbeing Augustine struggles with is absolute, and he insists on its absoluteness by suggesting that the problem to which it points has no logical resolution.

Augustine attempts to escape the bondage of the will and the nothingness that makes it possible by embracing the transforming power of what is infinite. A necessary condition for transformation is the positive self-concern that is natural to the psyche. This implies that the image of

God has not been effaced and points to the truth of the Neoplatonic thesis that a memory of God binds us to the source that generates us.[28] However, the continuity of Neoplatonic ontologism is not enough to bring redemption to the disoriented will. Just as the continuity that makes linguistic flexibility possible presupposes the discontinuity of creation *ex nihilo*, so an external source of deliverance is necessary that will restore the image of God to its original condition.

The descent from will to willfulness is not primarily intellectual, but volitional; and the character of this descent forces Augustine to move beyond his intellectual conversion to Neoplatonism to his more profound Christian conversion that transcends it. Like the Prodigal Son who takes a journey into a far country and squanders his inheritance, he must come to himself before he can go back home. This radical reversal of the human predicament not only involves a refocusing of the intellect, but also requires a reorientation of the will that allows Augustine to reestablish an imagistic relation with God.[29] The recreation of the image of God that occurs along the vertical axis of experience binds Augustine's intellect and will together and makes it possible for his being, his will, and his intellect to recover their relation to their Trinitarian origins.

The goal Augustine pursues is not identical with knowledge: intellectual deliverance presupposes that to know the good is to do it, while the reorientation of the will requires him to turn away from the willfulness that separates him from the source that creates him. Augustine's conversion to Christianity is not an exoteric expression of an esoteric doctrine, but an intellectual and moral transformation that requires a distinctive philosophical response. As Alfred North Whitehead says, Christianity is "a religion in search of a metaphysics."[30] Our fundamental task is to develop an Augustinian version of this metaphysics. The kind of philosophical system we need is not a metaphysics of presence, but a metaphysics of presence and absence that does not presuppose the Neoplatonic image of the fallen soul that returns to its origins, but requires the Christian image of a divine interjection that bridges the infinite chasm between God and one who has turned away from him. Augustine's experiential and reflective journey is not simply an odyssey of the soul along an ontological continuum of emanation, but a way of living with presence and absence that presupposes creation *ex nihilo* and that redeems human beings from the abyss into which we have fallen. If one ever encounters God, it must always be within a context of this kind; and it is only out of the richness of these encounters that faith seeking understanding can develop the metaphysics it needs.

To maintain this thesis is to reject some of the most astute Augustinian scholarship that moves in a Neoplatonic direction,[31] and we must face this fact at appropriate places in the book. However, even at this stage, we should focus our attention on this crucial fact: Augustine's deepest difficulty is not the problem of finitude, but the problem of fallenness;[32] his basic predicament is not the problem of ignorance, but the problem of willfulness. As a result, his most important task is to answer Paul's question, "Who shall free me from the body of this death?"[33]

As Augustine struggles with this question, he mobilizes our wills and touches both the conscious and the unconscious sides of our intellects. The author of the *Confessions* believes that a barrier separates God from the soul that it can never cross of its own initiative, but he also believes that God bridges the chasm that isolates us from him. This suggests that we should read his story, not only as a philosophical odyssey, but also as a religious journey that presupposes creation *ex nihilo* and that points to the problem of unity and separation in his thinking. This journey depends on the grace of God, which not only generates an ontological continuum along which we can move, but also points to the positive relation between God and the soul, that preserves the irreducible differences between them.

SPEAKING AND HEARING AS PRIMORDIAL PHENOMENA

Augustine's journey toward God unfolds within a temporal, spatial, and eternal framework; presupposes the centrality of the relation between God and the soul; and points to the linguistic dimension of the problems before us. Yet what more should we say about the linguistic pathway that the author traverses in binding God and the soul together and about the figurative uses of language that make it possible for him to do so? These questions are important, not only because they focus on the language of God and the soul, but also because they call our attention to speaking and hearing as primordial phenomena.

One of the most important things to notice about Augustine's use of language is that he often employs sensory metaphors to point beyond the fragmentation of time toward the stability of eternity.[34] In doing so, he establishes a linguistic pattern that ties language about God to sense perception rather than to the transcendental categories usually preferred by the scholastics. As his frequent reliance on the category of substance and on the concepts of being and truth suggest, Augustine is not indifferent to the power of categorial and transcendental discourse.[35] However, in following the Platonic rather than the Aristotelian tradition, he is aware that the richest language about God is rooted in the senses, linking the lowest level of cognition to the highest place the soul can reach in its efforts to give an adequate description of eternity.[36] In this coincidence of opposites, the depths of experience meet the heights of eternity, and the language of God and the soul becomes the language of the heart.

Augustine follows the Platonic tradition by emphasizing the importance of visual metaphors. However, only a few have noticed that auditory images are equally important in his account of the relation between God and the soul.[37] This is evident even in his early book about the freedom of the will, where Augustine places seeing and hearing on the same level because they are the only senses for which the corresponding object is accessible to everyone (7.17.23, 10.5.7, 10.23.33).[38] Publicity is one of the most important marks of truth, and the fact that seeing and hearing open out on a public world, and on the creative source to which it points, suggests that both of them are privileged modes of access to what lies beyond us.[39]

Augustine uses auditory images throughout his writings, but their crucial role in his search for God is especially evident in the *Confessions*. It is tempting to assume that the predominance of auditory language in Augustine's most well known book derives exclusively from his numerous quotations from the Psalms. Yet he uses auditory symbols, not only when he echoes the words of the Bible, but also when he speaks with his own voice.[40] The problem is not whether auditory images saturate the *Confessions*, but how we are to relate them to the more familiar visual metaphors that are so clearly present there. Indeed, the problem of relating visual and auditory ways of speaking is a linguistic version of how to connect Neoplatonism and Christianity in Augustine's thinking.

The Neoplatonic path to God depends on visual metaphors and produces a vision of Truth, while Augustine's Christian conversion allows him to respond to the voice of God with the voice of his heart. Augustine uses visual metaphors to express the significant role of the intellect in the search for God (7.17.23, 10.5.7, 10.23.33). He speaks of entering into his "inmost being," of seeing with the eye of his soul, of "an unchangeable light" (7.10.16), and of the "trembling glance" that finally gives him access to God (7.17.23). He also begs God not to hide his face from him and says, "Even if I die, let me see thy face lest I die" (1.5.5). Yet the great rhetorician uses equally powerful auditory symbols to express the longing of his soul for transformation. First he asks, "Let me learn from thee, who art Truth, and put the ear of my heart to thy mouth" (4.5.10). Then he writes: "Accept this sacrifice of my confessions from the hand of my tongue. Thou didst form it and hast prompted it to praise thy name" (5.1.1). Finally, he implores God to "trim away" all "rashness and lying" from his lips, to harken to his soul, and to "hear it crying from the depths" (11.2.3).

We can understand the story of Augustine's life most adequately by reading it aloud rather than by moving our eyes from place to place along a printed page. Proceeding in this way allows the cadences of his discourse to resonate in our ears, reflecting the original situation in which he speaks, and mirroring the linguistic interaction between God and the soul to which he responds. The richness of Augustine's rhetoric and the power of his thinking move us most when we hear him speaking; the oral culture in which he lives and the circumstances in which he dictates the *Confessions*[41] come to life as we listen to his story; and the conversation between God and his soul becomes accessible to us when we repeat the words he speaks and hears as he enters God's presence. The *Confessions* is not a theoretical account about God that Augustine formulates from a distance, for he knows that God has spoken to him directly and that he must respond to the voice of his creator from the center of his being. The response he makes to what he hears presupposes two kinds of word; on the one hand, it is the intelligible structure of the world that makes his reflections about God and the soul possible; on the other hand, it is an act of speaking in which God reveals himself to Augustine's fragmented heart.

One way to describe the distinction between visual and auditory language is to suggest that visual metaphors are active, intellectual, and a way of bringing the journey toward God to completion, while auditory images are passive, volitional, and expressions of the pilgrimage involved in the quest for unity by the fragmented soul. According to this account, the eye sends out a "visual ray" that touches its object, gives the soul an intellectual apprehension of it, and moves beyond glimpses of God to the capacity to gaze on him with steadfastness and stability.[42] In fact, some commentators suggest that it is tempting to assume when the soul makes the transition from time to eternity, the "eye of the mind" and the "eye of the body" converge and that we see God face to face in an intellectual and aesthetic apprehension of truth that mobilizes the soul and the body as a unified being.[43] The ear waits passively for someone to address it; the soul decides how and whether to make a volitional response to what it hears; and having made a positive response, the soul attends to the voice of God as a preliminary step to seeing his face. In this pivotal moment, hearing the call of God gives way to the vision of God, and faith that leads us toward him is transformed into sight that permits us to stand in his presence.

This way of proceeding suggests that the auditory dimension of Augustine's figurative use of language is preliminary and that he joins his Neoplatonic predecessors in giving pride of place to the "eye of the mind."

However, several important considerations count against this relatively straightforward picture of Augustine's conception of the language of God and the soul. First, though the eye of the soul makes contact with its object, their interplay with one another is mediated by a third term that not only binds the knower and the known together, but also holds them apart. The will connects and disconnects the eye from its object, driving a volitional element of Augustine's journey into the heart of its intellectual dimension. In addition, the brightness of the light he encounters sometimes overwhelms the eye of the mind that seeks to make contact with it. When this occurs, the pervasive discontinuity between God and the soul is more important than the visual continuity between them. Second, the will expresses its crucial role, not only by permitting us to glimpse and gaze on God, but also by transforming the vision of God into the love of God. In this special case, seeing issues in contemplation; and contemplation produces love that brings our knowledge of God to completion in a fashion that transcends intellectual comprehension. Third, though seeing and hearing are separated in finite contexts, they converge and interpenetrate in the journey toward God. On such occasions, the pilgrim hears and sees voices, just as the Light and the Word are dual aspects of the essence of God. Finally, metaphors of vision point toward a continuity between God and the soul, while analogies of hearing point toward an irreducible discontinuity between them. Even in the vision of God, unity is not identity, but is the richer community of similarity, likeness, and analogy in which a fundamental difference of essence remains between God and the soul. In this moment of unity, there is an imagistic correspondence between the soul and God that brings visual and auditory elements together and that permits the finite being to become a picture of both the word and the light that come from God. When this correspondence occurs, the knowledge of God that fulfills our intellect, and the love of God that fulfills our will, become the praise of God that fulfills our being. In this moment, the intellectual and volitional dimensions of the encounters between God and the soul express themselves as an auditory phenomenon, in which the voice of the soul unites with the voice of the heart in a song of praise that never ends.

PROBLEMS OF ACCESS TO THE TEXT

At this juncture, several important problems about Augustine's enterprise require special consideration. The first concerns the attitudes of typical readers to Augustine's encounters with God; the second relates to the historical reliability of the text; the third pertains to the truth of what Augustine has written; and the fourth focuses on the relevance of the *Confessions* to the postmodern predicament. Let us consider each of these issues in turn.

The most important thing to say about our initial attitude toward the text is that we are perhaps too close to what Augustine has written or too far away from it. On the one hand, we have heard his story before and believe we understand it without further reflection; on the other hand, his problems are unfamiliar or offensive, turning us away from them toward other questions that seem to be more pressing or congenial. As a consequence, a radical opposition emerges between positive and negative attitudes in almost any audience he addresses. When we read the *Confessions* for the first time, read it again because we know that it has an indispensable place in the Western tradition, or return to it with philosophical and theological maturity, it either arouses or irritates us by bringing us face to face with the inescapable relation between God and the soul.

Augustine deals with this problem by finding a middle ground between the divine and human realms and by speaking from it. In the process, he challenges his readers to find a place of their own between pious fascination and intellectual antagonism. The writer of the *Confessions* speaks in the first person singular; he does not simply talk about God, but addresses him directly; and when he speaks about his three encounters with God, he asks us not only to understand what he means, but also to feel what he feels. Augustine also encourages his readers to move back and forth between the immediacy of his experience and his attempts to describe it as a series of intelligible stages, making it possible for us to participate in the journey he undertakes at both the experiential and reflective levels.

The second question we should examine is the problem of the historical value of the *Confessions*. Though this question has been debated for decades and the results have been inconclusive, the fundamental issue is clear: during the six months after his conversion to Christianity, Augustine writes four dialogues that scarcely mention his conversion, saying only that he has decided to throw himself into the welcoming arms of philosophy.[44] In addition, in a letter to Nebridius he mentions a conversion to philosophy and continence, but does not refer to his Christian conversion explicitly.[45] Three of these dialogues are dialectical exercises designed to introduce young interlocutors to philosophy, and the tone of the dialogues and of the letter to his friend are utterly devoid of the

passion that precedes the transformation of his life. When we add that
Augustine writes the *Confessions* many years after the fact, it is not difficult
to understand why historians have doubted his memory or veracity. The
evidence from documents written soon after his conversion seems to
contradict Augustine's later recollections in the *Confessions*, making it easy
to conclude with Harnack, Alfaric, and others that Augustine is recon-
structing his past or lying about it for prudential purposes.[46]

The most obvious response to this indictment is to emphasize the fact
that Augustine is not a "scientific" historian, but a rhetorician and a story-
teller, living and writing in the oral culture of fourth- and fifth-century
North Africa. Among other things, this means that he does not share the
nineteenth-century historicist's conception of an autobiography. According
to this conception, the opposition between fact and fiction is absolute; and
the historian's task is to look for a connection between propositions and
states of affairs to which they correspond. When it is conducted in these
terms, the debate about Augustine's veracity becomes a confrontation between those who believe this correspondence obtains in the case of the
Confessions and those who claim that the more abstract and theoretical
character of his writings soon after his conversion makes this doubtful.

Whatever else can be said about it, we should not expect this problem
to be illuminated on the basis of historicist assumptions: Augustine's task
is not to produce a scientifically accurate account of his experience, but to
allow memory, forgetfulness, reconstruction, and providence to interplay
with one another to forge the story of a unified life. In this respect, he is
closer to postmodern approaches to the problem of historical narration
than to the majority of nineteenth- and twentieth-century commentators
on his text. On the other hand, Augustine's sensitivity to the eternal
dimension of experience and his dependence on the providence of God
sets him apart from contemporary thinkers, who often attempt to reduce
the past to an interpretive construction. Though Augustine does not seek
to establish a correspondence between statements and states of affairs, he
does express a willingness to stand before God as the standard by which
his thoughts and actions are measured. Living an authentic life in the
light of the truth that flows from God, surrendering one's will to the voice
of God, and bringing one's intellect, will, and being into correspondence
with the nature of God reflect the heart of Augustine's enterprise.

Both the psychology and the rhetoric of the Cassiciacum dialogues
and the letter to Nebridius are compatible with a dramatic conversion to
Christianity six months earlier. After his conversion, one should expect
Augustine to become calmer and to turn the philosophical side of himself

toward dialectical problems. Even in the *Confessions* he tells us that he experiences perfect peace immediately after his conversion (8.12.30). The nature of his interlocutors during this brief period of retirement also makes the abstract theoretical character of the Cassiciacum dialogues appropriate. In these texts, Augustine is addressing sixteen-year-old boys who need theoretical training rather than an extended account of a dramatic conversion. In addition, Augustine's friend, Nebridius, is a rigorous analytical thinker with whom he discusses the most abstract philosophical and theological questions; and those to whom he dedicates the dialogues are Neoplatonists who have not yet become Christians. Thus, we should expect the rhetorician who has abandoned his chair of lies, but who has remained sensitive to the power of a nuanced way of speaking, to emphasize the philosophical rather than the religious side of his conversion in what he says to them.

More fundamentally, it is doubtful whether Augustine understands what occurs in the garden until several years after the fact. Episodes that transform one's life should not be reduced to their least common denominator. Indeed, they are often so rich that the reflection of a lifetime is necessary to comprehend them. One of the most important lessons Augustine can teach us is that truth in the richest sense becomes accessible only when we return again and again to the moments that give space and time eternal significance. Speaking in a different situation, but to the same kind of audience, C. S. Lewis makes a similar point when he entitles his autobiography, *Surprised by Joy*. As he defines the term, "joy is an unsatisfied desire that is more desirable than any other satisfaction."[47] If this is so, the experiences that occasion it and the truth to which it points must be embraced as epiphanies to which we must return, rather than as episodes that can be captured in a finite set of propositions.

When we turn to the problem of the truth of what Augustine has written, we find a delicate interplay between memory, reconstruction, and the vertical dimension of experience that sustains his encounters with God. The episodes that Augustine recounts presuppose the power of his memory to recover the incidents that he has experienced. To this extent, his book is a recollection of previous events rather than a reconstruction of them and purports to be true in a relatively conventional sense. On the other hand, Augustine describes only some of the circumstances of his life, restricts himself to crucial episodes, and builds his story with such rhetorical power that the result is an account of a unified life. In this respect, the *Confessions* is a reconstruction rather than a recollection.

It is also important to notice that the events Augustine describes are not merely episodic. Rather, they are what they are and mean what they mean because they emerge from a divine ground; and the providential hand of God is in the background, weaving the stages of his life into a pattern. The relations among recollection, reconstruction, and the activity of God are interwoven in the text; the receptive and creative powers of the soul point to a ground that gives them ultimate significance; and the dimension of depth that lies beyond history and interpretation binds them together and holds them apart. When this occurs, God discloses himself to the rational agents he creates, demands an authentic response from those who become aware of his presence, and points to the possibility of a truthful relationship with his creatures within the vertical place his creation of the world establishes. In this sacred space, truth as disclosure illuminates the intellect, truth as authentic existence mobilizes the will, and truth as correspondence brings the will and the intellect together into an imagistic relation with God.

Within this context, our final problem is to understand how a contemporary reader can gain access to a text saturated in the thought forms of the late Roman Empire. It is easy to assume that the problems Augustine discusses are unfruitful ways of engaging in philosophical reflection; for whatever else may be said about the contemporary situation, it is clear that God and the soul no longer establish the context in which most of us live. Language is the new horizon for philosophical inquiry, and most philosophers have turned away from the problem of God and the soul toward the world reconstrued as a text. Though this "text" calls for interpretation, it is more a construction than a discovery; and it can be deconstructed only because an act of construction generates it.

If the world is a text, it is not a book written by someone who exercises authorial control over it; nor is it a book to be deciphered by anyone who can expect to encompass it. The shift toward language presupposes that the autonomous self of modern philosophy has been decentered, that the text with which we are confronted is as much absent as present, and that the meaning we can extract from the *Confessions* is not grounded by an interplay between signifier and signified that would give our approach to Augustine's intentions semantical stability. As a consequence, any contemporary approach to the *Confessions* faces a cluster of difficult questions: "How can we interpret a text of which neither the author nor the reader is the master?" "How can we acknowledge the fact that the text hides as much as it reveals?" "And how can we appraise Augustine's preoccupation with God and the soul without presupposing that what he says depends upon a referential connection between signified and signifier that anchors his enterprise?"

A careful reading of the *Confessions* points to several significant features about Augustine's use of language that permit him to answer these questions, and by doing so, to address contemporary readers. First, he uses language to address his readers directly, speaking from his own fragmentation to ours and acknowledging that neither he nor his readers can ever be in complete control of what we say or do. Second, his text is saturated with figurative discourse because he knows that both God and the soul are always present and absent, forcing him to stretch language to the breaking point to convey hints and suggestions about their meaning and proper relationship. Finally, he uses allegorical interpretation as a way of indicating that even God and the City that he is constructing never anchor our lives univocally. Instead, they open us up to the radical otherness of what will always lie beyond us, point to the infinite richness of our origins, and resist reduction to static contents of consciousness that would be incompatible with the ecstatic dimension of experience and reflection on which Augustine's enterprise depends.

As we approach the *Confessions*, we can understand Augustine's language from a descriptive point of view, watching his drama unfold before us as if we were spectators. Commentators often deal with the *Confessions* in this way, placing the text in quotation marks and insisting on preserving a proper measure of theoretical detachment. This is appropriate in a scholarly analysis of the book, for a bracketing device is necessary if we are to consider Augustine's way of understanding God and the soul as one approach among others. However, the author of the *Confessions* writes without quotation marks, not simply because Latin does not have such a device, but because his language resonates with figurative and performative richness. Augustine does not give us a theory about God, but God himself; he does not provide a theoretical account of the soul, but points to its need for deliverance; and he does not provide a systematic account of the relation between God and soul, but gives us a linguistic pathway that permits us to approach it only through figurative discourse. The most serious question about the text is the proper relation between the scholarly discussion of Augustine's intentions and their figurative and performative dimensions.

We might choose to maintain our academic distance, discussing the book in merely abstract terms. However, the quotation marks we place around the text might drop away, asking us to face the philosophical and religious implications of Augustine's life and thought directly. This is the existential and reflective risk one must take in any serious effort to study the *Confessions*. Since Augustine's deepest problem is not cognitive, but personal, a merely theoretical response to his fragmented condition is inappropriate. Our central questions become: "What power can make the quotation marks fall away, and what will allow us to respond to Augustine's journey as active participants?" Adequate answers can be found only if God speaks again in the words through which he speaks to Augustine, shattering our attempts to control our destiny, hiding in the moments in which he reveals himself, and challenging us to turn away from attempts to capture what is ultimate by using language as a tool to reduce it to a stable content of consciousness.

I agree with Kenneth Burke's suggestion that language is the key to the *Confessions*. However, Burke is wrong when he insists that we can leave Augustine's language about God in quotation marks and that we can approach it from a rhetorical point of view that ignores the existential claims it makes on us.[48] Since the most persuasive aspect of the text is its evocative and performative dimensions, my book does not focus simply on the typically philosophical aspects of Augustine's undertaking, but weaves experience, reflection, and evocative discourse together in an account of the relation between God and the soul that can never be frozen into a cluster of doctrines. Augustine breaks beyond the web of words to give us access to the presence and absence of God; and I will try to show how he does this, not only by discussing perennial theological and philosophical problems, but also by interpreting the *Confessions* in an Augustinian spirit.

As this book unfolds, I shall express some historical opinions, examine the philosophical and theological framework Augustine uses to unify his discourse, point to the linguistic richness of the text, and comment on the nuances of particular lines, words, and phrases that are central to Augustine's intentions. However, my primary task is to develop an account of the language of God and the soul that explains the richness and originality of Augustine's Christian metaphysics. In attempting to do this, I am more interested in what Augustine is becoming than in the historical and philosophical sources that influence him and more concerned with what is original in his thinking than with what is derivative. My goal is to develop an Augustinian metaphysics that is adequate to creation, the fall, conversion, and fulfillment; and I want my work to be judged by the extent to which it permits us to embrace the richness of the text as an existential, rhetorical, philosophical, and theological document.

1

The Philosophical Conversion (Book VII)

In Book VII of the *Confessions*, Augustine focuses his attention on the concept of God and considers his need for a mediator. In between, he struggles with the problem of evil and finds the pathway that leads to his intellectual conversion. Though the young philosopher has freed himself from dualism and has become convinced that God is incorruptible, he is still unable to conceive of a spiritual substance or to speak about God except as a being extended in space. Yet after he reads certain books of the Platonists, a vision of God enables him to overcome these problems,[1] permits him to make a constructive response to the problem of evil, and helps him understand why he needs a mediator between God and the soul.

The Neoplatonic vision in which Augustine participates is both an existential and an intellectual episode. From an existential point of view, it allows him to climb a Neoplatonic ladder from the visible to the invisible, see an unchangeable light, respond when God calls out to him from afar, and catch a glimpse of a spiritual substance that stands over against him. From an intellectual perspective, this same experience helps him understand why a spiritual substance cannot be conceived in spatiotemporal terms, teaches him that figurative discourse is necessary for making access to it, convinces him that the evil he fears is not a substance, and shows him that corruption is both a privation of the good and a perversion of the will. In this chapter, we begin with the problem of framing an adequate concept of God and turn to Augustine's struggles with the problem of evil. Then we analyze the Neoplatonic vision and consider why this experience makes it necessary for him to raise the problem of the incarnation.

THE CONCEPT OF GOD (7.1.1–7.2.3)

From a temporal point of view, Augustine is now passing into youthful maturity. According to the Roman conception of the life cycle, this means that he is emerging from a lengthy period of adolescence and moving into the fourth stage of life, which occurs between the ages of thirty and forty.[2] When he is a boy, time passes through Augustine as if he were an empty container; after the death of his closest friend, his temporal experience moves back and forth between events that are dispersed, but which he binds together by associating them with one another (4.6.11); eventually, time heals his wounds, but begins to slip away when he postpones his conversion (4.8.13); and only as he stands at the threshold of maturity does he move toward an ecstatic concept of temporality that stretches beyond itself toward the dynamic presence of God (7.1.1). This ecstatic concept of time, which Augustine develops in Book XI, begins to play a crucial experiential role for the first time in the account of his philosophical conversion.

Since he first begins to seek wisdom, Augustine knows that God does not have the form of a human body; but as a fallen creature trying to think about what transcends him infinitely, he does not know what else to believe about God except that he is incorruptible, inviolable, and immutable. Without knowing either how or why, he can see that the corruptible is inferior to the incorruptible, that the inviolable is superior to its opposite, and that the unchangeable is better than the changeable (7.1.1). Knowledge of this kind presupposes the work of a divine teacher,[3] whose existence Augustine has not yet acknowledged, but an understanding of whom will develop when he constructs the philosophical and theological framework that makes his intellectual and Christian conversions possible.

The distinctions between corruptibility and incorruptibility and between violability and inviolability generate moral and metaphysical polarities, where the first points to a contrast between what can and cannot degenerate, while the second points to an opposition between what can and cannot resist encroachment. By contrast, the superiority of what is unchangeable to what is changeable seems to be exclusively metaphysical, where the unchangeability of God presupposes a static conception of eternity and the changeability of creatures points to the vicissitudes of time. The first two polarities can be allowed to stand without further elaboration, but the third requires clarification if we are not to be misled about Augustine's philosophical intentions.

The distinction between the changeable and the unchangeable, and the corresponding contrast between time and eternity, point in two directions.

On the one hand, immutability sometimes means impassability; when this is so, the term suggests that what is immutable is perfect, where any change would be a change for the worse. In this case, to say that God is immutable would be to claim that he is eternal rather than temporal, where eternity not only implies impassability, but seems to imply a lack of internal dynamism as well. However, it is important to notice that immutability is compatible with dynamic interaction, where what is immutable has internal dimensions that interplay with one another in unexpected and unpredictable ways. In this case, to say that God is immutable is to claim that the Godhead never changes, but that the persons of the Trinity interact in spontaneous ways that express the most fundamental meaning of the love of God. Augustine uses the concept of immutability in both ways (11.7.9,13.5.6), and we can understand the concept of a spiritual substance only if we take both interpretations into account.

Augustine does not draw these distinctions explicitly at this stage of his reflections, but turns instead in an existential direction, crying out against phantasms and trying to brush away the "unclean images" that swarm around his mind (7.1.1). False images interfere with his capacity to understand the concept of God, leading him away from an adequate conception of God in an exclusively materialistic direction. Yet as he attempts to rid himself of phantasms, they are scarcely scattered before they gather again, fluttering against his face and clouding his vision (7.1.1).

Even though he knows that God does not have a human shape when he begins his quest for wisdom, Augustine is still distracted by phantasms and imagines that God is a body extended in space. The former Manichaean believes that this incorruptible, inviolable, and immutable being is either infused in the world or diffused outside it through the infinite space that surrounds it; for he is convinced that what is not in space is absolutely nothing and is even more insubstantial than the spacious nothingness of empty space (7.1.1). Once more we find that Augustine's relation to God exhibits a spatial dimension; but more fundamentally, we sense his horror in the face of absolute nonbeing. On this occasion, the only thing that prevents him from toppling into it is an inadequate concept of God, according to which the one he worships is an infinitely extended body diffused throughout a spatial medium.

The threat of nonbeing not only implicates God, but also entangles the soul; for as we have noticed repeatedly, God and the soul are related closely in Augustine's thinking. Just as he conceives of God as a body extended in space, so he conceives of himself as nothing but a body that occupies a determinate spatiotemporal region (7.1.2). Otherwise, he would have been forced to conceive of himself as absolutely nothing, facing the abyss of absolute nonbeing, not only in the case of God, but also in relation to himself.

Augustine does not understand that the act of thinking that gives him access to material objects is not itself material in the same sense (7.2.2). Yet he is correct in believing that thinking is a measurable activity, even if this belief eventually requires him to extend the concept of measurement beyond the physicalistic framework in which it is usually employed. This will be important when we turn to Augustine's discussion of the nature of time; for since he believes that the past, the present, and the future presuppose acts of thinking, measuring time will make it necessary for him to "measure" the mind in an appropriately analogical sense of the term (11.28.37). This will force him, in turn, to drive figurative discourse into the heart of metaphysics, not simply as a rhetorical embellishment, but as a necessary way of expressing his most important philosophical insights.

Before Augustine learns to speak the figurative language that will permit him to make philosophical progress, he imagines that his creator is a corporeal substance stretching out through infinite space, penetrating the mass of the world, and reaching out beyond it in all directions. As a result, he believes that the earth contains God, that the heavens contain him, and that he is present in everything else, where God, who is not limited at all, limits every finite being. This leads him to compare God with light rays that penetrate everything and fill it entirely, permitting all things to receive its presence without being restricted to a particular place (7.1.2).[4]

Until it is made possible by a Neoplatonic vision and until the fires of philosophical reflection refine it, this step toward the light is impeded by Augustine's tendency to transform spiritual entities into evanescent phantasms. Indeed, the young philosopher is unable to conceive of a spiritual substance until he encounters God, where only the *reality* of what he sees can convince him of its *possibility*. Truth is prior to meaning for Augustine; and for this reason, forging an adequate concept of God depends on experiencing his reality rather than the other way about.[5]

Augustine is reluctant to abandon thinking about God as a material substance; for as the Manichaeans understand so clearly, materiality gives solidity to substance and appears to provide a stable foundation for a metaphysical system. A literal definition of the concept of substance implies that it is a stable foundation standing underneath an entity; and it is this implication that makes it so difficult for Augustine to reject his Manichaean heritage intellectually, even after he has repudiated it volitionally. As his reflections unfold, the discovery of the importance of figurative discourse will enable him to move away from philosophical literalism, and from the dyadic way of thinking that undergirds it, to a new way of thinking that gives him access to the concept of a spiritual substance. According to this way of understanding the concept in question, a spiritual substance not only lies beyond dualism, but can only be expressed in a metaphor of infinite richness. However, at this stage of his life, Augustine is searching for stability; and he cannot understand how God construed as an immaterial entity can provide it.[6]

Despite the influence that the concept of material substance continues to exercise on him, Augustine remembers an important objection against the Manichaeans that comes from his friend, Nebridius, when they are still in Carthage several years before. At this relatively early stage of their involvement with the sect, Nebridius asks, " 'What would that unknown nation of darkness, which the Manichees are wont to postulate as a hostile mass, have done if [God] had refused to contend with it?' " (7.2.3). Nebridius concludes that if the power of evil could hurt him, he would be corruptible; but if this power were harmless, there would be no reason for him to fight. In either case, the Manichaeans are mistaken in claiming that the world is a battleground between Good and Evil in which goodness is defined in relation to its opposite (7.2.3).

Because of the impact of Academic Skepticism, Augustine has already turned away from Manichaean dualism through an act of the will; but now he sees the force of an argument that refutes it. If God is incorruptible, the story of a battle that embroils him with the power of evil is false; and if he is corruptible, this same story is false because it would entail that he would not be God at all. In either case, Manichaeism can be rejected, not only volitionally, but intellectually as well. As a consequence, the last vestige of Augustine's commitment to the Manichaean solution to the problem of evil collapses; and he moves beyond it to a new way of understanding the concept of God, the problem of evil, and the language appropriate to them.

THE PROBLEM OF EVIL (7.3.4–7.8.12)

Augustine begins his discussion of the problem of evil, not by focusing on it as an autonomous theoretical issue, but by placing it within the context of creation *ex nihilo*, by remembering the nature of God, and by pointing to a practical implication of the question that he is about to consider. Beginning with creation *ex nihilo*, he claims that God creates not only our *souls*, but also our *bodies*, and not only our souls and our bodies, but also our *beings* as composite entities embedded in the natural order (7.3.4). These claims are important because they imply that however central the problem of God and the soul may be, the soul and the body are united and have a natural place within the world as a product of God's creative act. In discussing the pivotal experiences that bring Augustine's journey toward God to completion, we must never forget this; for the transformation of the soul is connected intimately with the reorientation of the body and with a way of speaking that points beyond them to the ground of their existence. According to this way of reading Augustine, the relation between the soul and the body is depicted most adequately by figurative discourse that binds them together and holds them apart, rather than by metaphysical categories that construe them as separate substances that are somehow connected and separated from one another.

The metaphysical way of understanding Augustine's concept of the relation between the soul and the body construes the soul as a substance, the body as a substance, and the unity of the soul and the body as a substance as well.[7] According to this view, human beings are composites; the soul is the higher part of the composite; the soul uses the body as an instrument; and the soul is to be identified with the "true man." There can be no doubt that Augustine sometimes speaks this way, giving encouragement to those who wish to emphasize the dualistic dimension of his thinking.[8]

However, it is important to notice that he often speaks about the relation between the soul and the body in a radically different way. According to this way of speaking, the human being is to be understood rhetorically by using figurative discourse rather than by understanding it as a whole made up of parts (7.1.2). When Augustine speaks in this way, the person is identified with the soul, with the body, and with the soul and the body taken together, where in each case, we are what we are in different senses of "is." In addition, metaphors bind the soul and the body together; analogies hold them apart; and the interplay between these ways of speaking undergird the richly evocative use of language in which Augustine engages as he speaks about the relation between God and the soul.

We will return to Augustine's solution to the problem of the soul and the body in a later chapter; but for the moment, we must turn to his discussion of the problem of evil in relation to the concept of God and with reference to one of its most important practical implications. We have noticed already that by contrast with the entities that come to be and pass away, Augustine conceives of God as incorruptible, inviolable, and immutable; but against the background of this stable set of beliefs, he does not have an explicit and orderly knowledge of the cause of evil. Nevertheless, he knows that whatever its cause, his understanding of it must not entail that God is mutable, lest in trying to solve the problem of evil, he become evil himself by falling into the sin of presumption. The Manichaeans are mistaken in understanding evil as an independent principle that challenges the sovereignty of God, and their malice surfaces when they insist that the creator is subject to the encroachments of evil rather than admitting that they are responsible for the evil in their own actions. Thus, Augustine focuses on the problem of evil, recognizing that it is not an isolated theoretical problem, but a problem that has a bearing on his concept of the nature of God and that points to an existential predicament into which he must not fall as he attempts to deal with the perplexing issues it raises (7.3.4).

The philosopher takes a crucial step in struggling with the problem of evil when he remembers what he has often heard about the freedom of the will. According to this approach to the problem, an act of the will that originates within the open space between good and evil is the cause of evil doing; and the judgment of God in response to our negative volition is the cause of the suffering we experience as a result of our own actions. However, Augustine does not understand what he has heard about freedom; he cannot "draw the eye of his mind" out of the spiritual chasm into which he has fallen; and his failure to do so plunges him down again and again into an existential and theoretical abyss that continues to separate him from the light that flows from God (7.3.5).

Despite his failure to grasp the connection between the problem of evil and the freedom of the will, a single conviction lifts Augustine toward the light: he knows that he has a will just as clearly as he knows that he is alive and that when he wills or is unwilling to do something, it is he alone who is either willing or unwilling (7.3.5). As a consequence, he begins to understand that he is not a spectator observing the conflict between two competing principles within his soul, but a moral agent who is responsible for his own actions. He also concludes that what he does against his will is something done to him rather than something he does himself. This means that what he does against his better judgment is not his fault, but his punishment, and that because this punishment comes from God, it is just (7.3.5). Later Augustine will understand that even what he does against his will is an act for which he is responsible, not simply because he is the agent of the action, but because the acquisition of the habits to which he succumbs in such cases are his own responsibility (8.5.10–11). However, even at this preliminary stage of his reflections, facing the question of moral responsibility clears the ground for him to make progress in dealing with the theoretical and practical dimensions of the problem before him.

Augustine struggles with these issues, not by solving the problem of evil in a single stroke, but by raising questions about it that continue to perplex him as he tries to turn toward God. These questions reflect the dualistic tendencies that he still exhibits and implicate both God and the devil. If God has created Augustine and his creation is good, why does he sometimes will to do evil rather than good? And if the cause of his evil actions is the devil, who created him; and why does the devil who has been created good fall into evil himself? These persistent questions, and the infinite regress to which they lead, crush Augustine's intellect; but they do not force him to reembrace Manichaean dualism. The adherents of the doctrine he has repudiated prefer profession to confession, and Augustine denounces them for placing the blame for their mistakes on an evil principle that encroaches on God rather than accepting responsibility for their own actions (7.3.5). In doing so, the "Prodigal Son" who has wandered away from his origins is beginning to discover that only by saying, "I am to blame,"[9] will he ever be able to go back home.

Having begun to understand the incorruptibility of God, and having begun to bring himself into an existential correlation with it, Augustine attempts to establish further facts about God's nature to which he can commit himself without reservation. First, he anticipates Anselm by claiming that we cannot conceive anything better than God. Then he reasons that if what is incorruptible is better than what is corruptible, he could conceive something better than God if God were corruptible. On this basis, he claims that the incorruptibility of God follows as a necessary truth from his recognition of the facts that the incorruptible is better than the corruptible and that he is unable to conceive anything greater than God. Finally, he concludes that if he ought to seek God by focusing on what is incorruptible, he ought to seek the source of evil by looking in the opposite direction. This suggests that if God is good because he is incorruptible, evil can be understood by locating the source of corruption (7.4.6).

Augustine attempts to do this by interlacing penetrating comments about the nature of God and about the goodness of creation with equally penetrating questions about the origin of evil. First, he claims that God is good and that he surpasses everything he creates. Then he insists that because God is good, the finite products of God's creative act are good as well. Finally, he asks a series of questions that express the problem of evil more acutely than he has ever formulated it before:

Where then is evil, and whence and by what means has it crept in here? What is its root, and what is its seed? Or has it no being whatsoever? Why then do we fear and shun what does not exist? If we fear it without cause, that very fear is evil. By it our stricken hearts are goaded and tortured, and that evil is all the more serious in so far as what we fear does not exist, and still we are fearful of it. Therefore, either there is an evil that we fear, or the fact that we fear is itself an evil. Whence, therefore, is evil, since God the good has made all things good? (7.5.7)

Augustine's questions about the root and the seed of evil suggest that he is attempting to plunge into the heart of the problem and trace it back to its origins. Unfortunately, the attempt to do this encounters a seemingly insurmountable obstacle that expresses itself in the possibility that evil has no being at all. If this proves to be the case, the problem of evil would lead us to the problem of absolute nonbeing, where this problem is not to be solved theoretically, but to confronted experientially as a threat to our existence. Nevertheless, Augustine makes progress in answering his questions by noticing that if we fear what has no being at all, the fear itself is evil (7.5.7). This is an advance in the discussion because it shifts his attention away from the search for a substance and reinforces his earlier recognition that the orientation of the soul is the crucial element in the attempt to deal with the problem of evil. Augustine begins to see what he will elaborate later: the fear of what is *not*, and the existential disorientation it expresses, is evil, not because it is a substance, but because it points to a distinctive way of living that is *oriented away* from the ground of its existence.

Having considered the possibility that matter as an independently existing principle is the source of evil, and having rejected this view because it is incompatible with God's omnipotence, Augustine shifts abruptly from the theoretical to the existential level, overwhelmed by the fear of death and by the fear that he will never find the truth about the issue with which he is struggling (7.5.7). The fear of dying that emerges when he faces the death of his closest friend (4.6.11) and that he regards as the only obstacle that prevents him from becoming an Epicurean (6.16.26) continues to haunt him, this time as a way of bringing his attempt to understand the problem of evil to an impasse. Yet in spite of his fear of death, Augustine insists that faith in Christ that is to be found in the Catholic Church is "firmly fixed within [his] heart," and that though he is unformed and wavers on many points of doctrine, he not only does not turn away from it, but drinks more of it in day after day (7.5.7).

Augustine's reference to faith in Christ is important because it is the foundation of attempts to demonstrate that he is not only a catechumen of the Catholic Church, but that he has already become a Christian before he reads the books of the Platonists[10] and participates in the ascent toward God to be considered in the next section of this chapter. If this is so, it is reasonable to conclude that he reads these books from a Christian point of view, and that Neoplatonism is subordinated to Christianity in the three pivotal episodes that bring his journey toward God to an experiential culmination.[11] Before we try to reach a conclusion about these issues, let us reconsider the stages of Augustine's religious and philosophical development in which his relation to Christianity is a crucial factor.

The first significant stage is the occasion when Augustine begs his mother for baptism, for it suggests that the name of Christ is important to him and his mother even when he is a child (1.11.17). This suggestion is confirmed by the fact that after Augustine reads Cicero's exhortation to embrace philosophy, he is unable to commit himself to it completely because the name of Christ that he has drunk in "with [his] mother's milk" is not in it (3.4.8). After he decides to abandon the Manichaeans some eleven years later because he believes that the philosophers are superior to them in giving an account of the order of nature, he refuses to commit the cure of his soul to them because they lack "the saving name of Christ" (5.14.25). As a consequence, he decides to continue as a catechumen of the Catholic Church until something certain enlightens him.

Though all of these stages of Augustine's development are important, none of them is sufficient to make him a Christian. This becomes evident when we consider his reaction to the preaching of Ambrose soon after he refers to himself as a catechumen of the Church. On this occasion, he says that though he is in the process of being refuted and converted, he refuses to be cured and resists the healing hand of God, who has applied the remedies of faith to the diseases of the world (6.4.6). The obvious conclusion to be drawn from this passage is that the catechumen is in the process of becoming a Christian, but that this process has not been completed. Augustine also tells us that from this time forward, he prefers Catholic teaching (6.5.7). However, in the light of his refusal to be cured, this does not mean that he has become a Christian, but only that he believes certain Christian doctrines.

In listing these doctrines, the catechumen says that he believes that God exists and that God cares for us. However, he also tells us that he does not know what should be thought about God's substantial being, or which way leads up to God or back to him. Thus, even though the name of Christ continues to be an important element in his thinking, he is not yet aware of the fact that Christ is the pathway that leads to God (6.5.8). On the other hand, he commits himself to the authority of Scripture, claiming that God would have never given it such authority throughout the world unless he had wished for us to believe in and seek him within this context (6.5.8). In doing so, he takes a step toward the living Word of God to which he will respond in the garden in Milan by acknowledging the written Word that will give him access to it. Yet even so, Augustine says that he is still wretched, indicates that he has not yet been converted, tells us that his "very vitals" are torn apart by care, and acknowledges the fact that pride is the fundamental problem that separates him from God (6.6.10).

Augustine laments the fact that eleven years after he had been inspired by Cicero's book to seek wisdom, he is still unable to find it. Though the doctrines of the Church no longer seem to be absurd to him, and though he decides to turn toward the authority of the Church until he finds the truth he has been seeking for so long, he is unwilling "to abandon worldly hopes and devote [himself] wholly to seeking God and a life of happiness." Thus, he remains a catechumen who has not yet become a Christian, still vacillating and delaying "to be converted to the Lord" (6.11.19).

The tenuous state in which Augustine remains at this juncture is reflected in the uncertainty that he expresses at the end of Book VI about the ultimate causes of good and evil. There he says that he would have become an Epicurean if he had not believed in a life after death; and even given the assumption that the soul is immortal, he wonders why a life of perpetual bodily pleasure would not make him happy. In doing so, Augustine indicates once more that he has not become a Christian; and he confirms this conclusion by saying that his soul turns on its "back and sides and belly," unable to find rest until it finds rest in God (6.16.26).

At the midpoint of his discussion of the problem of evil in Book VII, Augustine returns to the turmoil with which Book VI concludes by claiming that he is overburdened with cares that spring from the fear of death and from a fear of not finding the truth about the problem of evil (7.5.7). However, in this same context, he writes the puzzling passage about his faith in Christ that has prompted us to retrace some of the earlier stages of his religious and philosophical development. Let me quote the crucial passage once more, this time in its entirety:

Yet the faith of your Christ, our Lord and Savior, the faith that is in the Catholic Church, was firmly fixed within my heart. In many ways I was yet unformed and wavered from the rule of doctrine. But my mind did not depart from it, nay, rather, from day to day it drank in more and more of it. (7.5.7)

The passage before us is important because it points to two ways of understanding Augustine's relation to Christianity. On the one hand, we might embrace the view that in the brief period between the end of book VI and the middle of Book VII, Augustine becomes a Christian without indicating either how or why this occurs. On the other hand, we might be convinced that his experience as a catechumen of the Catholic Church has given him sufficient time to reach the conclusion that Christ is the pathway to God, even though he has not yet decided to embrace it. I believe that the weight of the evidence points toward the second of these two conclusions.

To see why this is so, it is important to distinguish three kinds of commitment that characterize Augustine's relation to Christianity. First, when he reaffirms his status as a catechumen of the Catholic Church, he puts himself on an institutional pathway that leads eventually to faith in Christ. Let us call this first kind of relation to Christianity *institutional commitment*. Second, when he claims that he prefers Christian doctrine, that the faith of Christ is fixed firmly in his heart, and that he drinks in more of the Church's doctrine day after day, he begins to move along an intellectual pathway that leads back to God. Let us call this second kind of relation to Christianity *notional commitment*.[12] Finally, when we find that Augustine has no experiential warrant for accepting the religious direction in which he is moving, and when this continues to be the case until his conversion in the garden in Milan, it becomes evident that he has not yet embraced the faith to which he has begun to make an institutional and notional commitment. Let us call this third kind of relation to Christianity *existential commitment*.[13] To say that Augustine has not yet become a Christian is to claim that even though he has decided to pursue an institutional commitment to the Church, and has expressed a notional assent to some of its doctrines, he has not yet made an existential commitment to it.

At this stage of his development, Augustine believes four things that are relevant to his eventual conversion: first, he believes that God exists; second, he believes that God is immutable; third, he believes that God cares for human beings and passes judgment on them; and finally, he is convinced that in Christ and the Bible, God provides a way of salvation that leads to eternal life. Against the stable propositional background, he begins to speak to God from the center of his soul rather than to his friends about the religious and philosophical problems that perplex him

(7.7.11). This suggests that he is finally moving into a private realm of meditation analogous to the one presupposed by Ambrose's silent reading, the one into which he will move when he has the mystical experience that the Platonic books made accessible (7.10.16), the one he embraces when he reads the passage from the book of Romans in the garden in Milan (8.12.29), and the one he will share with his mother during their mystical experience in Ostia (9.10.23–26). In all these cases, there is no public confirmation of what occurs in terms that would satisfy a historian, but a vertical transaction between God and the soul that only those who have experienced something similar can appreciate.

To prepare the way for his resolution of the problem of evil, for his response to Neoplatonism, and for the Neoplatonic vision that he is about to recount, Augustine gives a visual formulation of his existential predicament. "Hordes and heaps" of images rush in on him from every direction; and as he turns away from them to return to himself, they mock him by asking where he is going (7.7.11). Then he formulates his predicament in a graphic metaphor that implicates both his soul and his body: "By my swelling wound I was separated from you, and my bloated face closed up my eyes." Finally, even though he is blind from bloated cheeks, he trusts that God will have mercy on him and reach down to reform his deformities; and he tells us that God arouses him by "inner goads" so he cannot rest until his creator stands before his "inner sight" (7.8.12). The need for inner vision is Augustine's overriding concern at this stage of his development, and it is this fact that makes him so receptive to the teaching of the Neoplatonists.

NEOPLATONISM AND CHRISTIANITY (7.9.13–7.9.15)

Before Augustine gives an account of his intellectual conversion and refers to the Neoplatonic books that make it possible, he draws a radical distinction between pride and humility. In doing so, he points to the eternal dimension of experience, where one's attitude toward God is the most important issue with which he is concerned. At the center of Book VII, God reveals himself to the eye of Augustine's mind; but the author of the *Confessions* insists that God also resists the proud and gives grace to the humble. Thus he tells us that the man who gives him the books of the Platonists is "puffed up" with "pride" and that this attitude stands opposed to the humility expressed when the Word " 'was made flesh, and dwelt among us' " (7.9.13).[14]

The contrast between pride and humility is important because it points to the limitations of Neoplatonism as a way of approaching the relation between God and the soul and calls our attention to the attitude required of those who want to participate in it. However, it is easy to overlook the limitations of Neoplatonism from an Augustinian point of view, and fail to understand the significance of the distinction between pride and humility. In fact, his reading of the books of the Neoplatonists and the intellectual conversion that emerges from it are the foundation for a way of understanding Augustine that overemphasizes the influence of Plotinus on his thinking.

This interpretation reflects the conviction that Augustine had extensive contact with a group of Neoplatonists in Milan long before his conversion to Christianity. According to this view, philosophical and social interaction with Neoplatonic intellectuals predisposes him to approach the distinctive doctrines of the Christian faith from a Neoplatonic point of view. Thus, the temporal and spatial parameters of Augustine's life come into play once again, where his transition toward philosophical maturity is mediated by contact with Neoplatonic philosophers, and where the reflective community in which he participates is saturated with Neoplatonic teaching.[15]

It is not surprising that the view in question has informed so many interpretations of Augustine, for the author of the *Confessions* suggests that Neoplatonism and Christianity share a cluster of important philosophical presuppositions. For example, in the books of the Platonists, he finds the thoughts if not the words expressed in the prologue to the Gospel of John:

"In the beginning was the Word, and the Word was with God, and the Word was God. The same was in the beginning with God. All things were made by him, and without him nothing was made." (7.9.13)[16]

In these books, he also reads that life is to be found in the Word of God, that this life is the light of men, and that though the light shined in the darkness, the darkness did not comprehend it. These latter two remarks come dangerously close to attributing his own doctrine of divine illumination to the Neoplatonists; and if he were not so determined to call our attention to the radical differences between Neoplatonism and Christianity, what Augustine says about the many similarities between them might be enough to convince us that from his perspective, they are virtually identical.

One commentator suggests that the author of the *Confessions* projects certain crucial doctrines of Christianity onto the Neoplatonic tradition. Gilson says that Augustine attributes the doctrine of creation *ex nihilo* to Plotinus and that he believes that the identity of the first and the second persons of the Trinity is a doctrine to be found in Plotinus as well. There is more than one way of insisting that Augustine is a Christian Neoplatonist; and this way of doing so not only acknowledges his participation in a community of Neoplatonists, but also suggests that he misinterprets Neoplatonism along distinctively Christian lines.[17]

The passage that Augustine quotes from the Gospel of John suggests that the relation between the first and the second persons of the Trinity can be correlated with the relation between the One and the Divine Intellect, if not in word, at least in thought. If we accept a sufficiently flexible conception of correlation, there is no reason to reject this view; for it is evident that a formal correspondence obtains between the persons of the Trinity and the Neoplatonic hypostases. However, formal correspondence does not entail material equivalence; and there is no reason to believe that Augustine does not grasp the difference between the identity and difference between the Father and the Divine Word, and the derivative relation between the One and the Divine Intellect in which the Word is derived from the Father by generation. However, the more important question is whether he knows the difference between emanation and creation *ex nihilo* when he writes the *Confessions*, leading us to ask about the plausibility of the claim that he projects the doctrine of creation onto the writings of the Neoplatonists.

Neoplatonists and Christians agree that God makes the world in a suitably broad sense of the term, but this scarcely entitles us to assume that Augustine believes that the way this occurs is identical in the two cases. For example, when he claims in Book XII that God creates prime matter *ex nihilo*, he takes an explicit stand against Plotinus, suggesting that he has read the *Enneads* carefully enough to know the difference between emanation from the One and creation from nothingness (7.9.13). Throughout the *Confessions*, Augustine gives adequate evidence for believing that he understands the doctrine of creation *ex nihilo* and that he grasps the distinction between creation and emanation as cosmological alternatives.

Augustine's primary purpose in drawing our attention to the parallels between Neoplatonism and Christianity is not to blur the distinctions between them, but to lay the groundwork for appreciating their differences. The first of these differences is expressed in the claim that the Word of God came unto his own, but his own did not receive him; and it is expressed more forcefully in the assertion that as many as received him, " 'to them he gave power to be made the sons of God, to them that believe in his name' " (7.9.13).[18] In both cases, the incarnational focus of Christianity sets it apart from Neoplatonism; and the acknowledgment of its centrality in Augustine's enterprise places a considerable strain on the suggestion that he confuses the doctrines of the Neoplatonists with the teachings of the Bible in his attempt to appropriate Neoplatonism.

The quotations to which we have referred launch a series of contrasts between the aspects of Christianity Neoplatonism anticipates and the parts it does not. The Neoplatonists know that the Word is the offspring of God, but they do not understand that the Word became flesh and dwelled among us. They also believe that the Word is equal to God in some appropriate sense of identity, but they do not know that he empties himself and takes the form of a servant (7.9.14). In fact, Plotinus never says anything even faintly comparable to the *kenosis* passage from Paul's *Epistle to the Philippians*:

"[He] emptied himself, taking the form of a servant, being made in the likeness of men, and in habit found as a man," and . . . "he humbled himself, becoming obedient unto death, even to the death of the cross. For which cause, God also has exalted him" from the dead, "and has given him a name which is above all names: that in the name of Jesus every knee shall bend down of those that are in heaven, on earth, and under the earth: and that every tongue should confess that the Lord Jesus is in the glory of God the father." (7.9.14)[19]

The incarnation and the humiliation to which this passage refers are crucial elements in Augustine's conversion to Christianity; and it is only by attending to both elements that we will be able to understand his claim in Book VIII that he puts on a new garment called, "Jesus, the Christ." However, this passage is important at this juncture because it allows Augustine to compare the pride of the Neoplatonists with the humility of Christ. The philosophers know that the Word of God is coeternal with the Father, and they understand that human wisdom is achieved by participation in it. Yet they do not realize that " 'Christ died for the ungodly,' " nor do they understand that God did not spare his son, but " 'delivered him up for us all' " (7.9.14).[20] Indeed, it is probable that Augustine has the Neoplatonists in mind when he insists that God hides these things from "the wise and prudent" and that he reveals them only to children (7.9.14).[21]

One of the best ways to point to the difference between the Neoplatonic and Christian dimensions of Augustine's thinking is to note what he does and does not do with Neoplatonism. Augustine's reference to our participation in the Word of God allows him to embrace a Neoplatonic continuum between God and the world and points to the permanent truth in the claim that he is a Christian Neoplatonist.[22] However, his unequivocal commitment to creation *ex nihilo,* and his suggestion that the incarnation, the death, and the resurrection of Christ bridge the chasm between God and the world make it evident that when he writes the *Confessions,* his Christianity takes precedence over his Neoplatonism from both cosmological and soteriological points of view. Indeed, Augustine departs from Neoplatonism in the realization that both creation *ex nihilo* and the redemptive work of Christ are expressions of the grace of God without which the metaphysical chasm between God and the world could neither be generated nor mediated.

By contrasting the wisdom and the prudence of the philosophers with the humility required by Christianity, the great rhetorician attacks the heart of Neoplatonism. According to the Neoplatonist, the two most important attributes of the philosopher are the theoretical and practical wisdom they display; and Augustine has both concepts in mind when he says,

But those men who are raised up on the heights of some toplofty teaching do not hear him as he says, "Learn of me, for I am meek and humble of heart, and you shall find rest to your souls."[23] "Although they know God, they do not glorify him, or give thanks, but become vain in their thoughts, and their foolish heart is darkened; for professing themselves to be wise, they became fools." (7.9.14)[24]

The criticism that Augustine levels against the Neoplatonists has both theoretical and practical implications. On the one hand, they do not know that the God they long to see has spoken to them in his son and that he has accommodated himself to the weakness of their intellects. On the other hand, their hearts are darkened because they fail to glorify and thank the creator for permitting the divine word to redeem their fallen wills. The principle defect of the Neoplatonists is their failure to understand that the Word of God addresses both their intellects and their wills, allowing him to speak to the sin that manifests itself in both contexts. This will become especially important in Book VIII, where the problem Augustine faces is both intellectual and volitional, and where the

Neoplatonic vision that we are about to consider is supplemented by his transformation in the garden in Milan.[25]

Despite the limitations of Neoplatonism, Augustine's last word about the philosophical position that makes it possible for him to become a Christian is positive. Though Neoplatonism falls short of Christianity in failing to embrace the incarnation, the death, and the resurrection of Christ, its teaching not only takes him beyond materialism, but also encourages the "eye of his mind" to catch a glimpse of the glory of God and of the immaterial substance he struggles for so long to conceive. The Neoplatonists realize that finite beings are tempted to transform the spiritual substance of God into idols and images; and because they know this, they seek the same "gold" God allows his people to take from Egypt to the Promised Land. When Augustine reads the books of the Neoplatonists, he learns about Egyptian gold, not from a Christian text, but through the natural revelation available to everyone (7.9.15).[26] Thus, it is almost impossible to overestimate the profound impact that the Neoplatonists make on Augustine's philosophical development.[27] The quotations in which he compares their writings with the Bible, and the philosophical concepts in which so much of his writing is saturated indicate this, however careful he may be to call our attention to the differences between Neoplatonism and Christianity.

One of Augustine's deepest philosophical problems is how to unify the power and the structure of the divine word in a single principle; and he finds a way of doing this by embracing the logos of the Neoplatonic tradition. This tradition binds the performative and the intelligible dimensions of the word together; for the Word that emanates from the One is not only an intelligible principle, but also a dynamic source from which finite beings unfold continuously. Neoplatonic emanation is a surrogate for divine creation; its dynamic conception of the Divine Intellect is an important dimension in the background of Augustine's thinking; and the dynamic word to which the Neoplatonic books call his attention makes it possible for him to embrace the Truth he has been seeking for so long.

THE NEOPLATONIC VISION (7.10.16–7.17.23)

Augustine responds to the dynamic word of Neoplatonism in a mystical experience[28] that unfolds in two stages.[29] In connection with the first of these stages, consider one of the most memorable passages in the *Confessions*:

Being thus admonished to return to myself, under [God's] leadership I entered into my inmost being. This I could do, for [God] became my helper. I entered there, and by my soul's eye, such as it was, I saw above that same eye of my soul, above my mind, an unchangeable light. It was not this common light, plain to all flesh, nor a greater light, as it were, of the same kind, as though that light would shine many, many times more bright, and by its great power fill the whole universe. Not such was that light, but different, far different from all other lights. Nor was it above my mind, as oil is above water, or sky above earth. It was above my mind, because it made me, and I was beneath it, because I was made by it. He who knows the truth, knows that light, and he who knows it knows eternity. Love knows it, O eternal truth, and true love, and beloved eternity! You are my God, and I sigh for you day and night! (7.10.16)

In continuing to describe this first stage of his vision, Augustine emphasizes its tenuous nature by claiming that God lifts him up so he can see that there is something to see, though he is not yet fit to see it. He also says that God beats back the weakness of his sight by sending dazzling beams of light on him, causing him to tremble in love and amazement. In this moment, the young philosopher realizes that he is still far away from God, hears God's voice from a distance, and begins to understand that he can draw closer to him only as he matures. Yet as he slips away from the relation that he longs to enter, God cries out to him from afar, "I am who I am"; Augustine hears the voice of God in his heart; there is no room for doubt about God's nature and existence; and the philosopher exclaims, "It would be easier for me to doubt that I live than that there is no truth, which is 'clearly seen, being understood by the things that are made'" (7.10.16).[30]

This stage of Augustine's Neoplatonic vision calls for careful reflection. First, when he turns inward, his vision of the light presupposes a Neoplatonic community; but this spatial context is counterbalanced by the fact that Augustine also participates in a solitary relationship with God that does not implicate this community directly. In doing so, he transcends space and time and encounters God along the vertical axis of experience. Second, Augustine says that the light he sees is not simply different in degree from all other lights, but different in kind; and he elaborates this difference by identifying the light in question with the creator who brings him into existence. This suggests that the light to which he refers is not on a continuum with him, but that it transcends him infinitely, pointing to an infinite chasm between God and the soul. Third, the fact that God lifts him up to see that there is something to see, though he is not yet able to see it, and the fact that the light he glimpses "beats back his feeble sight" suggests that it is not only an intelligible content to which he makes access, but also a principle of illumination and concealment that stands over against him. To the extent that Augustine is a (finite⊥infinite) being in whom the image of God has not been effaced, he has access to unchangeable light; but because he is also a (finite⊤infinite) being, who has fallen away from God,[31] God "speaks" to him from a distance, suggesting that he will be unable to sustain his vision until he is fully developed.

When Augustine sees the light, the language of seeing displaces the language of speaking and hearing, at least momentarily. However, he describes the light that transcends him infinitely in figurative language, suggesting that it cannot be reduced to either mathematical or scientific terms. This suggests that the turn inward and the principle of illumination that makes it intelligible are accessible only in the kind of metaphorical and analogical discourse that Augustine has been using from the outset. Finally, at the end of this state of vision, Augustine returns to auditory metaphors, claiming that God cries out to him from afar, "I am who I am," and suggesting that what he hears is even more important than what he sees when he glimpses the immutable light. In this moment, a hole is blown in the circle of the first stage of his Neoplatonic vision,[32] not only by Augustine's incapacity to contemplate what he glimpses, but also by the voice of God that addresses him from afar. At this crucial juncture, Augustine is not drawing a conclusion from an argument from God's existence. Rather he is responding to what he hears from what exists beyond his soul where the truth that stands over against him can be seen and understood through the things that are made.

The first stage of the Neoplatonic vision is not only an important part of Augustine's intellectual conversion, but also a crucial element in his response to the problem of evil. He does not first solve the problem of evil as a philosophical enigma, and on this basis, catch a glimpse of the light that flows from God. Instead, he locates the problem of evil in the sphere of corruption and incorruptibility, sees that there is something incorruptible to be seen, hears God calling to him from afar, and begins to resolve the problem of evil on the basis of his mystical experience (7.10.16). In doing so, he suggests that finite things are neither wholly real nor wholly unreal: they are real because they come from God, but unreal because they are mutable; they are real because they are created, but unreal because they participate in the relative nonbeing that defines their finitude (7.11.17). This not only leads Augustine to the privation doctrine of evil, but also points beyond it to a solution to the problem of evil in terms of the freedom of the will.

Augustine formulates the doctrine of privation against the backdrop of both the Neoplatonic and the Christian convictions that every finite being is good. In the Neoplatonic tradition, the goodness of finite beings depends on their having a positive place within a chain of being, however high or low they may be in reference to other things. By contrast, the Christian tradition begins with the doctrine of creation *ex nihilo*, where everything God creates is good after its kind. Yet in both traditions, the goodness of finite beings is presupposed when the privation of goodness is introduced as an explanation for the problem of evil.

Augustine considers four levels of existence about which considerations of the relation between good and evil are relevant. First, he maintains that all things are good insofar as they exist, even if they are subject to corruption. In this case, created beings are finite, mutable, and subject to degeneration, even if they never fall away from God (7.12.18). Second, he claims that most finite beings are not only *subject to corruption*, but have also *become corrupt* by turning away from God. The only exceptions to this are spiritual creatures that are subject to degeneration, but do not become corrupt because they cling steadfastly to God. Third, he says that the only being not subject to corruption is supremely good. In this case, he points to God, not only as the upper limit of an ontological continuum, but also as the source that creates it and as the ground that stands outside it altogether (7.12.18). Finally, he argues that if something were not good at all, there would be nothing in it to be corrupted; and if a thing were deprived of goodness altogether, it would not exist at all (7.12.18). In this case, absolute nonbeing stands underneath the ontological continuum as the negative principle toward which corruptible things can fall away.

Let me restate the differences among the four ontological levels Augustine distinguishes in the following way. First, his claim that finite beings are good insofar as they exist suggests that though they are mutable, participate in relative nonbeing, and are subject to corruption, the most important fact about them is that they reflect the goodness of their creator. This means that though most of them exist as this and not that, here and not there, now and not then, mutable beings that can be corrupted are good because they are concrete expressions of the goodness of God.

Second, though finite beings are good because God creates them, and though they are subject to corruption because they are mutable, they become corrupt only when they fall away from God. In such cases, beings that are subject to relative nonbeing make a transition from finitude to fallenness, no longer clinging steadfastly to God, but moving from the created time and space they were intended to enjoy to the fallen spatiotemporal matrix in which they are separated from God. The only exception to this are spiritual creatures who are finite, but do not exist in space and time. In this special case, to cling steadfastly to God is to be oriented toward eternity, and to fall away from him is to plunge into fallen temporality as a creature alienated from God. Third, the only being not subject to corruption is God, the supremely good creator of whatever else exists. In this case, God is the upper limit of the ontological continuum on which every created being has a place; but he is also outside this continuum as the creative source that brings it into existence. Finally, if a being is not good in any way, it is not created; and since to be is to be either a creature or the creator, to not be good is not to be at all. In this case, the "being" in question is the absolute *nihil*, which exists below the ontological continuum, is the abysmal "source" from which God creates the world, and is the absolute absence toward which beings that fall away from God are oriented.

In summary, God stands beyond the ontological continuum as its source; the absolute *nihil* stands underneath it as the abyss; and finite beings stand in between, either as oriented toward God or as separated from him. As the *Confessions* continues to unfold, it remains for Augustine to explain how beings that have fallen away from God by becoming oriented toward the absolute *nihil* can be transformed. In the process, he will indicate how they move from the fallen spatiotemporal matrix into which they have fallen toward the converted and fulfilled spatiotemporal contexts in which they recover their positive relation to the ground of their existence. As he does this, Augustine does not confuse Neoplatonism with Christianity, but adds a distinctively Christian dimension to the Neoplatonic framework that he presupposes.

The truth in the claim that Augustine projects Christian doctrines onto Neoplatonism is not that he conflates the two positions unconsciously, but that he adds dimensions of discontinuity to Neoplatonism that Plotinus never envisages. The first of these dimensions is creation *ex nihilo*; the second is the distinction between relative and absolute nonbeing; the third is the contrast between finitude and fallenness; the fourth is the incarnation, the death, and the resurrection of Christ that make redemption possible; and the fifth is the different roles to be played by the intellect and the will in reconciling fallen creatures with God. Taken by itself, Neoplatonism gives Augustine the continuity to which his intellect responds; but the Christian dimension of discontinuity is also necessary if his fragmented will is to be transformed.

Augustine claims that every finite being, "taken one by one," is good; but he also maintains that all finite things taken together are "very good" (7.12.18). The first claim permits him to defend the thesis that created beings are good without implying that every one is just as good as every other. This is important because Augustine knows that he must acknowledge the ontological goodness of every creature without denying the differences that permit us to make normative judgments contrasting one with another. The second claim allows him to consider the rich variety of lower and higher goods in which the goodness of the whole is greater than the goodness of the parts. This is important because Augustine realizes that the ontological goodness of every creature taken individually must be supplemented by the goodness that arises from the harmonious relation of one being to another within a larger totality.

The Neoplatonic side of Augustine's thinking surfaces when he claims that since evil is the privation of goodness rather than a negative principle that stands in polar opposition with God, from God's perspective, evil does not exist. In addition, he claims that evil does not exist for the universe as a whole, since nothing can break in from the outside to destroy the order that God has imposed on it (7.13.19). Though parts of the universe seem to be evil, they are good because of their coherence with other elements of the cosmos and because they are good in themselves. When he regards certain things in isolation, Augustine wishes that they might be better, but on reflection, he approves them even when they are taken alone. Indeed, Augustine claims that when he considers the world taken as a whole, he no longer wishes for individual things to be better; and he says that all things taken together are better than superior things considered by themselves.

These claims launch an intricate chain of reflections, beginning with the goodness of the material world, each element of which praises its creator; moving to the angels that praise God "in the heights," and culminating in the sun and the moon, the stars and the light, the heaven of heaven, and the waters that are above the heavens, all of which join one another in praising their creator (7.13.19). This reference to the heaven of heaven is an anticipation of the cosmology that Augustine develops in Books XII and XIII; and it remains to be seen how his conception of the spiritual beings who inhabit it can be related to the unformed material from which the universe is made. However, even at this stage of his reflections, the distinctively Christian side of Augustine's thinking points to the value of the lowest levels of the universe by insisting that if nothing but the material world had existed, its created goodness would make it appropriate for him to praise God for it.

Augustine claims that all things owe their being to God and exist in him, even though they do not exist there as they exist in space. Rather, God "contains" them because he holds all things together by his truth (7.15.21). Here Augustine adumbrates a concept of truth that has nothing to do with the correspondence between statements and facts, but with the value a thing displays simply because it exists. In this case, truth is equated with being, where to be and to be true are the same, and where to be true is to be a product of God's creative act.

This conception of truth enables Augustine to explain falsehood as what exists in thought but not in fact; but in making this claim, he does not mean that falsehood consists in the failure of a statement to correspond with a state of affairs. Rather, he is referring to the production of a phantasm that masquerades as genuine. Again, the concept of truth and falsity Augustine has in mind is not propositional, but ontological, pointing to a distinction between a created being that reflects the goodness of its creator and an imaginary construction that reflects the willfulness of its author. One of the most damaging kinds of construction Augustine has in mind is a lie, where lying is a failure to orient oneself toward the infinite richness of God. In this case, to lie is to fall away from the truth, where truth is to be equated with the being and the goodness we are created to express. Those commentators who accuse Augustine of fabricating parts of the *Confessions* should pay special attention to his account of the nature of truth and to his wish not to fall away from the truth in anything he does or says.

At this stage of his inquiry, Augustine asks once more about the nature of evil; but on this occasion, he not only claims that it is not a substance, but also says that it is "a perversity of will, twisted away" from God toward lower things (7.16.22). This is the definitive position that he adopts about the problem of evil; and it is clearly an advance, not only beyond dualism, but also beyond the Neoplatonic doctrine that evil is a privation of goodness. In embracing the view that evil is a twisted perversity of will, Augustine moves from a metaphysical to a volitional conception of evil, identifying it not with a substance, or with a privation, but with the distortion of a being that is oriented toward creatures rather than toward the source that brings them into existence.

Our freedom to do evil permits us to turn toward absolute nonbeing; and twisted perversity has pride at its roots, the punishment for which plunges us toward the absolute *nihil*. This does not imply that nonbeing is evil; for otherwise, creation *ex nihilo* would have a negative origin. Instead, absolute nonbeing is *nothing at all*, where Augustine's account of evil presupposes the capacity of the will to fall toward it. At the most fundamental level, evil is a negative orientation of the soul, the pride of which thrusts it back toward the nothingness from which it is created. The *absence* of being is neither the *negation* of being nor the *distortion* of being; and Augustine presupposes *absolute* nonbeing in the guise of radical absence by pointing to the negative orientation of the soul that seeks its own dissolution by twisting away from God toward lower things.

In the first stage of his Neoplatonic vision, Augustine has heard God calling to him from a distance, and he marvels that he is now able to love him as he is rather than as a phantasm. However, he quickly admits that he is not steadfast enough to enjoy the light of truth he has glimpsed. In a passage that reminds us of Plotinus, Augustine's says that God's beauty transports him to what transcends him, but that his own weight tears him away, causing him to sink with grief toward lower things (7.17.23).[33]

In anticipation of his later reflections about the distortion of the will, Augustine identifies the weight to which he refers with "carnal habit" (7.17.23). This is important; for if we assume that Augustine is simply a Neoplatonist, we might be tempted to identify the weight to which he calls our attention with the body and with the evil that derives from the fact that the soul falls into it. However, in referring to *habit* as the source of evil, the author of the *Confessions* points once more to a volitional analysis of the problem of evil, which is more obviously compatible with Christianity than with the Neoplatonic strand in his thinking that so many commentators have chosen to emphasize.

At this stage of his account, Augustine tells us that the memory of his earlier experience of God sustains him. As a consequence, he says, "I did not doubt in any way that there was one to cleave to, nor did I doubt that I was not yet one who would cleave to him" (7.17.23). But what precisely is the memory to which he is referring? Is it the experience of God he has just recounted, the memory of God from an earlier stage of his life, or life in Adam, both as a type in which he participates and as an individual beside whom he stands in a state of original innocence? Perhaps it is all three of these or only one, where from an eternal point of view they merge; and where from a temporal perspective, they diverge.

The eternal convergence of these options would allow Augustine to mean all three things at once, while their temporal divergence might suggest that he must choose among them. From a temporal point of view, it seems reasonable to believe that the memory to which Augustine is referring is a recollection of the experience he has just been recounting, mediated by the fact that he first learns about God as a child. The claim that the image of God in which he has been created has not been effaced, and the belief that he reflects the original innocence of Adam, either as a type or a token, are meaningless in temporal terms; and no other temporal episode except the one that we have been describing is dramatic enough to serve as the referent for his present recollection.

Though Augustine returns to the difficult theme of the origin of the soul in Book X, what will be discussed in a subsequent book, let me make the crucial point once more at this stage of our reflections. From an eternal point of view, life in Adam, the experience recounted in this chapter, and any earlier experience of God Augustine might have had come together on the vertical axis of experience. Yet in temporal terms, the most likely candidate for what he remembers about God is what he discovers in the first stage of the upward journey we have been considering, here mediated by the fact that he has already learned something about God in early childhood. In the first stage of his vision of God, Augustine encounters God the father; and he understands the content of his experience to be identical with the nonincarnational parts of the prologue of the Gospel of John.

The first stage of Augustine's Neoplatonic experience leads him to glimpse another world; for as he tells us in quoting a familiar verse from the first chapter of Romans, " 'God's invisible things, from the foundation of the world, are clearly seen, being understood by the things that are made' " (7.10.16).[34] Then Augustine tells us in the second stage of his vision that he appreciates the beauty of bodies, both heavenly and earthly; that he can make judgments of truth and falsity about mutable things; that he can distinguish between what ought to be and what ought not to be; and that when he wonders how he can make judgments of this kind, he realizes that he has found the unchangeable truth that exists above his changeable mind (7.17.23). During the early stages of his education, Augustine climbs the Platonic ladder from images, to objects, to mathematical structures; but he never reaches the higher level of value or the standard of truth that makes moral judgments possible. Now his recollection of the second stage of his Neoplatonic vision allows him to realize that he has made access to this standard, not only reaching the fourth level of the Divided Line, but also stretching beyond it to what Plato calls "the Good beyond being."[35]

On the basis of his recollection of the vision of unchangeable light, Augustine describes the second stage of his Neoplatonic experience in dynamic terms. In doing so, he combines the mathematical structure of the Divided Line with the dynamism of the Metaphor of the Cave,[36] moving through a series of stages that generates a ladder from the world to the source that creates it:

> Thus I gradually passed from bodies to the soul, which perceives by means of the body, and thence to its interior power, to which the bodily senses present exterior things, . . . and thence again to the reasoning power, to which what is apprehended by the bodily senses is referred for judgment. When this power found itself to be in me a variable thing, it raised itself up to its own understanding. It removed its thought from the tyranny of habit, and withdrew itself from the throngs of contradictory phantasms. In this way it might find that light by which it was sprinkled, when it cried out, that beyond all doubt the immutable must be preferred to the mutable. (7.17.23)

Finally, Augustine makes his inferences and brings the account of his Neoplatonic vision to a conclusion:

> Hence [my soul] might come to know this immutable being, for unless it could know it in some way, it could in no wise have set it with certainty above the mutable. Thus in a flash of its trembling sight it came to that which is. Then indeed I clearly saw your "invisible things, understood by the things which are made." But I was unable to fix my gaze on them. In my frailty I was struck back, and I returned to my former ways. I took with me only a memory, loving and longing for what I had, as it were, caught the odor of, but was not yet able to feed upon. (7.17.23)

Though he does not say so explicitly, Augustine repeats the first stage of his Neoplatonic experience in the second by turning inward, where by moving in this direction once again, he is following the Socratic dictum to know himself. As Socrates suggests in the *Phaedo*, we make access to what lies beyond us by turning away from the world toward the *logoi* our souls formulate about them; and we approximate the truth by examining the stages through which we develop in attempting to find it.[37] By turning inward toward the soul, Augustine does not embrace a domain of Cartesian subjectivity, but finds that the world is accessible only through the mediation of language. When he embraces this discovery, he takes his stand at the hyphenated place of interconnection between subject and object, which permits objects to become accessible to him as the soul filters them through its own erotic structure.

Turning inward also enables Augustine to move beyond the dualism of his earlier philosophical position: objects become accessible to the subject, but they do not do so because we place the subject and the object side by side. Rather, we make access to objects and to what lies beyond them, first by transforming the subject and the object into the knower and the known, then by moving from less to more stable levels of reality, and finally by transcending the contrast between knower and known altogether. Unlike the first stage of the Neoplatonic experience, this second stage does not involve a leap from the soul to the light that serves as a principle of illumination (7.10.16), but moves gradually through a series of levels from the finite to the infinite (7.17.23).

At this stage of the discussion, Augustine makes it clear once more that the dimension of transcendence to which the intersection between the subject and the object calls our attention is the *arche* that allows us to make intelligible judgments when we move to the highest level of the soul (7.17.23). These judgments presuppose that what is immutable is superior to what is mutable; and they also presuppose that when we turn inward toward our souls, we not only find truths, but also truth itself (7.17.23). The culmination of this experience leads once again to the themes of God and the soul, permitting Augustine to identify God with the standard of truth that makes all the other dimensions of human experience intelligible. From an ontological point of view, truth and being are identical; and it is this fact that makes the continuity of Neoplatonism an indispensable element of Augustine's thinking.

However, the dimension of discontinuity that Augustine grafts onto Neoplatonism also becomes indispensable when he finally sees *that which is*; for he does so only in the flash of a trembling glance, and is unable to sustain the vision that gives him access to it (7.17.23). His moral weakness dashes him back; he lapses into his customary ways; and only a loving memory of his vision sustains him (7.17.23). This recollection gives Augustine an appetite for what he can smell, but is not yet able to eat, suggesting that he must undergo a further stage of development that transcends intellectual apprehension (7.17.23). However, he does not do this until he hears the voice of a child in the garden in Milan and responds to it as if it were the voice of God (8.12.29). The truth that Augustine apprehends in the second stage of his Neoplatonic vision is an intelligible content of cognition, a standard by which judgments are measured, and a condition for Christian maturity, where the maturity in question depends on an encounter with the voice of God that transforms Augustine's life.

As the final stage of his Neoplatonic ascent unfolds, Augustine seems to move in a philosophical circle, the beginning and the end of which coincide. Yet what distinguishes them from one another is the memory of God that he retains as he slips back to the place where he begins. For a moment, it seems that the finite coincides with the infinite; but in this moment of unity, there is also a dimension of irreducible difference that forces Augustine to turn away from what he has encountered (7.17.23). The philosopher only sees God momentarily; the fear and trembling this produces throws him back on himself; and though the circle Augustine traces comes full circle, he comes to himself only because he can remember the ground of truth that lies beyond self-consciousness, and that must speak to him if he is to be redeemed.

What would have happened if Augustine had tried to stay in the sunlight? As his own account of his experience suggests, it would either have absorbed him or destroyed him. However, this generates a paradox: Augustine can either stay in the sunlight and lose his sight, or go back to the cave with nothing but a loving memory. He can either merge with what lies beyond him, or preserve his integrity by falling away from it. If he does the first, he loses himself; if he does the second, he loses everything but a memory of his highest good. This is not as debilitating as the Manichaean dualism of good and evil, but it poses a serious problem for anyone who wants to make access to the ground of his existence. We either hold onto the content of our vision and lose ourselves, or we turn away from it and preserve that content only as a memory. This suggests that even the second stage of Augustine's vision is unstable and cannot bring rest to a soul that wishes to remain in the presence of God. In this case, the upward movement toward God experiences a counterthrust that turns Augustine back on himself.

A question arises quite naturally about whether Augustine can find a way of living that will allow him to remain in the presence of God? As he says of himself at the beginning of Book VIII, "It was not to be more certain concerning you, but to be more steadfast in you that I desired" (8.1.1). Yet how will this be possible, and what steps must Augustine take to actualize this possibility? Part of the answer depends on a proper understanding of the relation between seeing and hearing in his thinking, and part of it hinges on understanding his claim that he requires a mediator between God and the soul if steadfastness is to be achieved. Before we turn to the second issue, let us develop in more detail the relation between visual and auditory metaphor that undergirds the account of his mystical experience.

Visual metaphors dominate Augustine's account of both stages of his Neoplatonic ecstasy: he sees the immutable light with the eye of his soul (10.10.16), does not derive this vision from the flesh (10.10.16), and arrives at *that which is* with the flash of a "trembling glance" (10.17.23). In the first stage of his mystical experience, God cries to him from afar, "I am that I am" (10.10.16); but after he ascends the Neoplatonic ladder that begins with the senses, he sees rather than hears the invisible things of God (10.17.23). Thus, speaking and hearing retreat into the background; and Augustine seems to replace them with the visual apprehension of God. What are the implications of this attitude toward vision and visibility for our claim that auditory metaphors stand at the center of the *Confessions*, and what is its bearing on Augustine's need to find more steadfastness in God?

These questions become more acute when we notice that in several places in his works, Augustine orders the senses in a typically Neoplatonic fashion. First he mentions touching and tasting, then smelling, and finally hearing and seeing. This order reflects the relative distance between the knower and the known. Since it usually involves a closer contact between the subject and the object, we might think that tasting should come before touching. Augustine admits this, and he sometimes modifies his ordering principle accordingly. However, his model for touching is the sexual act; and as a consequence, he quite naturally places touching before tasting in the hierarchy of our access to things (10.30.41). Augustine also follows the Neoplatonic pattern in ordering the senses by placing seeing highest on the list. In his discussion of the "the sins of the eyes" in Book X, he gives seeing priority over the other senses; and in that context, he says that when we are seeking knowledge, we apply seeing to the other senses by analogy (10.35.54). Here it seems evident that Augustine is simply repeating the conventional wisdom of the Neoplatonic tradition.

Yet Augustine orders the senses in this way for a more important reason. As one moves up the ontological hierarchy, the object of consciousness enjoys a higher degree of publicity. We can touch and taste things in the same place only one at a time; and since more than one individual can smell the same odor, smelling is higher than touching and tasting. Yet hearing and seeing are higher still because their objects are the most accessible of all. Sometimes Augustine places hearing and seeing side by side in his assessment of the relative value of different modes of access to truth. For example, in On Free Choice of the Will, he says that the other senses do not behave exactly like the eyes and ears because the former make direct contact with the object.[38] Later in that same text, he places hearing higher in the hierarchy than seeing, saying that the objects "we touch, taste, or smell are less like truth than the things we see and hear."[39] In both cases, the eyes and the ears stand over against the objects of consciousness as public contents of cognition that are accessible universally.

The dominant visual metaphor in Augustine's writings is "the eye of the mind," and his most important auditory metaphor is "the ear of the heart." Yet how does he bring these two metaphors together? As I have suggested already, one theory about the relation between them is that hearing is a preliminary phenomenon, and that as Augustine's thought develops, he subordinates the auditory dimension of his experience to the intellectual vision of God. This view is grounded in the claim that hearing is more passive than seeing; and though its proponents admit that the "the ear of the heart" listens to God in passive obedience, they insist that the more significant "eye of the mind" sends out a "visual ray" to grasp God's essential nature.[40]

David Chidester claims that Augustine weaves visual and verbal metaphors together from his earliest to his latest works.[41] Verbal metaphors emphasize the pilgrimage of the Christian life, while visual metaphors point to the decisive moment of illumination when the soul glimpses and finally gazes on the goal of its journey. Nevertheless, this theory suggests that seeing is the more important of the senses; that hearing is a preliminary phenomenon that must be replaced with the vision of God; and that steadfastness in God eventually moves Augustine from the "trembling glance" of Book VII to a vision of God that the soul can sustain.[42]

These considerations raise serious questions about our thesis that auditory metaphors dominate Augustine's thinking, and they generate problems for our claim that speaking and hearing are primordial phenomena in the Confessions. We might be inclined to believe that the experiential culmination of the text is to be found in Book IX, where Augustine has a mystical experience with his mother, and where this experience gives them visual access to eternity before it becomes their permanent possession. As Augustine expresses the crucial point at the conclusion of the City of God, "There we shall be still and see [my emphasis]; we shall see and we shall love; we shall love and we shall praise."[43]

This view of the primacy of vision in Augustine's writings points in a Neoplatonic direction, and it raises a fundamental issue about the proper way of understanding the relation between God and the soul. At the culmination of its ascent, and in the endless reaches of eternity, does the soul merge with the ground of its existence; or do God and the soul remain separate, not only in time, but also in eternity? These questions concern the relation between continuity and discontinuity in Augustine's thinking, where vision emphasizes the first and where hearing focuses our attention on the second.

If we read the *Confessions* with this problem in mind, we find that though seeing is fundamental if we are to have a vision of God, the trembling glance with which Augustine apprehends the invisibility of God underlines the presence of radical discontinuity in his thinking. Discontinuity is not only an auditory phenomenon, but a visual one as well, where even though God can only be encountered in the present, seeing God never implies that he is completely present to consciousness. In the Christian conversion of Book VIII, and in the mystical experience of Book IX, we shall also find that speaking and hearing reemerge as the pivotal elements and that Augustine's final word about the relation between God and the soul is not visual, but verbal. This implies that steadfastness in God is possible for Augustine only if he moves beyond the first and the second stages of his Neoplatonic vision into the place where God speaks to his fragmented heart, and it also suggests that speaking will remain a central element in his experience even when he stands before God in eternity.

In this connection, it is instructive to notice that at the end of *The Trinity* and *The City of God*, a verbal dimension resurfaces. In the epilogue of *The Trinity*, Augustine says,

> So when we do attain to you, there will be an end to these many things we say and do not attain, and you will remain one, yet all in all, and we shall say one thing *praising* [my emphasis] you in unison, even ourselves being also made one in you.[44]

And on the last page of the *City of God*, Augustine tells us that resting in God leads to seeing, seeing leads to loving, and loving expresses itself in *praising*. In both books, the voice of the *Confessions* that focuses so often on Augustine's sins reappears as the voice of adoration, resounding dynamically in the eternal "resting place" to which it gives him access.

THE NEED FOR A MEDIATOR (7.18.24–7.21.27)

At this stage of his account, Augustine claims that he can find the steadfastness he seeks only be embracing a mediator between God and the soul. He says,

> I sought for a way of gaining strength sufficient for me to have joy in you; but I did not find it until I embraced "the mediator between God and man, the man Christ Jesus." (7.18.24)[45]

At earlier stages of his narrative, Augustine has mentioned four contexts in which he has been unable to mediate the positive and the negative aspects of his experience. After he embraces Manichaeism, he cannot conceive of a spiritual substance that transcends the distinction between Good and Evil as substantial principles; when he meets Faustus, he encounters a Manichaean bishop who does not know anything, but is a friendly man; in Ambrose, he meets a Catholic bishop who knows something, but is unable to reach his heart; and in his encounter with Academic Skepticism, he finds a doctrine that calls his Manichaean superstitions into question without being able to offer anything positive in their place. In all these cases, Augustine cannot find a middle ground in which he can bring the positive and the negative dimensions of his experience together.

In the two stages of the Neoplatonic vision, positive and negative aspects of Augustine's experience continue to remain separated; for he is unable to balance his glimpse of God with the fact that he returns to his "former ways" with only a "loving memory" of what he is unable to contemplate (7.17.23). This motivates him to seek a mediator who can overcome the opposition between the upward and the downward dimensions of his encounter with God, giving him steadfast knowledge of the truth, and also making happiness in God possible. Augustine must learn to use every aspect of the finite order, including the insight he gains from the Neoplatonic vision, to find enjoyment in God, where the joy he seeks can emerge only when he clings to God with the whole of his being.

Writing from the standpoint of a Christian bishop looking back on the past, Augustine points to the mediator he needs by calling him "the man Christ Jesus"; but he also focuses on the auditory dimension of the word by saying that Christ calls out to him, " 'I am the way of truth, and the life' " (7.18.24).[46] Earlier, the creator speaks to Augustine from afar, saying to him, "I am who I am." Now the word that speaks in the act of creation and in the voice that identifies itself in the mystical experience becomes the pathway that gives him access to the truth, and to the new life that he has not been able to find.

Christ becomes the mediator by standing in the middle ground between God and the soul and by mingling the heavenly food we are unable to eat with our humanity so that wisdom might become "milk for our infant condition" (7.18.24). As Augustine understands it, the incarnation is an emergency measure,[47] made necessary by the fact that we have wandered away from God, both intellectually and volitionally, and are unable to go back home unless Christ takes our fragmented condition on himself. In doing so, he makes the word accessible in human terms and participates in our humanity to make it possible for us to participate in his divinity.

At this stage of his development, Augustine does not understand the doctrine of the incarnation, nor is he humble enough to embrace the humility to which the death of Christ calls his attention. The philosopher is too proud to humble himself, and he is unable to cling to the humility of the one who seeks to redeem his fragmented soul. Though the Word of God that is exalted above the highest levels of creation has already lifted Augustine up to itself in the Neoplatonic vision, Christ can fashion the content of this vision into a dwelling place for fallen beings only by building a house of clay for himself. In doing so, the incarnated word enables us to cast ourselves upon it as "it arises and lifts [us] up" to eternity (7.18.24). What begins as the incarnation of the Word in a human body ends as the resurrection of the embodied Word that returns to the father, and Augustine invites us to participate in both dimensions of this process as a way of being reconciled with God.

It is difficult to understand how those who believe that embodiment is evil can avoid extending a pejorative conception of the body to the incarnated Christ. However, to do this would miss Augustine's point that the incarnation makes redemption possible, not because the body is evil and Christ shares in it, but because it has been created good, has fallen away from its original status, and can be redeemed only by one who is embodied without negative connotations. To be sure, Christ must be crucified to take Augustine's sins upon himself; but this only means that he permits the unfallen body he inhabits to become disfigured in order to redeem the distorted condition into which Augustine has fallen because he participates in Adam's sin. If anything should explode exclusively Neoplatonic approaches to the *Confessions,* it is the doctrine of the incarnation, and the picture of the death and the resurrection of Christ to which the mature Augustine commits himself. According to this position, the lowly dwelling place that Christ builds for himself is good; and it is only for this reason that it can become the site of redemption.

By contrast with the author the *Confessions*, the sinner in the drama that we have been presenting is careful to admit that he does not understand the incarnation, both before and immediately after he makes his Neoplatonic ascent toward God, however much he insists that the faith of Christ is firmly fixed in his heart. In Christ, the philosopher only sees a man of wisdom with whom no one else can compare; and though he believes in the virgin birth, he also believes that God sends Christ into the world simply to serve as an example of virtue for other human beings to follow. According to this view, the divine word teaches us to despise worldly things so we can attain immortality (7.19.25).

Since Augustine believes this, he also believes that Christ merits his authority as a leader; but in the rarified atmosphere generated by the two stages of his Neoplatonic experience, he is unable to grasp the significance of the incarnation. At an earlier stage of his development, Augustine cannot conceive a spiritual substance; and only a Neoplatonic vision finally enables him to do so. Now he cannot understand the mystery expressed in the claim that the Word becomes flesh, suggesting that only a different kind of experience, mediated by writings that diverge from Neoplatonism, can overcome this difficulty (7.19.25).

From his reading of the Scriptures, Augustine has learned that Christ eats, drinks, feels emotions, and speaks; and he concludes from this that in Christ, there is not only a bond between the word and the body, but also a link between the word and the soul. Indeed, he acknowledges that Christ is a perfect man and that the body of Christ cleaves to God, together with a human soul (*anima*) and mind (*animus*) (7.19.25). This point is important because it suggests that both the soul and the body can cleave to God, and that Christ is the perfect expression of the way in which the first Adam cleaves to God before he falls away from him.

As I have indicated repeatedly, Augustine identifies the true man with a composite of a soul and a body, suggesting that a "true man" is a "complete man," rather than a soul that inhabits a body from which it longs to separate itself. However, it is equally clear that he gives precedence to the soul in describing the bond that obtains between the word and the perfect man. This bond obtains, not because the word and the perfect man are identical, but because the soul of Jesus is a form of truth, displaying the perfection of human nature because it participates in wisdom. Here the perfect man is not the incarnation of the divine word, but the highest creature in a chain of finite beings that participates in it. Once more, Augustine does not understand that the word has become flesh, and he believes that the bond between Jesus and the word is important only because it permits him to embody the truth and to participate in wisdom (7.19.25).

Augustine's friend, Alypius, is convinced that Catholics believe that there is no soul or mind in Christ; and because he knows that only a rational creature could perform the acts the Bible ascribes to him, he moves more slowly than Augustine toward the Catholic faith. Yet when Alypius learns that he has mistakenly attributed the Apollinarian heresy to the Church, he is "pleased with the Catholic faith and better disposed to it" (7.19.25). In his own case, Augustine admits that he also learns about the meaning of the incarnation only at a later stage of his development; and he suggests that even the church becomes clear about this doctrine only in its battle with heretics. These remarks raise the question about whether Augustine begins to understand the incarnation, the death, and the resurrection of Christ before his conversion in Milan or only several months or even years afterward. This question is crucial; for if he has no grasp of the significance of these issues before the famous episode in the garden, it is almost impossible to regard the moment in which he puts on Christ as anything more than a ritualistic act[48] or a rhetorical construction[49] from his perspective as the author of the *Confessions*.

Before Augustine makes suggestions that will enable us to deal with this question, he emphasizes once more that he does not know God as he is revealed in Christ, that he desires to seem wise, that he does not mourn his ignorance, and that he is "puffed up with knowledge" (7.20.26). The philosopher has not found the *caritas* that can only be expressed when he humbles himself, and the Neoplatonic books are unable to teach him about it. Because this is so, Augustine wants to make it clear that his reading of the Neoplatonists precedes his study of the Scriptures.

Augustine needs to remember the difference between what he learns from the philosophers and what he learns from the Bible; for this allows him to "detect and distinguish how great a difference lies between presumption and contrition" (7.20.26). This difference coincides with the distinction between those who see where they are going without knowing the way and those who know the goal of their journey, as well as how to get there. As Augustine formulates the point, it is important to know "the way that leads not only to beholding our blessed fatherland, but also to dwelling there" (7.20.26).

The order in which Augustine's religious development unfolds is of crucial significance. If he had begun with the Bible instead of with the

Neoplatonists, he might have thought that the writings of the philosophers are an improvement on the Scriptures. Or if he had become a Christian first, and had read the books of the Neoplatonists later, he might have thought that wisdom could have been acquired by reading these books alone. However, by turning to the Scriptures after he reads the books of the philosophers, he realizes that he must move from a philosophical to a Christian transformation (7.20.26). The first path leads from insight to presumption, while the second leads from presumption to humility. Indeed, it would not be mistaken to suggest that Augustine's Christian "infancy," and his Neoplatonic "adolescence," becomes Christian "maturity" only when he turns to the linguistic embodiment of the Word become flesh by reading the Bible.

Yet what does the incarnation have to do with the transformation of the soul, and why should it be necessary to focus on it if we are to make progress beyond a momentary glimpse of God? The answer returns us to the will as the central Augustinian category; for the problem he faces is how to find redemption, not only intellectually, but also volitionally. The difficulty with the Neoplatonic vision is that it threatens to absorb Augustine's soul in what lies beyond it, and that he must fall away from it if he is not to lose himself in an eternal moment of philosophical insight.

Augustine is not simply a finite being who needs to stand in the sunlight, but also a fallen creature that needs redemption by the grace of God. As a consequence, he focuses his attention on the incarnation to point to the love that will heal his fragmented predicament. If finitude had been Augustine's only problem, an understanding of the incarnation would not have been necessary; nor would it have been important for him to read the Neoplatonists before he begins to understand the Bible. By proceeding in this way, Augustine discovers that Christianity is not simply an exoteric version of Neoplatonism, but a way of calling his attention to the fallen rather than the finite will as the source of the human predicament.

Augustine understands the incarnation as a way of merging the finite and the infinite without destroying either element, and he knows that embracing it can be a way of binding God and the soul together while also holding them apart. Accepting and responding to the incarnation makes it possible for him to encounter God directly, but it also permits him to preserve his integrity as a finite center of will that stands in contrast with God. Only if God presents himself to Augustine as an incarnated individual is it possible for him to stand over against him as an embodied being; and only in this case will it be possible for him to preserve both the closeness and the distance that are necessary to bring wholeness to his soul.

Augustine begins to pursue the theme of the incarnation by turning his attention to the writings of Paul. This is the later stage in his development to which he refers two paragraphs earlier, for it is from the writings of Paul that he begins to understand the incarnation, the death, and the resurrection of Christ. Earlier Augustine despises the Scriptures because of their defective style and believes that the writings of Paul both contradict themselves and do not agree with the Law and the Prophets. Yet now he begins to realize that these contradictions are more apparent than real (7.21.27).

One commentator suggests that the "contradictions" in question appear in Romans 11.3 and in 1 Corinthians 5.16, where both passages involve references to the incarnation of Christ.[50] If these are the passages Augustine has in mind when he refers to apparent contradictions in the Pauline epistles, and if reading the Apostle at this juncture causes these contradictions to vanish, he must understand something about the incarnation when this occurs. Indeed, this way of understanding the text suggests that Augustine had begun to come to grips with the problem of the incarnation before his conversion in the garden in Milan.

Paul's epistles not only admonish Augustine to find God, but also to hold fast to him, where grace makes it possible for him to overcome the law of sin and death that is raging within him. Indeed, both Paul and Augustine subscribe to the view that we have been delivered over to the hands of the devil because he has persuaded us to be like him and because he has induced us to stand outside the truth that flows from God. Thus, when both of them cry, " 'Who shall deliver [us] from the body of this death,' " the only answer points to the grace of God that is made available " 'through Jesus Christ, our Lord' " (7.21.27).[51] The one whom the Father has "begotten coeternal with [himself] and created in the beginning of [his] ways,"[52] has been put to death unjustly by the lord of death, making it possible for the sentence of death that has been passed upon us to be blotted out (7.21.27). Christ not only makes God accessible, but also pays an unjust penalty for sin; and it is the ransom he pays that enables both Paul and Augustine to exclaim that they have been freed from the body of this death through Christ their Lord.

Two theories of redemption have dominated theological reflection about the crucifixion of Christ. The first is the ransom theory that Augustine presupposes here, and the second is the sacrifice theory that Anselm elaborates 700 years later in *Cur Deus Homo*.[53] The first theory is juridical; the second is priestly and penitential; and both have much to commend them as ways of understanding what redemption means in the Christian theological tradition. Without discussing either theory in detail, it is perhaps enough to begin to bring these two theories together by indicating that since both spiritual and bodily death are the penalties for sin, the only person who can pay a ransom for it, and who can satisfy the justice of God by making a sacrifice for it, is the incarnated son who is altogether innocent.

The idea that God pays a ransom to the devil might seem implausible, especially if it is thought to imply that the devil has rights that God must acknowledge and overcome by a willingness to sacrifice his son. However, as Eugene TeSelle has indicated, the focus should not be on the rights of Satan, but on the dramatic battle between God and the devil for the souls and bodies of individuals who have been created to reflect the infinite richness of God.[54] Indeed, when sin occurs, the one who commits it is justly put to death; and the only remedy for his predicament is for the one who is without sin to stand in his place. Since the devil sees that Jesus is innocent, but puts him to death in spite of this fact, the innocent death of God's son can serve as a ransom for the justified death of those who have chosen to rebel against him. Thus, it is only when he is nailed to the cross that the handwriting of the sentence of death that has been passed against them can be blotted out.

It is not surprising that a rhetorician who had planned to become a lawyer and a government official should find the ransom theory plausible; and if we join Augustine in the courtroom where our own life is at stake, we might find it plausible as well. Though it is true that the crucifixion involves a sacrifice, it is also a juridical transaction in which the devil's unjust act in punishing a righteous man becomes the means by which those who are worthy of death are redeemed. It is also crucial to notice that the death from which Augustine is set free is not only physical, but spiritual as well; for the death of his body is a punishment for the death of his soul that results when he turns away from God. The ransom that Jesus pays for sin involves both a spiritual and a physical dimension,[55] the first of which transforms Augustine's soul and the second of which transforms his body. As TeSelle formulates the point,

> The single death and resurrection of Christ is, so to speak, reduplicated in its significance for other men, for they are subject to the *double* death of both soul and body and have need of a double resurrection. Consequently Christ's death and resurrection is both a *sacramentum* of the current death and renewal of the inner man and an *exemplum* of the future death and resurrection of the outer man.[56]

In both cases, the ransom Christ pays takes away Augustine's sin and makes it possible for him to stand before God as a resurrected being, whose soul and body are finally bound together in perfect harmony.

Augustine is correct in claiming that none of this is to be found in the writings of the Neoplatonists and to suggest that the writings of Paul point beyond Neoplatonism to his need for a volitional as well as an intellectual transformation. Yet if this transformation is to occur, he must hear the living word speaking through the written text and must respond to what the words in which it is embodied command him to do. This will not occur until the most decisive moment of his life, where reading what Paul writes about accepting the incarnation will transform his fragmented heart. For the moment, Augustine points one final time to the radical contrast between the books of the Platonists and the writings of Paul. Unlike the epistles, to which he has already called our attention, the pages of the Neoplatonists do not contain the

> face of piety, the tears of confession, [the] sacrifice [of Christ], a troubled spirit, a contrite heart, the salvation of [God's] people, the city that is like a bride, the pledge of the Holy Spirit, [and] the cup of our redemption. (7.21.27)

In those books, no one hears Christ saying, " 'Learn of me, for I am meek and humble of heart, and you shall find rest to your souls.' "[57] Indeed, the Neoplatonists scorn the one who calls because he is "meek and humble of heart," and because he has " 'hid these things from the wise and prudent, and [has] revealed them to little ones' " (7.21.27).[58] In all these ways, the books of the Platonists, which lead Augustine to a vision of God, fall short of the simpler, but more profound import of the New Testament. As a consequence, Augustine turns away from the pride of the Neoplatonists to the humility that the Scriptures invite him to embrace.

In his final appraisal of the books that have enabled him to catch a glimpse of God, and as a way of contrasting them with the writings of Paul to which he turns soon after his mystical experience, Augustine says,

> It is one thing to behold from a wooded mountain peak the land of peace, but to find no way to it. . . . It is a different thing to keep to the way that leads to that land, where no deserters from the heavenly army lie in wait like bandits. They shun that way, like a torture. In a wondrous way all these things penetrated my very vitals, when I read the words of that least of your apostles, and mediated upon your works, and trembled. (11.21.27)

In the second stage of the Neoplatonic vision, Augustine sees his highest good with a trembling glance. At that ecstatic moment, no one else is present; and we find only the dialogue of the soul with itself, the Neoplatonic vision, and the subsequent reading of Scripture as a preparation for deliverance. By contrast, when Augustine reads a passage from the book of Romans in the garden in Milan, he not only trembles at the voice of God, but also finds the deliverance he seeks while his friend, Alypius, is sitting beside him (8.12.30). From this experience, a Christian community emerges (8.12.30); and the structure it exhibits not only overcomes the philosophical isolation of the Neoplatonic vision, but also expresses the new creation that God generates within Augustine's soul. It is to the account of these themes that we now turn.

2

Augustine's Christian Conversion
(Book VIII)

The central existential Book of the *Confessions* begins with Augustine's hesitation to become a Christian and ends with the emergence of a Christian community. In between, his conversion to Christianity makes his transition from hesitation to community possible. At the beginning of Book VIII, Augustine tells us that his intellectual conversion is complete but that the volitional transformation that reorients his life has not yet occurred. In this chapter, and against the background of the intellectual certainty that he achieves in the Neoplatonic vision, we shall focus our attention on the transformation of the will that occurs in the garden in Milan and on the reorientation of Augustine's life that results when he responds to the voice that addresses him there.

As Augustine describes his own situation at the beginning of Book VIII, he does not seek greater certainty about God, but greater steadfastness in him (8.1.1). However certain the Neoplatonic vision may be, it is unstable from an existential point of view, pointing to Augustine's need to stabilize the upward and downward dimensions of his relation to God. If this is to occur, he must move from a mystical encounter with the Father to an existential response to the Son, making a transition from the transformation of the intellect to the conversion of the will.

The pivotal question to be faced in this chapter can be formulated in two ways. First, "What does Augustine reject, and what does he accept during his conversion to Christianity?" Second, "What does he embrace, and what does he repudiate as he moves beyond the Neoplatonic vision to the Christian faith?" The most familiar answer is that for Augustine, becoming a Christian involves the abandonment of sexuality, the repudiation of worldly ambition, and the acceptance of the ascetic life of a monastery, first as a layman and then as a priest. However, this answer is inadequate because it focuses on the surface rather than the center of Augustine's existential transformation.

It is true that after the decisive moment in the garden, Augustine abandons his search for a wife and repudiates worldly ambition; but his conversion to Christianity points beyond these relatively superficial phenomena to the transformation of his will. Augustine's attitudes toward sexuality and toward the advancement of his career are symptoms of an addiction that expresses a radical distortion of the will. Thus, when he responds to the voice of God in the garden, he not only relinquishes sexuality and renounces ambition at the surface of life, but also abandons the willfulness at the center of his being. It is to the story of this transformation, and the stages that lead to it, that we now turn.

INITIAL HESITATION (8.1.1–8.1.2)

Augustine begins the account of his conversion to Christianity with a prayer and with a confession about the mercies of God to the one who has bestowed them on him (8.1.1). Once more, he is making his confession, not to inform God about something, but to praise the source of his being and to focus the attention of his readers on the one who redeems him. Augustine also wants God to transform his entire being, asking that his bones be filled with love and that he be permitted to praise his creator for breaking his bonds asunder (8.1.1). In Book VIII, Augustine intends to narrate the stages in which God breaks the bonds of sexual addiction and sets him free from the deeper bondage of the will, suggesting that the redemption he needs transforms not only his soul, but his body as well.

In the intellectual transformation considered in the previous chapter, God has spoken to Augustine, has encompassed him on every side, has given him certainty about eternal life, and has removed his doubts about the existence of an incorruptible substance and about the fact that it is the source of every other substance (8.1.1). As a consequence, he moves up the Neoplatonic ladder and beyond it, catching a glimpse of God as *He Who Is* before he returns to his customary ways. In this moment of illumination, the intellectual journey that begins with Cicero's *Hortensius* and that stretches over a dozen years of intellectual conflict comes to fruition. The Neoplatonic vision brings Augustine's intellectual quest for wholeness to completion in an aesthetic and spiritual apprehension of God; but as he stands on the cusp between the spatiotemporal matrix into which he has fallen and the converted space and time he longs to enter, he tells us that he needs to move beyond the transformation of his intellect to the conversion of his will.

The steadfastness that Augustine seeks is moral rather than intellectual because it is temporal rather than eternal. At this stage of his journey, he does not seek more light, but a reorientation of his will that brings what he does into accord with what he knows. This is a practical rather than a theoretical problem, justifying the conviction that Augustine's conversion in the garden is an ethical phenomenon. My only hesitation about embracing this view is that it suggests that the transition from the intellectual to the moral conversion is more continuous than it is. If to know the good is to do it, it is only a matter of time before knowledge leads to appropriate action. However, Augustine breaks decisively with the Neoplatonic tradition about this issue, suggesting that his moral conversion is a volitional way of crossing a chasm that the intellect can never bridge.

The shift from knowledge *about* God to a desire for more steadfastness *in* God leads beyond the Neoplatonic vision of *He Who Is* to a volitional transformation that makes participation in the City of God possible. As Augustine suggests in Books XII and XIII, steadfastness in God is the original relation we are created to exemplify; and when we fall away from it, God calls us to return to him through a process of conversion that cancels our sin. However, at this stage of his life, Augustine cannot find the salvation that he seeks because everything about the temporal dimension of his experience is uncertain. He tells us that though the pathway to God has become pleasing to him, he is reluctant "to tread its narrow passes" (8.1.1). This suggests that the doctrines of the Church and his reading of Paul's epistles have convinced him that the incarnation, the death, and the resurrection of Christ are the way to reach God, even though he is not yet ready to walk in it.

God begins to override Augustine's reservations about becoming a Christian by prompting him to turn to Simplicianus for advice. Simplicianus has been a servant of Christ for many years; the grace of God shines through his life; and Augustine wants to avail himself of the wisdom the old man has acquired in a life devoted to following Christ. He also wants to talk with Simplicianus on more personal terms than he had ever been able to talk with Ambrose, laying his problems before him and asking about the most fitting way to follow Christ in his own case.

Augustine could not be more explicit about the frame of mind in which he approaches Simplicianus: he sees people in the Church going in many directions;[1] the life he is living no longer satisfies him; his hopes for honor and wealth no longer delight him; but his "love of women" keeps him in bondage to an addiction that has plagued him since adolescence. Augustine's chief problem at this stage of his development is not pride or curiosity, but sensuality; and it blocks the pathway that leads from his fallen predicament to the salvation he seeks (8.1.2). Augustine knows that the Apostle Paul does not forbid him to marry, but Paul's admonitions only heighten his tensions by suggesting that celibacy is better than marriage, even though it is clearly the more difficult alternative.[2] Thus, when Augustine chooses the easier path, he exclaims,

> For this single reason my whole life was one of inner turbulence and listless indecision, because from so many influences I was compelled—even though I was unwilling—to agree to a married life that bound me hand and foot. (8.1.2)

By calling our attention to the bondage in which he languishes, Augustine points beyond the intellectual dimension of his predicament to the will as a center of power that requires transformation. Augustine's intellect no longer separates him from God; for he has abandoned the Manichaean dualists who worship creatures rather than the creator and has encountered the eternal Word through whom God creates all things by participating in the Neoplatonic vision described in the previous chapter. After his Neoplatonic vision, the writings of the Apostle Paul influence him to move in a distinctively Christian direction; and when he does so, he turns away from those among the Neoplatonists who know God without glorifying him, prefer wisdom to piety, and embrace profession rather than confession. Nevertheless, Augustine remains separated from God because of his incapacity to orient his will toward the one who creates the world and who dies to set him free. As he formulates the point in the second paragraph of Book VIII, "I had now found the good pearl, and this I must buy, after selling all that I had. Yet still I hesitated" (8.1.2).

It is easy to assume that the moral conversion of Book VIII is continuous with the intellectual conversion of Book VII and that it brings it to a natural culmination. According to this way of understanding the text, the only pearl that Augustine buys is chastity and continence; and when he does so, the ascetic price he pays makes it possible for his fallen soul to return to God. Yet such a view fails to understand the significance of Augustine's claim that he has separated himself from some of the Neoplatonists; and it fails to recognize the fact that his present predicament is not defined by the problem of ignorance, but by the problem of sin.

After his intellectual conversion, a transformation of Augustine's will is necessary that not only leads beyond his bondage to sensuality, but also beyond the stain of sin that taints his entire existence. The problems that arise here are more fundamental than issues about continence and chastity; and they come to focus in the questions, "How can Augustine overcome his willfulness?" "And how can he find a source of power beyond himself that can transform his fragmented heart?" The pearl that Augustine seeks is not chastity and continence, but the transformation of the will that will allow him to embrace the grace of God. Yet as he faces this crucial issue, he hesitates.

It is easy to assume that the hesitation Augustine mentions is only the first of many mythological elements that the rhetorician has woven together to construct an exoteric version of his move beyond Neoplatonism. No doubt, allusions to Greek and Roman literature are in the background as Augustine reconstructs the stages that lead to the episode in the garden, and perhaps we should acknowledge that they are present in his account of the episode itself. However, the crucial question is whether these allusions are instruments in Augustine's hands for expressing his conversion, or whether they are ways of speaking to which the distinctively Christian dimension of the text can be reduced.

My own position is that this kind of reduction is inappropriate, not only because the conversion in the garden comes to focus on the incarnation, but also because Augustine begins his account of moving toward it with a biblical allusion. It is not by accident that Augustine's account of his conversion to Christianity begins, not only with hesitation at the crossroads, but also with hesitation to buy the pearl that Jesus offers in the gospels,[3] and which Augustine finally purchases when he puts on a new garment called, "Jesus, the Christ" (8.12.29). Just as he claims that the children of Israel escape captivity with Egyptian gold in hand, so Augustine uses the gold of the classical tradition to speak about the pearl at the heart of the gospel. In the following sections, our fundamental task is to trace out the stages in which the great rhetorician subordinates his classical education to this overriding intention.

THE CONVERSION OF VICTORINUS (8.2.3–8.4.9)

Augustine goes to Simplicianus, the spiritual father of Ambrose, to recount his wanderings. When he mentions the fact that he has read the
books of the Platonists that Victorinus has translated, the old man congratulates him; for he is pleased that Augustine has not fallen on the
writings of other philosophers that might have led him astray (8.2.3).
Simplicianus is a Christian Neoplatonist, who approves the introduction
of God and his Word in the Neoplatonic writings. However, he is also a
humble follower of Christ, opposing other philosophers who focus only
on the physical world, and diverging from proud Neoplatonists who ne-
glect the pathway that leads to God.[4]

As Colin Starnes has argued in responding to Courcelle, Augustine
does not go to Simplicianus because he is a Neoplatonist, but because he
is a Christian.[5] What the young philosopher needs at this stage of his life
is not instruction in Neoplatonism, but a sympathetic ear, and the wisdom
that can lead him beyond the spiritual abyss into which he has fallen.
Augustine is capable of understanding difficult philosophical texts without
any instruction, and it is unlikely that he needs to discuss Plotinus and
Porphyry with Simplicianus in order to decipher them. What he needs
instead is a spiritual adviser, who can respond to his existential predicament
and can help him move beyond his conversion to Neoplatonism to the
transformation of his will. The name of the man Augustine visits points to
simplicity and to the need for a philosopher trained by Neoplatonists to
embrace the humility of the cross.

Simplicianus understands why Augustine has come to see him; for
instead of engaging in philosophical discussion, he encourages him to
become a Christian by describing the conversion of Victorinus, a scholar
and rhetorician whom he had known in Rome. Victorinus had mastered
the liberal arts; had read, criticized, and explained many of the writings
of the philosophers; had been the teacher of many senators in Rome; and
had been a worshiper and defender of idols for most of his professional
and intellectual life. Yet in spite of this, Victorinus becomes a Christian,
"bending his neck under the yoke of humility," and lowering "his brow
before the reproach of the cross" (8.2.3).

Victorinus moves from paganism to Christianity by reading the Bible
and by studying the Christian writings at his disposal. Then he tells
Simplicianus that he has become a Christian, though he wants to be a
Christian in secret rather than acknowledge his conversion openly. In
responding to him, Simplicianus points beyond the conversion of the

intellect to the transformation of the will by saying that he will never believe him until he sees him in the Church. However, Victorinus indicates that he does not appreciate the difference between notional and volitional assent by asking, " 'Is it walls, then, that make men Christians?' " (8.2.4). This pattern repeats itself on many occasions: Victorinus is afraid to offend his influential friends, and he knows that a storm of hostility will descend on him if they discover he has become a Christian. Yet as Victorinus continues to inquire into the meaning of the Christian faith, he becomes even more afraid that Christ will deny him if he refuses to confess him openly (8.2.4).

"Suddenly and unexpectedly," the great rhetorician says to Simplicianus, " 'Let us go to the church. I wish to become a Christian' " (8.2.4). In referring to this crucial moment, Augustine anticipates the objections of his readers to his own sudden conversion in Milan, preparing the way for it by mentioning the unexpected decision of Victorinus to become a Christian. In this case, Simplicianus goes with Victorinus to the Church and is scarcely able to contain his joy. The priest in charge admits him to the first stage of instruction; and not long afterward, he submits his name for baptism. In response, Rome marvels, the Church rejoices, the proud are enraged, but Victorinus pays no attention because his hope is finally focused resolutely in God (8.2.4).

Since Victorinus is a famous man, the officials of the Church offer to allow him to make his profession of faith privately; but he decides to make it in public. Even though there has been no salvation in the rhetoric he teaches, he has professed it openly; and he concludes that when salvation is at stake, he should not be ashamed to embrace it before the entire congregation. As Victorinus ascends the platform, many in the crowd recognize him; and those who know him begin to whisper his name. When they see him standing before them, there is a sudden outburst of joy; but as he begins to speak, the crowd hushes so they can hear what he says. Finally, when he embraces Christianity clearly and forcefully, the people surrounding him take him into their hearts immediately prior to his baptism (8.2.5).

Simplicianus' description of the conversion of Victorinus is not simply an incident to be recounted, but an occasion for Augustine to raise a philosophical question. This is a pattern in the *Confessions*, where an unexpected episode often interrupts the flow of the narrative and becomes an occasion for philosophical reflection. At this juncture, Augustine asks why people in the Church rejoice more at the salvation of a person God delivers from danger than over one who has never lost hope; and he reminds us that even God rejoices over one lost sheep that repents rather than over ninety-nine that need no repentance. Indeed, there is joy in the house when the Prodigal Son comes home; for as the Gospel of Luke describes the episode, the "younger son was dead and is come to life again, was lost and is found" (8.3.6).[6]

Why do Victorinus, Augustine, and the Prodigal Son find it so hard to return to the one who brings them into existence? A Neoplatonic interpretation might suggest that the heart of the problem is the bondage of the soul to the body from which it struggles to return to a preexistent state. By contrast, Augustine suggests that the problem is not that the soul has fallen into the body, but that the will has become willful and that in its negative form, it keeps him in bondage. Toward the end of his journey toward God, Augustine is a captive against his will (8.5.10-8.5.12), but he also suggests that he cannot escape the bondage into which his willfulness has led him except by responding to a divine interjection with the whole of his being. Thus, the author of the *Confessions* exclaims,

> Lead us, O Lord, and work within us; arouse us and call us back; enkindle us, and draw us to you; grow fragrant and sweet to us. Let us love you, and let us run to you. (8.4.9)

In reflecting on the example of Victorinus that Simplicianus sets before him, and in reminding us of the story of the Prodigal Son, Augustine anticipates his own transformation as he returns to the father from whom he has been estranged.

THE BONDAGE OF THE WILL (8.5.10–8.5.12)

When Augustine hears the story of Victorinus, he is eager to imitate him; and indeed, this is the purpose Simplicianus has in mind in relating it to him. The man to whom Augustine turns for spiritual advice tells him that Victorinus responds to a law forbidding Christians to teach literature and rhetoric by choosing to abandon his "school of words" rather than the Word of God. In doing so, Victorinus is not so much brave as happy, having finally found a reason to devote himself fully to God. This is what Augustine wants to do, and thus he longs to imitate Victorinus by embracing the happiness he has been seeking so long (8.5.10).

Imitation is a central theme in the *Confessions*. First, it leads from icons to objects, then to intelligible structures, and finally to standards of value these lower levels presuppose. The Christian tradition supplements this Neoplatonic hierarchy by claiming that man is created in the image of God; and in the pear-stealing episode, Augustine plunges beneath the hierarchy by becoming a negative imitation of omnipotence. Yet at this stage of his life, Augustine wants to return to God by imitating the transformation of another person: the young professor is a rhetorician, and it is appropriate that he should seek to imitate a man who represents what he is and what he wants to become. It is also unlikely that he fails to notice the name of the person he wants to imitate. "Victorinus" points to *victory*, and by implication, to the conquest of the predicament from which Augustine needs to extricate himself.

Augustine wants to find the wholeness that he seeks through an act of the will, but the habits he has developed over the years prevent him from doing so. This does not mean that there is a negative principle working in him, but points to the bondage of the will that his own actions have produced. Here Augustine begins to deal with the problem of evil for the last time and to move toward the account of his conversion by focusing on the opposition between freedom and bondage (8.5.10). In doing so, he not only moves beyond Manichaeism, but also transcends the Platonic doctrine of privation by emphasizing the role of the will in generating his negative condition.

Augustine depicts the crucial point by describing the chain that enslaves him for so long:

The enemy had control of my will, and out of it he fashioned a chain and fettered me with it. For in truth lust is made out of a perverse will, and when lust is served it becomes habit, and when habit is not resisted, it becomes necessity. By such links, joined one to another, as it were, . . . a harsh bondage held me fast. (8.5.10)

As Augustine discovers, the remedy for the bondage of sin, and for the addiction that expresses it, requires more than the freedom of the will. It also requires the grace of God.

The transition from will to willfulness leads from lust, through habit, to necessity; and in doing so, it moves beyond the (finite↔infinite) structure of the person who has been created in the image of God toward an infinity of its own that seeks to leave its finitude behind.[7] The best way to explain the presence of evil is not to posit two competing principles, as the Manichaeans do, or to appeal to the privation of goodness to which the Neoplatonists call our attention, but to point to the transition from finite freedom to willful captivity. In the human realm, the problem of evil is not dualistic or ontological, but existential; and it expresses itself most profoundly in the bondage of the will.

In describing the opposition between freedom and bondage, Augustine speaks about two radically different directions in which the will develops:

> A new will which had begun within me . . . was not yet able to overcome that prior will made strong with age. Thus my two wills, the one old, the other new, the first carnal, and the second spiritual contend with one another, and by their conflict they laid waste my soul. (8.5.10)

As Paul expresses the point, "the flesh lusts against the spirit, and the spirit lusts against the flesh";[8] and as Augustine suggests in this passage, the one who had become a wasteland, and who is now a battle ground between two competing orientations, understands the opposition between the flesh and the spirit from his own experience.

When the will moves in a spiritual direction, it reaches for a spiritual substance that can sustain it; but when it moves in a carnal direction, it infinitizes itself. The contrast between flesh and spirit is not intended to call our attention to the distinction between the soul and the body, but points to conflicting orientations that tear the person apart. When he distinguishes between flesh and spirit, Augustine is not formulating a new version of Manichaeism, but describing two radically different ways of living, one of which is the positive expression of freedom, while the other issues in the bondage of the will. Both the saint and the confessor have this opposition in mind when they distinguish between the bondage of the flesh and the freedom of the spirit.

At this stage of his development, Augustine's will moves toward the spirit rather than toward the flesh; and his attraction to the flesh is something that he suffers rather than something he does. Nevertheless, he does not deny that he is responsible for his habits; for he has willingly become what he now finds himself to be (8.5.11). This insight enables him to understand Paul's remarks about the nature of sin, in contrast with the Manichaeans, who reach the mistaken conclusion that Paul is a dualist.

When Paul claims that it is not we who sin, but sin that dwells in us, the Manichaeans assume that he is pointing to a force over which he has no control. By contrast, Augustine claims that the law of sin is the tyranny of habit and that Paul's apparent dualism is simply a graphic way of pointing to the opposition between two competing dimensions of the soul. The battle within Augustine's soul is not between two independent principles, but a confrontation between the spirit of life and a cluster of habits that have congealed into the bondage of necessity. Thus, an evil will that Augustine is unable to control results from the transition from will, through habit, to necessity (8.5.10).[9]

After the two stages of the Neoplatonic vision, Augustine can no longer claim that he is uncertain about the truth. Nevertheless, his flesh binds him to the earth, and he carries the baggage of the world about him as if he were asleep (8.5.12). On all sides, God shows Augustine that his words are true; but even though he is convicted by the truth, he can only reply with the drowsy words:

> "Right away. Yes, right away." "Let me be for a little while." But "right away—right away," was never right now, and "Let me be for a little while" stretched out for a long time. (8.5.12)

Augustine concludes that he is a

> captive in the law of sin which was in [his] members. For the law of sin is the force of habit, whereby the mind is dragged along and held fast, even against its will, but still deservedly so, since it was by its will that it had slipped into the habit. (8.5.12)

Finally, the writer exclaims with the Apostle Paul, "Unhappy man that I was! Who would deliver me from the body of this death unless your grace, through Jesus Christ our Lord?"[10]

If we take this passage literally, we might assume that the principal conflict with which Augustine is concerned is the radical opposition between the soul and the body. According to this way of understanding the text, the soul longs to return to God, but the body restrains it. However, since Augustine knows that the flesh and the spirit differ from the body and the soul, it should be evident that the *body of this death* is a metaphorical way of describing the bondage of the will, and the death of both the soul and the body that results from it. Augustine does not seek freedom from the body, nor does he speak the kind of literal language that suggests that freedom of this kind is desirable. Rather, his use of metaphorical discourse points to the fact that the will moves in two directions simultaneously and that his deepest problem is the disintegration into which he has fallen.

STAGES OF LIBERATION (8.6.13–8.11.27)

When Augustine turns to the account of his conversion, he does not do so abruptly, but moves through a series of stages that he must endure before the decisive moment comes. These stages give us access to the conditions in which he lives and to which his transformation must be related if the episode in the garden is to have existential significance. How much Augustine remembers and how much he reconstructs about this episode cannot be distinguished with the accuracy as the historicist demands; for what the author recounts is not merely a spatiotemporal episode, but an encounter with the Word of God along the vertical axis of experience. Space, time, and eternity intersect in the Garden in Milan; and our conception of the truthfulness of the author must be rich enough to bind these dimensions together. Indeed, only if we acknowledge the interplay among the three axes along which Augustine moves can the significance of his Christian conversion transcend and be connected with the concrete circumstances in which it occurs.

Augustine's way of expressing the truth of his life is to construct a narrative that respects the facts, gives us access to his interpretations of them, and leads us to a place beyond space and time that makes demands of its own on the spatiotemporal order. What Augustine remembers and what he reconstructs must be subordinated to what he becomes, where he becomes an authentic individual when he returns to the ground of his existence. In the Neoplatonic experiences considered in the previous chapter, Augustine sees the light of truth with a trembling glance; but in the account of the conversion toward which he is now leading us, he becomes *true* by aligning himself with *the truth*, where this correlation expresses itself existentially. As he has reminded us already, what he needs is not greater certainty about the truth, but greater steadfastness in it. This becomes possible only when Augustine embraces the truth that incarnates itself in space and time and that binds memory and reconstruction together by transforming his life into genuine as opposed to counterfeit coin. The standard to which his memory and his interpretations must conform is the standard of God, who will only accept the confessions of a contrite heart, even from a gifted rhetorician.

As he begins his confessions to the one who redeems him, Augustine reminds us that the "chain of sexual desire" and the "slavery of worldly business" prevent him from becoming a Christian (8.6.13). These metaphors are important because they point to the chain of sexual addiction that he has been unable to break and to a desire for professional success that enslaves rather than liberates his extraordinary abilities. Yet at a more fundamental level, both addictions point to the bondage of the will from which he is unable to extricate himself. Augustine is not a slave because he is embodied, nor embodied because he is enslaved, but enslaved as an embodied being; and the bondage of the will that results from this fact leads him to cry for redemption that only the grace of God can provide.

Before the grace he needs can begin to do its work, Augustine alludes to his increasing anxiety and to the friends whose companionship sustains him (8.6.13). The individualism that characterizes so much of our thinking can blind us to the support our fragmented hearts can derive from our friends, while Augustine points to both the individual and the community by acknowledging his fragmentation within the larger context in which it develops. As he moves toward Christianity, the chain of sexuality, the slavery of worldly business, and the anxiety of sin issue in the bondage of the will; but friendship and the love of wisdom it helps to enkindle continue to sustain him.

While Nebridius is absent, Ponticianus, a fellow countryman and a servant of the emperor, visits Augustine and Alypius at their house in Milan. Augustine does not remember what his acquaintance wants with them; but he does remember that when they sit down to talk, the visitor notices a book on the table before them. When he finds that it is not a textbook of rhetoric, but a letter of the Apostle Paul, he looks up with a smile because only this book is before Augustine's eyes. Earlier, Simplicianus congratulates Augustine for reading the books of the Platonists. By contrast, Ponticianus, is delighted that Augustine is reading the (Epistle to the Romans); and he begins their conversation by mobilizing the specifically Christian dimension of Augustine's interests in religion (8.6.14).

The symbols embedded in the previous paragraph warrant more detailed reflection. First, the absence of Nebridius from the conversation is important; for as Augustine tells us earlier, he is an acute analyst of the logical structure of theoretical issues. This trait is valuable on other occasions, but it is irrelevant to the Christian conversion Augustine is about to undergo. At this stage of his life, what Augustine needs is existential transformation rather than philosophical reflection about his fragmented situation. Second, the presence of Alypius is significant; for the young man is not only dependent upon Augustine, but is also more chaste than erotic in temperament. He therefore provides a contrast term to Augustine, whose powerful conversion narrative stands out in bold relief against the relatively placid background that his philosophical companion provides. Third, the friend who visits Augustine and Alypius is not only a servant of the emperor, but also a Christian; and this leads immediately to a question about which emperor Augustine ought to follow. The young rhetorician has been seeking a royal appointment; and in the conversion and in the years that follow, he will receive it. Finally, the book that Ponticianus finds on the gaming table is not a rhetorical text, but a letter of the Apostle Paul that will lead to Augustine's transformation. This biblical text not only points beyond the game of rhetoric, but also points beyond the game of life; and it leads Augustine beyond the books of the Neoplatonists to the Word of God that heals his fragmented heart.

As a way of trying to persuade Augustine and Alypius to become Christians, Ponticianus tells them the story of Anthony, a well-educated and well-respected Egyptian monk who embraces Christianity and decides to live in the desert. When Ponticianus learns that his friends have never heard the story, he lingers on the topic, telling them the details of the conversion of the desert father (8.6.14). Ponticianus is also surprised that Augustine and Alypius do not know about the existence of monasteries or about the monastery in Milan under the care of Ambrose (8.6.15). Until he hears these stories, Augustine's search for wisdom is primarily intellectual; but now it begins to shift in a voluntaristic direction. Examples of Christians in the desert and of monks in a monastery are crucial elements in this transition, turning Augustine away from theoretical abstractions to the transformation of his will.

Ponticianus comes closer to Augustine's heart, not only by moving from the desert to the monastery in Milan, but also by telling him a story about himself and his friends, who are members of the emperor's court that Augustine aspires to join.[11] One day while the emperor is attending the circus, he and his friends take a walk in the gardens that are located close to the wall of the city. As they walk in pairs, one of the group strolls away with Ponticianus, while the other two walk by themselves. These other men soon come to a cottage of Christians and find a book about the life of Anthony; and when one of them begins to read it, he considers embracing a life like Anthony's in the desert. He and his friend are secret service agents who have been loyal to the emperor; but as the young man continues to read, love and shame engulf him. Suddenly, a radical contrast emerges between being a servant of the emperor and being a friend of God; and the one who reads decides to act on the difference between them (8.6.15).

The secret service agent with the book in his hand turns to the friend who is standing beside him, claims that he has decided to enter the service of God, and asks that even if he might be reluctant to imitate him, he at least be willing to refrain from opposing him. Yet his companion quickly becomes a Christian as well, shifting his loyalty from the emperor at the circus to the one who addresses him through his friend. When Ponticianus and his friend who have been walking in the other part of the garden come searching for them, the two converts tell them what they have decided to do and beg them not to reject them; and though Ponticianus and his comrade do not turn away from their own way of life, they commend the other two for their decision. When they turn their attention back to the palace, the new converts remain in the cottage, where their fiancées dedicate "their virginity" to God (8.6.15).

There are three features of this episode that require special attention. First, the story presupposes a pair of crucial references to entertainment. Ponticianus finds a letter of the Apostle Paul on a gaming table; and this discovery becomes the occasion for his narrative about Anthony, the desert fathers, the monastery in Milan, and the secret service agents. One of the agents of the emperor also finds a book about Anthony, and reads it while the emperor is attending the circus. These references to recreation suggest a radical contrast between two ways of reading the *Confessions*: on the one hand, it might be nothing more than an aesthetic and rhetorical game Augustine is playing with his readers; on the other hand, it is an irreducibly religious document, where the gaming table and the diversions of the emperor contrast with the book on the table and with the conversion of the emperor's servants. The second point to notice is that the emperor's servants become Christians after one of them reads about the conversion of Anthony. This raises a crucial question about what reading a text has to do with hearing the voice of God. If speaking and hearing are at the center of Augustine's *Confessions*, what is the relation between hearing and reading that makes conversion possible? Finally, there is a sexual dimension in the conversion of the secret service agents that affects their fiancées. The women's decision to dedicate their virginity to God points to a connection between Christianity and asceticism, raising a question about whether a decision to follow Christ requires a commitment to an ascetic way of living.

The contrast between aesthetic and religious approaches to the *Confessions* is important, and Augustine will face the problems it raises in the conversion experience he is about to relate. In that context, the question he asks is whether what prompts him to read a passage from the Bible is a children's game or the voice of God that seeks to address him in silence (8.12.29). Augustine knows the difference between aesthetic and religious experience, and it is important to both him and his readers to decide whether his response to God falls under the first or the second category.

The second question about the relation between reading and hearing is also a crucial issue in Augustine's account of his conversion. At the decisive moment, Augustine will make a transition from hearing the voice of God to reading a biblical text. Yet in this case, reading and hearing are closely connected: when Augustine reads the Word of God, he hears it speaking to his heart; and as his eyes move along the page in silence, he responds to what he hears from the center of his being. Augustine believes that the Word of God speaks directly to his soul through the words of the Bible, where in this special case, there is no chasm between hearing a voice and reading a text.

Finally, the question of sexuality that emerges in the conversion of the secret service agents might seem to point in a Neoplatonic direction, tempting us to assume that one cannot become a Christian without embracing an ascetic way of life. What else could account for the decision of the fiancées of the converts to dedicate their virginity to God? Augustine himself endorses an ascetic pathway; and it is not to be denied that he soon adopts this way of living for himself. Nevertheless, we must not assume that sexuality is the primary issue in Augustine's return to God. Sexuality under the conditions of his fallen predicament is a symptom of a deeper problem: when the will turns away from God, it makes a transition from finitude to fallenness; and one of the clearest ways in which sin expresses itself is in the context of sexual desire. This is not an accident, for we are sexual beings who are incomplete until we have found companionship with another. As a consequence, it should be expected that the distortion of creation and of the community that the fall disrupts would express itself in sexual terms.

For some people, sexual activity becomes an addiction that requires a radical remedy; and this certainly seems to be so in the case of Augustine. For others, the abandonment of sexuality is a symbol for the transformation of the will. Perhaps this is the case for the secret service agents and for their fiancées. However, in every case, the basic problem is the distortion of the will that leads away from God rather than the sexual dimension of experience that sometimes expresses it. Conversion requires the radical reorientation of the will; and at the deepest level, this transformation moves us from our fallen predicament into the converted spatiotemporal matrix where we can become a new creation.

The problems of aesthetics and religion, hearing and reading, and sexuality and asceticism prepare us for the conversion of Augustine; for by focusing on each of these themes, the great rhetorician is leading his readers toward the most important moment of his life. The most comprehensive way to make this point is to notice the subtlety with which Augustine constructs his narrative. He builds his account around a series of examples, nesting them inside one another like Chinese boxes: first we have the *Confessions,* then the story of Ponticianus, then the story of Anthony, next the story of the secret service agents, and finally, the story of their fiancées. The first contains the second, the second contains the third and the fourth, and the fourth contains the fifth. In all of these ways, Augustine is spinning a web of words that will eventually lead us to raise the question about the way out of the labyrinth.

An interplay between aesthetic unity and religious transcendence is central to Augustine's intentions, and this interconnection surfaces in the labyrinthine structure of his narrative. The series of concentric circles and the aesthetic circularity it represents presuppose a transcendent dimension that stands over against them. Not knowing what Ponticianus wants with him generates a dimension of indeterminacy that surrounds Augustine's story, and this story includes other stories as elements of itself. However, the story also points beyond itself to a source of power that breaks in on it from beyond the human realm. The book on the table will finally free Augustine from the aesthetic circularity of his narrative by addressing him directly; and when this occurs, the words in the book leap off the page, making it possible for God to reveal himself to Augustine's fragmented heart.

Anthony's biography is instrumental in the conversion of the secret service agents, which takes place in a garden and results from reading a book. It is not by chance that the book on the gaming table that prompts the recollection of this episode is instrumental in Augustine's conversion, and it is also not a coincidence that this conversion occurs in a garden. By allowing Ponticianus to speak in a garden, and to do so by pointing to a desert, a monastery, and another garden where a conversion takes place, Augustine is generating the context in which his own conversion occurs. Yet he is also pointing beyond his narrative to the word of God that will address him from beyond the garden wall. The desert through which Augustine has wandered, the garden wall that encircles him, and the word that addresses him point to the unity and the separation of Augustine's enterprise. In the decisive moment in the garden, Augustine breaks beyond the circularity of Neoplatonism by responding to the voice of God, and by relying on a source of power that is discontinuous with the human realm it generates.

Augustine makes the transition from aesthetic circularity to religious transformation by saying that while his friend is speaking, God turns him toward himself. In doing so, he approaches Augustine from behind his back, where the rhetorician has placed himself by refusing to exercise self-scrutiny. God does not allow Augustine to hide his shame, but sets him face to face with himself so he can see how ugly he is. Religious alienation sometimes produces aesthetic and moral disfigurement, and this certainly seems to be so in the case of Augustine. When the one who is finally facing himself tries to turn his gaze away, his friend continues his narrative. Then God opposes Augustine to himself and forces him to look at himself so he can see his iniquity and hate it. Finally, Augustine responds to his discomfort by playing a game of his own by praying, "Grant me chastity and continence, but not yet" (8.7.17).

Augustine's shame intensifies as Ponticianus continues to speak, and hidden dimensions of himself of which he has been unaware for so long begin to emerge from behind his back. When his friend has finished his story and leaves Augustine standing in the garden with Alypius, the young rhetorician begins to talk to himself. He lashes his soul to make it follow his will; and the ethical side of himself no longer winks at his sin (8.7.18). Yet in this moment of perplexity and indecision, he continues to turn away from the transformation he seeks. Augustine begins to speak in short sentences about his fragmented condition: his soul draws back; it refuses to respond; it will not make an effort; its arguments are exhausted; it continues to resist. In speechless dread, what Augustine fears most is death; and his anxiety expresses itself in the fear that the addiction by which he has been enslaved will finally lead to the death he fears (8.7.18). Yet as the battle that agitates both his soul and his body continues to rage within him, he begins to emerge from the conflict because the time for transformation is at hand.

At this decisive moment, Augustine turns inward to continue his struggle. Yet on this occasion he does so, not to have a Neoplatonic vision, but to face the fragmentation of his will. Augustine's earlier intellectual conversion is not sufficient to set him free because it does not address the opposition between the flesh and the spirit or enable him to come to grips with the bondage of the will that has resulted from acts of its own. This self-transcendent being, who has attempted to become infinite for so long, is now at war with himself; and he must finally confront his internal conflicts directly if he is to hear the voice of God from beyond the garden wall.

When Augustine turns inward, he experiences bodily changes over which he has no control (8.8.19). He also describes their common predicament to his friend, Alypius, first by asking a series of questions, then by comparing their situation unfavorably with the joy of others who are much less sophisticated, and finally by suggesting that they are bound together in the same kind of "unfriendly friendship" he had experienced sixteen years before in the pear-stealing episode. Yet at this juncture, Augustine scarcely knows what he is saying; and he flings himself away from his companion, who gazes at him in silent astonishment. In doing so, the philosopher does not sound like himself; and his face, eyes, color, and tone express his meaning more clearly than his words (8.8.19).

There is a garden attached to the house where Augustine and Alypius are living; and the turmoil in Augustine's heart drives him out into it where no one can interrupt him. Yet Alypius follows him step by step, and they sit down as far away from the house as possible. Once more, the powerful rhetorician is at work: the house beside the garden points to the center of Augustine's soul, and in moving away from it, he turns away from the surface of himself. The young man is angry with himself for not obeying the will of God, and even his bones cry out for him to embrace it. The distance he must travel to do so is not as far as he has traveled already in moving from the house to the garden. Yet what he needs to make this journey is a united will; and what he must transcend is a divided and fluctuating will, wrestling with itself while one part rises as another falls (8.8.19).

Bodily movements express Augustine's agitation and the bifurcation of his will that threatens to tear him into pieces:

In the shifting tides of my indecision, I made many bodily movements, such as men sometimes will to make but cannot, whether because they lack certain members or because those members are bound with chains, weakened by illness, or hindered in one way or another. If I tore my hair, and beat my forehead, if I locked my fingers together and clasped my knees, I did so because I willed it. Yet I did not do that which I wanted to do with an incomparably greater desire, and could have done as soon as I willed to act, for immediately, when I made that act of will, I would have willed with efficacy. In such an act the power to act and the will itself are the same, and the very act of willing is to do the deed. (8.8.20)

Augustine's predicament is so fundamental that it implicates his whole being: both the voluntary and involuntary parts of his nervous system respond to it; and like Achilles in the *Iliad,* he strikes himself, seeking relief for his desperate predicament.[12] Behind this act is a literary tradition with which Augustine is familiar and over which he exercises rhetorical control.

Nevertheless, his erratic behavior suggests that his problem lies deeper than the power of his intellect. Originally finite, and now fallen, Augustine seeks redemption; and the infinite dimension of his soul that expresses itself in bodily movements that he cannot control requires the transformation, not only of his soul, but of his body as well. If this is to occur, he must engage in a performative act in which willing and doing are the same. Like the Prodigal Son, who demands his inheritance prematurely and squanders his possessions so tragically, Augustine needs to go back home.

Before he tells us how this happens, Augustine makes a philosophical digression. This is typical of the structure of the *Confessions*, where experiential episodes and abstract reflections often stand side by side. This digression accomplishes three purposes: first, it increases the suspense of Augustine's narrative by delaying its conclusion; second, it allows him to discuss the nature of the will as the central factor in his conversion to Christianity: finally, it permits him to attack the Manichaeans by pointing to the radical contrast between dualism that bifurcates him and redemption that transforms his fragmented heart.

Augustine cannot understand why his will does not obey his commands: when the mind commands the body, it obeys; but when it commands itself, it resists. Yet the philosopher dissolves this paradox by concluding that in giving commands to itself, the will is not exercising the whole of its powers. It is not strange "partly to will a thing and partly not to will it," for this opposition expresses the conflict between habit that presses us down and the truth that sustains and supports us. Augustine concludes that there are two wills at war within him because neither of them is whole and because what is present in the one is lacking in the other (8.9.21).

Augustine rejects the Manichaean doctrine that because there are two wills within us, there are two kinds of mind, one good and the other evil. The duality he has in mind is between two *acts of willing* rather than between *two faculties of the will*; and as a consequence, he describes the conflict within himself as a confrontation between two competing wills rather than between two opposing principles.[13] He also suggests that he is an individual who is engaged in deliberation and that he is paradoxically identical, both with the side of himself that wants to follow Christ, and with the side of himself that turns away from him. Thus, he points to a conflict within himself for which he himself is responsible by claiming,

> When I deliberated . . . , it was I myself who willed it and I myself who did not will it. It was I myself. I neither willed it

completely, nor did I refrain completely from willing it. Therefore, I was at war with myself, and I was laid waste by myself.
(8.10.22)

Augustine also implies that this internal conflict reflects the original sin
that he inherits from Adam. He says,

This devastation was made against my will, and yet it revealed
not the nature of a different mind within me, but rather the
punishment of my own nature. Therefore, it is no more I that did
it, but sin that dwells in me, sin that issues from punishment of
a more voluntary sin, for I was Adam's son. (8.10.22)

Though Augustine participates in Adam's freedom because he has been
created to reflect the goodness of God, he also participates in the sinful
predicament that the fall of Adam generates. The fall produces a bifurcated
consciousness in which two sides of the person are in conflict with one
another, and Adam's sin is more voluntary than ours because it is the first
occasion when a unified consciousness becomes divided against itself. In a
nontemporal formulation of the same point, the sin of Adam is the proto-
typical "moment" in which consciousness divides into two sides that stand
opposed to one another, where Adam is the type of which we are tokens,
and where the unity of original innocence is contaminated by the division
of original sin. Our own sin that is less voluntary that Adam's and that
manifests itself in a divided consciousness is a function of our sinful nature,
which is ours by virtue of the fact that we exist "after the fall." From this
point of view, "all [of us] have sinned and fallen short of the glory of
God."[14] From the point of view we must adopt when we deliberate, we act
freely; but Augustine insists that our freedom is always qualified by the fact
that we participate in Adam's sin. Thus, even our free acts are tainted by
original sin; and it is for this reason that he says that the sin dwelling in us
is responsible for the sins we commit.

In Adam, Augustine shares both the unity of original innocence and
the divided consciousness of original sin; and if he is to find the wholeness he seeks, he must move beyond these competing dimensions of his
nature toward transformation by the second Adam. In doing so, he can
identify himself with the deepest desire of his heart that expresses itself
in a unified will. Unity of this kind is not merely intellectual, but involves the reorientation of the entire person. It also expresses the grace
of God, and results from a divine interjection that allows us to renounce

our desire to become divine and to embrace a new way of living. Having moved from creation to the fall, Augustine now needs to move from fallenness to redemption, where the transformation he seeks will eventually set him free.

As Augustine twists and turns in his chains, he tries to break them by saying to himself again and again, "Let it be done now; let it be done now"; and as he does this, he almost decides, but not quite (8.11.25). He does not fall back into his earlier predicament, but stands aside for a moment to catch his breath. Here is the first step toward receptivity; for in this moment, Augustine begins to breathe the breath of life that creates him and to breathe the breath of grace that will create him anew. Again, he tries to reach God by his own initiative; he almost succeeds; he tries again, gets closer still, and all but grasps the goal he seeks. Yet he is not quite able to do so because he hesitates "to die to death and to live to life" (8.11.25). Up to the moment in which he becomes a new creature, the more he approaches the goal he seeks, the more horror he feels. In this crucial moment, God does not strike him back, or turn him aside, but holds him in suspense; and the only thing that will remove his suspense is the voice of God that addresses him directly.

Augustine attempts to reach the goal he seeks by saying, "Let it be done now; let it be done now." In doing so, he attempts to move toward redemption through a performative utterance. In the act of creation, utterance and act are identical. In the pear-stealing episode, "Let's go, let's do it," precipitates the action. However, on this occasion, performative discourse is unable to achieve its result. A chasm opens up between the transformation Augustine seeks and the power of his will to achieve it. This does not imply that Augustine's will is not an indispensable factor in the conversion experience he is about to describe. However, his conversion cannot result from an act of his own; and it must reflect the fact that the (finite⟶infinite) structure of the psyche ceases to accentuate itself, and becomes receptive to the voice of God.

At the penultimate moment, Augustine's old mistresses keep him from listening; for though he has begun to regard them as trifles and vanities, he admits that they continue to enthrall him. Indeed, his mistresses tug at his "fleshly garment" and whisper:

> "Do you cast us off?" "From that moment we will no more be with you for ever and ever!" and again, "From that moment no longer will this thing and that be allowed to you, forever and ever!" (8.11.26)

Augustine prays that God will guard him from what these voices are suggesting; but at this stage, he can scarcely hear them speaking. His passions do not challenge him face to face, but mutter behind his back, plucking at him as he is leaving and trying to make him look back at them. Yet as his desires continue to clutch him, he hesitates to break free and leap to the place from which God is calling. Indeed, the chain of habit keeps saying to him, "Do you think that you can live without them?" (8.11.26).

Augustine does not identify his mistresses, but he clearly suggests that he has more than one. Perhaps he is referring to the mistress with whom he lives for sixteen years and to the one who replaces her soon after the one he loves has been torn away from him. More probably, he has in mind the two things that keep him from becoming a Christian. Earlier, he calls these impediments "the chain of sexual desire" and "the slavery of worldly business." These obstructions are beginning to lose their attractiveness, but they continue to whisper to Augustine from beneath the level of consciousness. The power of his will cannot leap across the chasm that separates him from God; the chain of habit constrains him; and the transformation of his life is not an achievement that lies within his own power. Augustine's realism forces him to acknowledge that he cannot sweep the past away with a single stroke; and as he will discover in Book X, even after God has swept it away and remembers it against him no more, the marks of sin continue to distress him.

Nevertheless, Augustine is drawing closer to God; and as he hesitates to cross the threshold, "the chaste dignity of continence" appears to him (8.11.27). She holds a multitude of examples in her hands and challenges him to join them. Yet the passions that swell up within Augustine's heart stand in radical contrast with "the chaste dignity of continence." His passions drive him backward, and she lures him forward. His habits forge a chain that binds him, and continence projects a goal that draws him gently toward herself (8.11.27).

Though continence challenges Augustine to embrace chastity, it is important to remember that chastity and continence are not the same. The first refers to sexual abstinence; and the second is a broader conception that points to self-control. Continence is also more fundamental than chastity because it involves a modification of the will from which chastity can emerge. The examples of others lead Augustine to embrace it, but continence is a gift that expresses the grace of God rather than an achievement that reflects a natural capacity for self-control.

When he hears the voice of self-control, Augustine blushes; for he can still hear the muttering of his mistresses, and he still hangs in suspense between God and the world (8.11.27). Yet at this point, Continence speaks a final time:

> "Turn deaf ears to those unclean members of yours upon the earth, so that they may be mortified. They tell you of delights, but not as does the law of the Lord your God." (8.11.27)

At this crucial moment, the auditory dimension of Augustine's experience is once more the central theme. Though he sees Continence smiling at him, the more important aspect of their interaction is that he hears her speaking to him. The words of Continence are precursors of the voice of God; for though she asks him to abandon sexual activity, the focus of her message is the transformation of the will. At this crucial juncture, Augustine is seeking a unified will, while his friend, Alypius, keeps close beside him, awaiting the outcome of his agitation in silence (8.11.27).

THE DECISIVE MOMENT (8.12.28–8.12.29)

When Augustine turns inward, he plunges into the depths of his soul and heaps up his misery "in full view of [his] heart" (8.12.28). The task of "deep reflection" he undertakes requires him to turn away from theoretical abstractions and to move beneath the level of ordinary consciousness (8.12.28). The sinner does not skate along the surface of his experience, unaware of the demons underneath; and when he finally faces them directly, the storm breaks and the tears come (8.12.28). Augustine expels the ocean that has engulfed him through a flood of tears; the dry land that he has been seeking is in sight; and the wood of the cross that will lead him to it is in view. Yet since solitude rather than continued conversation with Alypius is more appropriate for weeping, Augustine leaves his friend behind him to be alone in another part of the garden, abandoning the negative community in which both of them stand (8.12.28).

    Immediately prior to his conversion, Augustine flings himself under a fig tree and allows his tears to flow; and though he uses different words, he cries, " 'And you, O Lord, how long? How long, O Lord, will you be angry forever? Remember not our past iniquities' " (8.12.28).[15] Yet Augustine's sins still enthrall him; and he asks, " 'How long, how long? Tomorrow and tomorrow? Why not now? Why not in this very hour an end to my uncleanness?' " (8.12.28). Alone in the wasteland, Augustine abandons his willfulness and opens himself to a source of power that lies beyond him. This does not mean that he renounces either his will or his friends, but that he is willing to stand alone before God. In this moment of solitude, he finally exercises the will of absolute receptivity rather than the willfulness of self-accentuation.

A wall surrounds the garden where Augustine sits, and he has no visual access to what lies beyond it. Yet from the house beyond the garden wall,[16] he hears the voice of a child, whose gender he cannot determine. The voice chants, *"Tolle, lege. Tolle, lege."* "Take and read; take and read" (8.12.29). It is important to notice that these words come from a place beyond Augustine's reach and not simply from the "house of his soul." The self-enclosed garden in which Augustine weeps, the inner life to which it calls our attention, and the self-reflexivity of the soul to which it points cannot generate the transformation he needs. Rather, an encounter with a transforming source of power from beyond the circle of self-consciousness is necessary if Augustine is finally to come to himself. Yet since God not only transcends him infinitely, but is closer to him than he is to himself, God's voice can reach beyond the garden wall to address Augustine directly; and the abruptness with which it does so on this occasion should not surprise us. Augustine has been moving toward this moment for many years; he has heard stories of other conversions that happen spontaneously; and the unexpectedness of the sudden transformation he undergoes is typical of the way dramatic conversions often occur.

Augustine's first response to what he hears is not active, but reflective. He ceases to weep and "thinks intently" about whether he has ever heard these words before as part of a children's game (8.12.29). His life has been a sequence of diversions; and when the decisive moment comes, he wants to know whether it is aesthetic or religious. If it is the first, he remains a pagan rhetorician; if it is the second, he can respond to the grace of God. Augustine longs for deliverance, but he will not accept a routine occurrence as an expression of divine intervention. Only when he realizes that he has never heard these words before does he imitate Anthony in "assuming" that the "voice" he hears is the voice of God (8.12.29).

There are five places in the text where an act of speaking is crucial, outstripping the priority we usually give to propositional discourse. First, God says, "Let there be light," pointing to the moment in which the world comes into existence through creation *ex nihilo* (e.g., 13.8.9, 13.10.11, 13.19.25). Second, Augustine and his adolescent companions say, "Let's go, let's do it," initiating the pear-stealing episode in which they fall away from God by making the fatal transition from will to willfulness (2.9.17). Third, Augustine says, "Speak so I may hear" (1.5.5), but also "let me speak" (1.6.6), pointing to the open space between God and the soul where a conversation between two centers of power and meaning can occur. Fourth, Augustine tries to bring about his own conversion by saying repeatedly, "Let it be done now"; but the bondage of his will, and the willfulness that has generated it, prevents him from doing so (8.11.25). Finally, when he hears the words, *"Tolle, lege," "Tolle, lege,"* his inability to determine the gender of the child who chants them not only places their content beyond sexuality, but also points to the place where God begins to gather the fragments of his fragmented heart together (8.12.29). The voice from beyond the garden wall explodes the Neoplatonic circularity of the soul's conversation with itself and brings Augustine face to face with a source of power and meaning that stands over against him. As a consequence, he moves into the vertical space between God and the soul where he can respond to a voice that wants to transform him rather than merely to inform him of something.

Damming the torrent of his tears, Augustine gets to his feet; for he believes he has heard a divine command to open the Bible and read the first passage he sees (8.12.29). He is like the man beside the pool of Bethesda who has been lame for thirty-eight years, but who arises, takes up his bed, and walks when God speaks.[17] The example of Anthony also encourages him, for he has heard that the desert father is converted when he comes into a church accidentally and hears a passage from the gospel that he believes is intended especially for him. In that case, the text says, "Go, sell what you have, and give to the poor, and you shall have treasure in heaven, and come, follow me."[18] In this case, Augustine is prepared to imitate Anthony, but does so by responding to words intended specifically for him.

Augustine returns to the bench where Alypius is sitting and snatches up the book he has left there. He opens it and reads the first paragraph he sees, where in the fifteenth chapter of Romans, Paul writes,

"Not in rioting and drunkenness, not in chambering and impurities, not in strife and envying, but put you on the Lord Jesus Christ, and make not provision for the flesh in its concupiscences."[19]

Then Augustine says,

No further wished I to read, nor was there need to do so. Instantly, in truth, at the end of this sentence, as if before a peaceful light shining into my heart, all the dark shadows of doubt fled away. (8.12.29)

This episode is the turning point of the *Confessions*, and its decisive impact on Augustine's life is undeniable. Yet having said this, it is important for us to interpret it within the hermeneutical context in which it occurs. Augustine reads the word of God in silence; and in doing so, he imitates the silent reading of Ambrose that puzzles him so much when he wants to speak with him. He also imitates the secret service agent who reads the story of Anthony; where in both cases, God speaks in silence with "a still small voice." On the other hand, reading the Bible on this occasion differs from the earlier episode in which the physician tries to turn Augustine away from astrology by suggesting that a book we pick up at random often supplies the information we need because we are guided by a higher instinct. In that case, intuition is the ground of the behavior the physician describes; in this case, providence is the source to which Augustine attributes the transformation he seeks.

We should also remember four gardens as we respond to Augustine's story about his conversion to Christianity. The first is the garden where Adam and Eve eat the forbidden fruit and attempt to become gods.[20] The second is the orchard where Augustine and his friends steal the pears and imitate omnipotence (2.6.14). The third is the place where Jesus prays before the crucifixion.[21] And the fourth is the garden where Augustine leaves his friend behind to listen to a voice that speaks to him alone (8.12.28–29). Augustine binds the Garden of Eden, the garden of his neighbor, and the garden where Jesus prays together in the garden in Milan.

The trees in all these gardens are also significant. In the Garden of Eden, God reserves the tree of the Knowledge of Good and Evil for himself.[22] In the orchard near his home, Augustine and his friends recapitulate the fall by stripping a pear tree. In the garden where Jesus prays, he separates himself from his disciples by falling on his face under an olive tree.[23] And in the garden in Milan, Augustine finds the solitude he needs by turning away from Alypius and by flinging himself under a fig tree (8.12.28).

The fig tree points in four directions. First, it reminds us of the olive trees under which Jesus prays. Second, it points to the fig tree from which the Manichaeans refuse to allow their followers to eat. Third, it symbolizes the fig tree in the gospels that Jesus condemns for not bearing fruit.[24] Finally, it reminds us of the tree under which Nathaniel sits in the Gospel of John and where Jesus sees him waiting for redemption.[25] As in the case of Nathaniel, God sees Augustine lying under a fig tree before he calls him; and when God speaks, the sinner sees the heavens open and the angels descend.

Listen first to the words that come from beyond the garden wall. The words Augustine hears are two Latin imperatives—*tolle, lege;* and these words mean, "Take up and read." However, we can also translate the passage, "Destroy and read." *Tollo* is irregular and its principle parts are *tollo, tollere, sustuli,* and *sublatum.* As Hegel points out in the *Phenomenology,* sublation has four stages: it means to take up, to destroy, to move beyond, and to embrace in a higher unity.[26] The Latin *tollo* carries this significance as well. God not only asks Augustine to take up a book, but also to put off his old nature and to accept transformation by something new.

Nevertheless, there is a crucial difference between Hegelian *Aufhebung* and Augustinian sublation. Hegel insists that when we move beyond an earlier stage of our experience, we must preserve both the positive and the negative elements of what is essential in it at a higher level of consciousness.[27] By contrast, the salvation that Augustine seeks demands that he repudiate his willful nature and become a new creation. In this special case, he must reject the infinite self-accentuation that has led him away from God. Instead, Augustine must accept a rupture in the flow of his natural consciousness that reflects the original discontinuity of creation *ex nihilo* and embrace the finitude from which he has turned away so persistently.

Turning away from self-accentuation to embrace one's finitude does not imply that an individual is no longer the same person in an empirical sense of the term. Many of the same traits that enable one person to be distinguished from another remain in place, even after conversion; and the traits that change in the process often do so only gradually. In addition, the individual who moves from infinite self-accentuation to finite self-acceptance has a (finite-infinite) structure, both before and after conversion. This (finite-infinite) structure is characteristic of every stage of the journey Augustine undertakes, beginning with creation in the image of God (finite-infinite) moving to his fallen predicament (finite-infinite), turning to his conversion in the garden in Milan (finite-infinite), and seeking fulfillment (finite-infinite) in the one who brings him into existence. However, one element in the transition from Augustine's fallen condition to the salvation that he seeks must not be preserved and taken up into a higher unity and that is the orientation of the soul that turns away from God.[28]

The content of the verses that Augustine reads reflects the form of the verb in which he is told not only to take up and read, and also to destroy and read. In suggesting that we turn away from behavior that leads to destruction and in demanding that we embrace Christ who gives us access to a new way of living, Paul's point is that we renounce the negative orientation of our nature and put on a new garment in its place. When we do so, we turn away from self-accentuation to accept the finite dimension of our nature that we are created to express.

It is tempting to assume that the crucial part of the passage from Romans is the one that tells Augustine to abandon the lusts of the flesh. Those who do so argue that Augustine gives up his plans for marriage and his public occupation, but does not abandon his studies or turn away from his circle of friends. Interpreters who move in this direction also insist that Augustine's ideal remains a society of wise men, who are devoted to the writings of Cicero, Plotinus, and Porphyry, and that his break with his past is limited entirely to his worldly ambitions and to his renunciation of the flesh.[29] Indeed, it is easy to argue that all his conversion requires is the repudiation of the body and the consequent return of the soul to its origins. If this is so, his Christian conversion is a disguised redescription of his earlier conversion to Neoplatonism. However, an adequate interpretation of the episode points in a different direction, requiring us to take the entire passage into account.

Before we examine this passage in more detail, it is important to notice that the Christian conversion in the garden differs radically from the Neoplatonic conversion examined already. First, though the conversion described in Book VII presupposes a Neoplatonic intellectual community, the conversion we are now considering presupposes a multifaceted community, including philosophers and theologians, government officials, children, Christian saints, old men and women, Augustine's mother, and his closest companions from childhood (8.6.15, 8.12.29, 8.12.30). Second, the Christian conversion is volitional rather than intellectual, requiring a change of direction before Augustine can build a philosophical system that reflects the richness of the existential transformation he undergoes. Third, the conversion in the garden allows Augustine to bring himself into a positive relationship with God without canceling his uniqueness. Finally, the conversion experience we are analyzing not only transforms Augustine's soul and his body, but also brings him into a new kind of community that expresses the Christian conception of the proper relation to God.

In the passage before us, Paul urges Augustine to embrace this kind of relationship by putting aside rioting and drunkenness, chambering and wantonness, and strife and envying (8.12.29). The first two defects do not apply to him, while the second pair points to sexual indulgence and is clearly pertinent to his situation. Yet strife and envying are also defects that continue to plague him. Augustine not only labors under "the chain of sexual desire," but also under "the slavery of worldly business"; and taken together, these symptoms force us to broaden our conception of his fallen predicament.

We must not restrict our attention to sexuality, but must drive beyond it to the moral, political, and religious slavery that constrain him. In the Epistle to the Romans, the flesh stands in contrast with the spirit and is not identical with the body. References to the flesh are Paul's way of pointing to the willfulness of the human situation. The lusts of the flesh transcend the body and point to the will that separates itself from God. These lusts not only include sexual desire, but also the strife and envy that disrupt Augustine's journey toward God.

Putting off the lusts of the flesh stands in contrast with putting on Christ. Yet what are we to say about this pivotal injunction? Most interpreters pass over it without comment, or suggest that it points to baptism as a cultic act, where we exchange the "bodily flesh" of our fallen predicament for the "divine flesh" made accessible to us in the incarnation.[30] However, unless we can interpret this passage at a more profound level than this, it can become an incantation; and if it does, one could scarcely blame a philosophical audience for ignoring it and for assuming that the earlier Neoplatonic vision is superior to the Christian conversion.

The Neoplatonic vision in Book VII and the Christian conversion in Book VIII are mirror images, where the first is intellectual with a religious dimension, and the second is religious with an intellectual dimension. It is easy to miss the second dimension of each, overlooking in particular the intellectual dimension of the moment in which Augustine exchanges the lusts of the flesh for a new garment. However, this phrase is the heart of Paul's admonition and points to the central role of the incarnation, the death, and the resurrection of Christ that Augustine has been trying to comprehend. Unfortunately, a failure to understand the use to which he puts this phrase prevents most interpreters from illuminating the most important episode in the text.

In the phrase, "Put on Christ," the words "put on" translate *induo*. *Induo* sometimes means to put on a costume, but it also describes the moment when a Roman boy becomes a man by receiving a toga from his father. Augustine assumes many guises, not only in childhood, but also throughout his intellectual development. Now he must put these earlier stages behind him if the old costumes are to become a new creation. The need for a new creation leads us to the center of Augustine's transformation. However, the most perplexing part of the story is Augustine's reference to the words that finally make redemption possible. These words are the scandal and the stumbling block that tell him to put on "Jesus, the Christ."

What can a philosopher say about this injunction that will allow us to uncover its significance? How can Augustine's conversion to Christianity give us access to a place that unaided philosophical reflection can never reach? Earlier Augustine says that all that remains to make his intellectual conversion complete is a willingness to embrace the incarnation. Now he reveals a willingness to do this when he listen to words that not only transform his life, but also provide a solution to one of his deepest reflective problems. As we shall discover, the phrase to which Augustine responds not only brings salvation to his fragmented heart, but also flowers into the philosophical theology that sustains the *Confessions* and that separates him from his Neoplatonic origins.

The incarnation, the death, and the resurrection of Christ invert the relation between the finite and the infinite dimensions of the psyche. Because the soul is an image of God, it is both finite and infinite. However, it deals with this fact by denying its limitations and by attempting to become infinite in its own right. In the Garden of Eden and in the orchard of Augustine's neighbor, human beings storm the gates of heaven through self-accentuation. Both Adam and Eve and Augustine and his adolescent companions fall away from God by embracing their own willfulness. By contrast, the incarnation, the death, and the resurrection of Christ involve a double transition from the infinite to the finite and from the finite to the infinite. In doing so, they demonstrate that infinitude need not detach itself from what is finite, but can embrace it as a realm in which it can express itself fully.

The incarnation is a way of embracing finitude; accepting an unjust death is a way of taking sin on oneself; and the resurrection is a way of indicating that the one who dies on our behalf makes conversion and fulfillment possible. When Jesus prays, "Let this cup pass from me," he turns away from death.[31] Yet the crucial fact about this prayer is that he also says, "Nevertheless, not my will, but thine be done."[32] In this moment, the incarnation reaches its richest expression. Here we see a picture of what it means, not for finitude to infinitize itself, but for the infinite to embrace finitude, and to accept an unmerited death that results from sins that he did not commit. After the crucifixion, the resurrection indicates that a (finite-infinite)[33] being can be fulfilled if it participates in the power of God that raises the one who takes our sins on himself from the dead.

If Augustine is to participate in this redemptive power, he must accept the reversal of the natural consciousness that moves from finite self-acceptance to infinite self-accentuation. He must also accept his fallenness, embrace his finitude, and be converted to a new way of living in which the infinite dimension of his nature can receive a finite expression. In Augustine's conversion in the garden in Milan, the will that had been willful for so long becomes a will again by accepting fallenness and embracing finitude; and freed from the bondage of the will, he begins to reflect infinitude as a gift of God's grace.

Embracing the incarnation, the death, and the resurrection of Christ brings peace to Augustine's fragmented heart; and it does so by causing his doubts about the role of Christ, the mediator, to flee away (8.12.29). Responding to Paul's injunction also permits Augustine to stabilize the upward and the downward movements that occur in the course of his mystical experience, giving him access to a third term that mediates the chasm between God and the soul. This middle term empties itself in the incarnation, becomes obedient to death on the cross, and is raised from the dead; and Augustine participates in this process by embracing his finitude, by accepting his fallenness, and by being set free from the bondage of the will that has enslaved him so long. Putting on Christ is not only a way of embracing the incarnation and sharing the crucifixion, but also a way of participating in the resurrection. Thus, Augustine can now move downward and upward simultaneously in the middle ground between the positive and the negative dimensions of his mystical experience, moving in the process toward the infinite richness of God he has been created to share.

The new garment that Augustine puts on, and the new way of living to which it leads, replaces the garments worn by adolescent thieves. It also takes us back to the original garden that makes the pear-stealing episode possible. Adam and Eve try to hide from God by clothing themselves in fig leaves. When he comes walking in the garden, he asks, "Where are you?"; or more literally, "Why are you where you are?"[34] Adam speaks for them both by answering with an excuse, but the fig leaves they wear cannot camouflage their negative condition. God tells Adam and Eve to take off the clothes they have made; and in exchange, he provides new garments of his own making.[35]

God places garments of skin around his children; and as they wear them, Adam and Eve can talk with him again.[36] By analogy, God puts a new garment on Augustine when he puts on "Jesus, the Christ," and this new garment brings him back into a positive relation with God by canceling his sin. In this case, the finite being who has sought to become infinite for so long undergoes a radical inversion; and when he puts on the one who can bind his finite and infinite dimensions together, he finally begins to live in the place where infinity can express itself fully.

In terms of our earlier analysis, the conflict between desires that tear Augustine's soul apart is first mediated by examples of conversions he longs to imitate. Then he attempts to bring about his own conversion by saying, "Let it be done now, let it be done now"; and when he fails, Continence appears and challenges him to do what so many others have done already. Finally, having separated himself from his friend, Alypius, and having thrown himself under a fig tree, he hears the voice of a child that brings the spatiotemporal dimension of his life to a standstill. This voice tells him to take something up and read it; and when he finds the book that he carries out into the garden, he reads a passage of Scripture that calls on him to embrace the mediator. When he does so, Augustine returns to the place where the conflict of his desires emerges and begins to undertake a distinctively Christian journey toward the infinite richness of God.

A final way to describe the decisive moment in which Augustine participates in the garden is to understand it as the conquest of an addiction. On many occasions, Augustine speaks of himself as if he were enslaved; and he often claims that his chains reflect the bondage of the will to which Paul's distinction between the flesh and the spirit call our attention. This is the kind of bondage with which an addict is familiar; and as a consequence, it is possible to compare the stages through which Augustine moves toward conversion with the stages an addict must negotiate in moving from bondage to liberation. First, the addict must be convinced that he ought to abandon his addiction, where the moment in which this conviction occurs may be called an "intellectual conversion." Second, it is important that the person in bondage be given examples of a wide range of individuals who have conquered their addictions so he can become acquainted with some of the pathways that lead beyond addiction. Third, a desire to imitate at least one of the individuals whose stories he has heard is necessary as the penultimate stage that must occur before the decisive moment. Finally, when conversion comes, it will do so in an instant, where the one who experiences it realizes that the source of transformation lies beyond himself, and where he knows that he has participated in a moment of grace that can neither be coerced or fabricated. In the garden in Milan, and in the stages through which Augustine moves in order to get there, this is precisely what occurs; and when it does, it is the transformation at the heart of the episode that generates the peaceful light that shines within Augustine's soul.

THE CHRISTIAN COMMUNITY (8.12.30)

The conversion of Augustine's will from infinite self-accentuation to finite self-acceptance occurs in private. However, he does not remain isolated, but quickly returns to his friend to tell him what has happened to him. In this way, Augustine recovers his relation to the community from which he has separated himself momentarily. The community he now embraces is not the positive community of parents and nurses, the negative community between a student and deceptive teachers of rhetoric who flog him for not studying as much as he should, or the natural friendship he shares with adolescent companions; but it also differs from the community of thieves in which every member stands alone. Indeed, it is a new kind of community that overcomes the negative community of the pear-stealing episode, points away from the nothingness to which it leads, and generates a context in which Augustine and his friends not only stand alone before God, but stand alone *together*.[37]

Alypius responds to Augustine, not by commenting about what has happened to him, but by telling him what has happened in his own case. The events he describes occur simultaneously with the more famous episode on the other side of the garden. Yet these separate events do not remain separate. After Alypius tells Augustine what he has experienced while he has been alone, he asks to see what Augustine has been reading. When Augustine hands him the book, Alypius finds that the next sentence is uniquely appropriate to himself. It says, "Now him that is weak in the faith take unto you."[38] When Alypius responds to these words, he also becomes a Christian, thereby joining Augustine within a community that does not cancel his individual integrity (8.12.30).

Earlier Augustine gives a detailed account of the character of Alypius. There we find that Alypius is a spectator who does not share the sexual passion of Augustine and whose stability stands in radical contrast with the Eros that drives Augustine from stage to stage. The verses Augustine and Alypius read reflect these differences. The first tells Augustine to put off the lusts of the flesh and put on Christ; the second admonishes Paul's readers to accept those who are weak in the faith.

Augustine summarizes the conversion of Alypius and formulates his understanding of its implications:

> He applied [this verse] to himself and disclosed [it] to me. By this admonition he was strengthened, and by a good resolution and purpose, which were entirely in keeping with his character,

whereby both for a long time and for the better, he had differed greatly from me, he joined me without any painful hesitation. (8.12.30)

The great rhetorician expects a sensitive reader to notice the differences between himself and his friend, but he also wants us to understand that they have made the same commitment.

The conversion of Alypius is derivative on the experience of Augustine. This is appropriate; for throughout the *Confessions*, Augustine has been the teacher and Alypius the pupil. However, both conversions display their uniqueness, and each reflects the character of the one who undergoes it. There is enough content in the source of power Augustine touches for more than one. It is true that the conversion of Alypius is not as dramatic as Augustine's; but because Alypius interprets his situation as an example of weakness of will, there is a connection between them.

In the case of Alypius, fallenness expresses itself in weakness rather than in self-accentuation; in the case of Augustine, this same predicament expresses itself in erotic power rather than humility. However, in both instances, the grace of God inverts the structure of the soul. The transformation of Alypius differs from the conversion of Augustine, but each has an internal structure that mirrors the other: the weakness of Alypius becomes the strength to accept a divine gift, and the strength of Augustine becomes the weakness to embrace his limitations. The same inversion that has transformed Augustine transforms Alypius as well; and when this occurs, the internal structure of their separate experiences binds them together.

When their conversion is complete, Augustine and Alypius tell Monica what has happened; and when they explain *exactly* what has occurred, she leaps for joy. She also praises God for being about to accomplish more than she could ever ask or think. As Augustine says,

For you had converted me to yourself, so that I would seek neither wife nor ambition in this world, for I would stand on that rule of faith where, so many years before, you had showed me to her. You turned her mourning into a joy far richer than that she had desired, far dearer and purer than that she had sought in grandchildren born of my flesh. (8.12.30)

We might be tempted to embrace a Neoplatonic interpretation of Augustine's concluding remarks by emphasizing the fact that his conversion turns him away from marriage and makes it necessary for Monica to

abandon her desire for grandchildren. In this case, chastity and continence are not only results of Augustine's conversion to Christianity, but
also the essence of the experience he relates. However, this narrow reading
of the conversion narrative suppresses other elements of it that are far
more important. Augustine not only forsakes "the chain of sexual desire"
and "the slavery of worldly business," but also takes his stand on the rule
of faith that Monica has dreamed about.

Faith in Christ stands at the center of Augustine's conversion; and
despite her desire for him to achieve professional success by marrying a
Roman heiress, finding Augustine on the rule of faith becomes the single
aspiration Monica cherishes more than having grandchildren. Indeed, it
would be appropriate to suggest that Monica is "converted" when she
hears about the conversion of her son, turning her back on the worldly
ambitions she entertains for her son, and accepting the fact that Augustine has now become God's son in a richer way than she could have ever
imagined. Earlier Monica has wanted marriage, legitimate grandchildren,
and professional success for Augustine, together with his conversion to
Christianity. Now she is "converted" when she becomes willing to accept
Augustine's Christian conversion to the exclusion of everything else.

A new kind of community emerges from this foundation. It is not a
collection of role players like the adolescent community with which Augustine begins, nor is it a negative community in which participants become isolated from one another. Rather, it includes an indefinite number
of individuals that are (finite$\stackrel{1}{-}$infinite) images of one another in relation
to God. The imaging relation that binds them together creates an analogical unity, where the analogical unity that binds them together cancels
the negative community of the pear-stealing episode and overcomes the
absolute *nihil* into which Augustine falls away from God. Augustine,
Alypius, Monica, and other members of this new community are identical
in certain respects, but also different. The transforming Word of God that
the Bible makes accessible does not cancel their differences; for though it
is rich enough to individuate them, it also gives them common ground in
relation to God. When Augustine interprets the meaning of creation in
Books XII and XIII, he emphasizes the infinite richness of the biblical
text. In the present case, this richness creates a Christian community,
where the identity and difference that defines it sustain the interaction of
its members.

The infinite must become finite to allow the finite order to come to
itself. In some cases, we must abandon our desire to become God; in
others, we must exchange our weakness for God's strength; and in still

others, we must give up our longing for grandchildren. Monica, Alypius, and Augustine, who have been friends before, become friends within a new kind of community. In this new community, each member stands alone; each experiences the grace of God in his own way; each stands alongside the others as a (finite$\perp$infinite) image of God that has returned to itself; and each interacts with the others as they stretch out toward God in a communal quest for fulfillment.

Friendship is a crucial thread that runs throughout the *Confessions*. It begins in adolescence, appears in a negative form in the pear-stealing episode, and contracts into the frozen isolation of an adolescent wasteland. Now friendship resurfaces, generating an imagistic relation that grounds a new kind of community. Friendship of this kind presupposes that those who have stood alone before God stand together. The pear-stealing episode leads from a positive community of friends to a negative community of isolated individuals. By contrast, conversion leads from individuating experiences with God to a community that not only holds its members apart, but also binds them together. It is also important to notice that this is not simply a promissory note about an eschatological future, but a down payment on what Augustine means when he points beyond the city of men to the City of God.

The city to which Augustine points presupposes that a community of individuals with a common orientation toward God is our natural condition. As he understands the issue, the individual and the community are an irreducible polarity, where God has created hearts that remain restless until they find rest in him. With this conception in mind, Augustine envisages a community in which we are bound together by a common object of affection. Unlike Plato, who holds the community together with a noble lie,[39] and unlike Hobbes,[40] Rousseau,[41] and Locke,[42] who bind it together with a social contract, Augustine suggests that communities arise naturally when separate individuals are oriented positively toward the same object. Thus, he suggests that the love of God binds Augustine, Alypius, and Monica together, where they mirror one another as (finite$\perp$infinite) beings, where they turn away from merely finite objects of affection, and where they are oriented toward what is infinite in its own right. In doing so, they move from creation *ex nihilo*, and from the existential predicament into which they have fallen, to conversion; and after they have been converted, they move toward fulfillment in the city that they have been created to inhabit.[43]

3

Mother and Son
A Shared Mystical Experience (Book IX)

This chapter begins with the birth of Augustine into a new way of living; and it ends with the death of his mother in Ostia, which brings her work in the world to completion. This implies that Augustine is just beginning to live when his mother dies, and it suggests that the death of the person who has smothered him for so long might be necessary if he is ever to embrace a life of his own. Yet at a deeper level, this part of the text focuses on a spiritual transition from death to life, not only for Augustine, but for his mother as well. At the beginning, we trace Augustine's development from redemption in the garden to baptism in the church; and at the end, we describe the transition of his mother from death in the world to life in God.[1]

These two parts of Augustine's narrative are images of one another, where the birth of Augustine and the death of Monica point to corresponding developments from death to life within their souls. Augustine's birth leads from bondage to the flesh to life in the spirit, while the death of his mother points beyond the loss of life on earth to life in heaven. The spiritual import of both transitions is reflected in the fact that they occur when Augustine is thirty-three (9.11.28). In the Roman world, this means that he has made a successful transition from adolescence to youthful maturity; but in Christian terms, it suggests that he has begun to participate in the life, the death, and the resurrection of Christ. Though Augustine lives and his mother dies, they are bound together by the fact that they celebrate their citizenship in the City of God a few days before her death in Ostia.

From a spatial perspective, this chapter comes to focus on the interplay between Augustine and his mother as members of the body of Christ; and by implication, it returns us to the problem of the individual and the community with which we have been occupied from the outset. Though one begins to flourish while the other prepares to die, what binds Augustine and his mother together is that both of them pass from death to life within the sustaining context of the Christian community. The analogies between Augustine and Monica bind them together and hold them apart, pointing not only to similarities that permit them to participate in the same community, but also to differences that require them to play distinctive roles in it.

When Augustine dies to his old way of life, he enters a new way of living that he must struggle to understand. By contrast, when Monica dies in a world where she can see only "through a glass darkly," she anticipates a new life in which she will see God "face to face." Monica participates in Augustine's journey from faith to understanding by sharing a mystical experience with him a few days before her death in Ostia, but the task of reflection Augustine undertakes in response to this experience stands in contrast with the relatively unreflective apprehension of the truth his mother embraces. Though they both touch the truth, the philosopher must reflect on what Monica accepts as a disclosure of what life with God will be like; and this crucial difference produces a reflective separation between them.

Augustine participates in the death of his mother by undergoing a spiritual death of his own, for her death issues in an existential separation between them that crushes his heart on "a pillow of tears" (9.12.33). In the end, what mediates the chasm between them is neither their temporal development nor their spatial interaction, but a communal orientation toward God that emerges along the vertical axis of experience. God's ears are near Augustine when he cries; God's heart is near Augustine's mother when she dies; and the infinite richness of God sustains them both, where their shared mystical experience gives them access to eternity from which neither life nor death can separate them. What begins as a vision of the Father in Book VII, and as an encounter with the Son in Book VIII, becomes life in the Spirit in Book IX;[2] and the spiritual community as it is actualized in the experience that Augustine shares with his mother gives them a foretaste of eternal life.

RETIREMENT AND BAPTISM (9.1.1–9.7.16)

Augustine's prayer at the beginning of Book IX echoes the desire to praise God with which the *Confessions* begins. Earlier he exclaims that God is great and greatly to be praised and that he desires to praise God as a part of creation and in spite of his sin. Now having put on a new garment and having become a servant of God, first his heart, then his tongue, and finally his bones praise God, asking his creator to respond by assuring him that he has brought salvation to his soul (9.1.1). On the first page of the text, Augustine asks whether he should first invoke God or praise him; and he answers by claiming that those who seek God shall find him, and that those who find him shall praise him. Now he praises the one he has found; and his heart, his tongue, his bones, and his soul are bound together in the desire to hear God say, "I am your salvation" (9.1.1).

Augustine deepens his analysis of the sin from which he has been delivered by asking who and what he is and by suggesting that the evil in which he participates pervades his entire being. First, it expresses itself in his deeds; then it manifests itself in his words; and finally it reaches the center of his will. Yet the recent convert to Christianity is confident that God is merciful and that he has reached down into the depth of his death, removing "an abyss of corruption" from his heart (9.1.1). The death that Augustine faces is not only the death of his body, but also the death of his soul; and his prayer of thanksgiving comes to focus when he says, "This was the sum of it: not to will what I willed and to will what you willed" (9.1.1). The united will that eludes him for so long, and that overcomes the willfulness that separates him from himself, finally expresses itself when his will coincides with the will of God.

Augustine wonders where his free will hides for so many years and from what deep and hidden pit God calls it forth in a single stroke. Though he had been seeking God since childhood, the suddenness of his conversion startles him, suggesting that some of his commentators are not the only ones to wonder about the radical reversal in the garden in Milan. Yet Augustine is clearer than most of us about the nature of his conversion: he is happy to abandon the lusts of the flesh, but he is happier still that a new garment takes their place. The infant of Book I who cries for satisfaction becomes a new creation; and with a mind that is free from seeking favors, from striving for gain, from wallowing in the mire, and from scratching the itching sores of lust, Augustine speaks like a child to the one who becomes his light, his wealth, his salvation, and his Lord (9.1.1).

Against this background, and along the vertical axis on which his soul is related to God, Augustine reaches a prudent decision. Instead of making a boisterous break with the past by snatching his tongue abruptly from the "language marts," he resolves to withdraw quietly. Fortunately, it is only a few days before the long vacation;[3] and Augustine decides to endure them rather than to withdraw from teaching before the vacation begins. Though one of his reasons for abandoning his profession is that his weakened lungs make it impossible for him to use his voice effectively, the reason that matters most is that God has ransomed him and that he does not intend to put himself up for sale again. The innocent victim whom the devil slays sets him free from the law of sin and death, and Augustine is happy to have an excuse to free himself from slavery to his students in order to embrace a new way of living (9.2.2).

Augustine is careful to insist that though God knows his plans for retirement, men, with the exception of his closest friends, do not know them. Critics who believe that Augustine's writings immediately after his conversion are more reliable than the *Confessions* contend that the only reason he relinquishes his position as a professor of rhetoric is the precarious condition of his health. Indeed, this is the only reason he gives in those earlier writings, leading these commentators to conclude that he is fabricating a spiritual explanation for his action in what he says about it as the Bishop of Hippo.[4] However, to proceed in this direction is to mistake a symptom for a cause, where the surface malady of exhausted lungs points to the deeper predicament from which the new garment he is wearing sets him free.

Augustine and his friends agree not to make the fundamental reason for his decision public, for they anticipate opposition from two directions. On the one hand, the "unfriendly friends" who help Augustine achieve his professional ambitions would reject him (9.2.2). On the other hand, Christians who hear about Augustine's decision might praise him for it, encouraging others to believe that by making a radical break from his public profession, Augustine is trying to glorify himself (9.2.3). Flanked by both alternatives, the author of the *Confessions* emphasizes the vertical dimension of his situation by saying that he and his friends are "mounting up from the vale of tears," singing a "gradual canticle" as they approach Jerusalem, and that as citizens of the City of God, they are armed with "arrows" and "consuming coals" against deceitful tongues (9.2.2). The ocean that has threatened to engulf them is expelled through their tears; the psalms they sing sustain them as they approach dry land; and the arrows and coals God gives them enable them to defend the

City they seek against the uncharitable thoughts and actions of citizens of the City of Men.

Yet the arrows that God supplies them to fend off critics pale by comparison with the arrow of God's love that pierces their hearts. In the garden in Milan, the voice of God breaks across the chasm that separates Augustine from him; and in the Christian community that emerges from this transformation, Augustine and his friends are transfixed in their "inmost parts" by the transforming word of God that sets them free (9.2.3). Indeed, Augustine indicates that he still has his Christian conversion in mind by reminding us of the examples of other people who have led him to embrace the grace of God (9.2.3). He also tells us that the words of God reach his body as well as his soul, that the living word transfixes his vitals, and that the transformation of others from death to life bring flaming fire into his mind (*animus*) (9.2.3). These are not the words of a disembodied soul, but the shout of victory from a transformed being; and they allow Augustine not only to abandon the deceitful tongue of a rhetorician, but also to resist the tongues of his detractors.

Though the teacher of rhetoric endures twenty days in his "Chair of Lies" until the long vacation comes, he finds it a strain to continue. The greediness that had sustained him is gone, and continuing to teach would have overwhelmed him if patience had not taken its place (9.2.4). This single word points to an open space that Augustine enters, where the silence and the convalescence he must endure are necessary conditions for becoming an instrument through which God can speak. The great psychologist acknowledges the fact that he must surrender words of his own to the Word of God; but he also discovers that as a result of the silence he endures, God will speak through him more powerfully than he could have ever spoken with words of his own.

Augustine indicates that he is making the transition from speech to silence, and from his own words to the Word of God, by expressing concern that his fellow Christians who read the *Confessions* will believe that he sins by continuing to teach rhetoric even for a single hour. Yet he remains true to the vertical axis along which he is moving by not entering into a dispute with them, and by expressing confidence that the waters of baptism wipe away "sins" of this kind, as well as deeds that lead toward destruction. The vertical axis of experience is more important to Augustine than the horizontal; and he expects other Christians to stand with him there, rather than to criticize the details of his behavior (9.2.4).

Friendship is crucial to Augustine, not only as it defines his relation to the Christian community, but also as it expresses itself in interaction with his closest companions. Thus, he considers the effects of his decision to abandon his profession on some of the friends who sustain him during his practice of it. For example, Augustine tells us that his abrupt decision tortures the man who is one of his most ardent financial supporters; for though his wife is a Christian, this friend is convinced that he cannot join Augustine in his commitment to Christianity because he is enslaved by the chains of matrimony. The slavery that had bound Augustine hand and foot is slavery of a much more innocent kind for Verecundus; but at the moment, slavery in this second case, and the ascetic ideal it expresses, prevents one of his closest friends from becoming a Christian (9.3.5).

In spite of this, Augustine's wealthy friend makes an important contribution to the new convert, inviting him and his companions to use his country house at Cassiciacum as a place for rest and contemplation. After Augustine and his friends return from their retreat, and while they are absent from their friend in Rome, Verecundus dies; but Augustine is consoled by the fact that before his friend "departs," he becomes a Christian, and by implication, a friend of a deeper kind than before. Augustine does not want to remember the kindness of Verecundus without also remembering that their friendship is sustained at a higher level. The house at Cassiciacum where Augustine finds rest is a heaven on earth; and he is thankful that as a reward for the gift of a time of rest to his friends, God gives Verecundus eternal rest, where his sins are forgiven, and where he reaches the mountain from which the infinite richness of God overflows (9.3.5).

At the moment, Verecundus is unhappy when Augustine becomes a Christian; but his friend Nebridius is not. Though he is not yet a Christian, and though he had fallen into the belief that the body of Christ is a phantasm, he emerges from this error about the incarnation, pointing once more to the importance of the birth, the death, and the resurrection of Christ in the account Augustine is giving of the meaning of the Christian faith. Indeed, freed from his error about Christology, Nebridius becomes an ardent seeker after truth; and not long after Augustine's baptism, he becomes a Christian himself, serving the church in North Africa before he dies (9.3.6).

Augustine's description of the death of Nebridius points in an unexpected direction. He tells us that this acute analyst of abstract questions, who is not present at his conversion, and who had been enslaved by the docetic heresy, is released from the flesh. Yet the "flesh" he has in mind is not the body, but a metaphorical way of expressing the negative orientation of the will that had separated his friend from God. Thus, Augustine says that Nebridius now lives in Abraham's "bosom" (9.3.6). Whatever kind of abode this bodily symbol signifies, the crucial distinction to which it calls our attention is not between the soul and the body, but between sin and redemption. When Augustine contrasts the flesh from which Nebridius is liberated with Abraham's bosom in which he dwells, he replaces a bodily metaphor for sin with an equally powerful bodily metaphor for salvation. In doing so, he implies that his friend is free from bondage to sin, and that he becomes an adopted son of God.

In anticipating the death of Verecundus and Nebridius, Augustine returns to the narrative present by turning his attention in two directions. First, he comforts Verecundus, attempts to reconcile him to his conversion, and exhorts him to become a Christian even though he is married (9.3.5). By contrast, he looks forward to the moment when Nebridius will follow him in renouncing the flesh; and indeed, the time when he will do so is near at hand (9.3.6). Once again, the flesh has two meanings in Augustine's philosophical vocabulary: though it points to the celibate life that Augustine prefers for himself and his friend, Nebridius, he does not hesitate to make room in the Christian community for Verecundus, who has no intention of abandoning his wife.

Having reflected on the death and the conversion of two of his friends, Augustine now shifts his attention from the past to the future. He has endured twenty days in the rhetorical desert, waiting for the moment when freedom will come; and when he finally abandons the Chair of Rhetoric in Milan, it is appropriate for him to use an auditory metaphor to mark the occasion. The great rhetorician exclaims,

You set free my tongue, as you had already freed my heart from that profession. I blessed you, and joyfully, together with all my household, I started out for that country place. (9.4.7)

In speaking about the moment when emancipation from his teaching duties finally comes, Augustine describes his life at Cassiciacum in one of the most controversial parts of the text. He tells us that his books testify to what he writes during his retirement; and he classifies them under three categories: dialogues with students and friends, a silent soliloquy in the presence of God, and letters to Nebridius that contain some of the most profound philosophical reflections in which he ever engages. Nevertheless, Augustine adds a qualifying phrase that places brackets around all of his literary work at Cassiciacum: "During this period as it were of rest it still breathed forth the school of pride" (9.4.7).

Many commentators emphasize the difference between the *Confessions* and Augustine's writings immediately after his conversion.[5] Yet the most striking fact about his recollection of his time at Cassiciacum is that he does not hide the differences between what he writes there and his evaluation of it from the standpoint of the *Confessions*. This evaluation points to the pride of the Neoplatonists from which he had not recovered completely in the aftermath of his conversion in the garden and during his final days as a teacher of rhetoric.

Some of Augustine's critics conclude that he is a Neoplatonist rather than a Christian at Cassiciacum, and the evidence to which they point takes three forms. First, the dialogues focus primarily on philosophical topics, and they express a degree of philosophical skepticism that seems inappropriate in a recent convert to Christianity. Second, Augustine does not mention his conversion in Milan in letters to his friend, Nebridius; and when he refers to it in one of the dialogues, he speaks about embracing Continence rather than Christ at the pivotal moment in the garden. Finally, he says that his illness is the reason for his retirement from the Chair of Rhetoric, not mentioning the fact that his deeper motive is to move away from the bondage of the will from which Christ sets him free.[6]

As in every scholarly controversy, there are always replies to critics that point in the opposite direction. The dialogues written at Cassiciacum are philosophical exercises that imitate a Ciceronian pattern; and in writings of this kind, we should expect a rhetorician to accommodate himself to the needs of his students. These dialogues are also explicitly Christian in spite of their Neoplatonic dimension, presupposing faith in Christ, acknowledging the authority of the Church, and illustrating Augustine's dictum that faith should be engaged in the task of seeking understanding. Finally, Augustine tells us his reasons for mentioning his conversion to Christianity only to his closest friends; and his failure to describe it in detail, even to Nebridius, tells us more about Nebridius than it does about him. The rhetorician always says what is appropriate to the character of those whom he addresses; and in this case, he waits until later to reveal what he now keeps hidden.[7]

The most startling fact about those who believe that a longing for chastity and continence is the most important factor in Augustine's conversion is their philosophical and historical literalism. These critics think in dichotomies; and in this respect, they resemble the Manichaeans from whom it takes Augustine eleven years to disassociate himself. Commentators of this kind separate historical events from subsequent interpretations, maintain that Augustine is either a Christian theologian or a Neoplatonic philosopher, and insist that he retires from teaching either because of a physical illness or because he decides to become a Christian. In all these cases, the critic asks us to choose between incompatible alternatives with no logical space in between.

This way of proceeding will never put us in touch with the mind of a thinker as complex as Augustine, who always remains a rhetorician, speaks in figurative language, merges historical events with imaginative interpretations, and immerses himself in a life in process rather than languishing in a torture chamber of rigid distinctions. If we are to understand the pattern of Augustine's development, we must plunge into the stream of his life; and if we do this, the following picture emerges. Though Augustine puts on Christ in Milan, and though he has a preliminary understanding of what this means when the decisive moment occurs, he does not have an adequate set of categories to express the theological significance of his existential transformation, either in Milan, or when he arrives in Cassiciacum. As a consequence, he not only conceals the distinctively Christian motivation for his actions from those who would not understand it, but also uses the only language available to him to express the significance of his religious experience in what he writes during his retirement. As he develops, other philosophical and theological categories will become accessible to him; but this does not mean that he is a Neoplatonist at Cassiciacum and that he becomes a Christian only after his baptism. To believe this would be to embrace dichotomies that Augustine would have never accepted.

My account of Augustine's development emphasizes his use of rhetorical and figurative discourse to describe the pivotal moments of his life, and it focuses on his appreciation of the dimension of difference as a crucial aspect of human experience. The first allows him to move from stage to stage without bifurcating his experience, while the second points to what is distinctively Christian in the story of his life. Rhetoric allows him to hide and to reveal what is appropriate on particular occasions, and figurative discourse permits him to talk about the relation between God and the soul by transcending the dichotomy between the continuity of Neoplatonism and the discontinuity of Christianity. In addition, the use of auditory metaphors allows Augustine to introduce and mediate a chasm between God and the soul that is much more radical than the dimension of difference to be found in the teachings of Plotinus and Porphyry. As a consequence, the one who puts on a new garment in the garden in Milan is able to use rhetoric, figurative discourse, and auditory metaphors to generate a space in which the infinite richness of the relation between God and the soul can express itself.

Augustine discovers part of this infinite richness at Cassiciacum; for even here, he insists that putting on Christ is essential for his transformation. This becomes clear when Alypius, who is reluctant to have the name of Christ included in Augustine's writings, finally assents to its inclusion, making it clear that both he and his teacher are committed to the Christian community (9.4.7). The prayer with which Augustine begins the *Soliloquies* and which records his private philosophical reflections at Cassiciacum also prefigures the existential passion of the *Confessions*. Here he is free of the rhetorical constraints his students impose upon him, and the forceful language he employs prepares the way for the language he uses later to describe his conversion.[8] Finally, the burden of Augustine's remarks in the *Confessions* about his retirement at Cassiciacum is that he meditates on the Psalms and cultivates a devotional life during the period immediately prior to his baptism (9.4.8). Though he engages in philosophy in public, he meditates on the Scriptures in private; and his account of his retirement puts us in touch with the existential dimension of his life that undergirds both activities.

In an age when philosophy and theology often follow different paths, it is not surprising that scholars should impose a radical distinction between them on Augustine. Yet he insists that philosophy is the love of wisdom, that he finds the incarnation of it in the garden in Milan, and that he begins to understand what this means in the private meditations he undertakes at the villa of his friend. One indication that this is so is that Augustine discovers the value of a life of humility during his retirement at Cassiciacum. During the wakeful nights he spends alone, the one who humbles himself in the incarnation, and who becomes obedient to death on the cross, subdues him and brings him low. As a consequence, the recent convert to Christianity begins to be conformed, not only to the image of God, but also to the image of Christ (9.4.9–10).

At Cassiciacum, Augustine cries when he reads the Psalms; and as he does so, he finds that these hymns of faith leave no room for pride. As he reflects on these earlier days in the *Confessions*, Augustine admits how far he has to travel, pointing out that he is still a novice in his relation to God and is simply a catechumen on a holiday at a villa. Yet the most important dimension of Augustine's meditations at Cassiciacum is the passion they generate, where the Psalms he reads set him on fire, and where he burns to repeat them against the pride of the Manichaeans (9.4.8).

The passion Augustine feels in private spills over into his attitude toward his enemies; for he is still indignant with the Manichaeans, even though he also pities them. Indeed, he wishes that they could have been close by to see his face and hear his voice as he pours over the fourth Psalm, where his facial expressions and his intonations reveal how he feels more clearly than his words. Augustine even wishes that the Manichaeans might have heard his comments about the Psalm without his knowledge; for under such conditions, they would not have thought that he speaks as he does simply on their account. In addition, the rhetorician is careful to point out that he would not have said "those same words, nor would [he have said] them in the same way" if he had known they were listening (9.4.8). The reason he gives for this way of proceeding is not that he wants to say only what others want to hear, but that if he had spoken to the Manichaeans about what he is feeling as he meditates, what he would have said would not have meant the same things to them as it does to him (9.4.8). The language of God and the soul is not a private language, but those who speak it can only communicate with others who want to learn how to speak it themselves.

Augustine trembles with fear; he warms with hope; he rejoices in the mercy of God; and when he listens to the Spirit of God, all these feelings express themselves in the expression in his eyes and in the sound of his voice. And even though the author of the text admits that he had loved vanity and had sought falsehood, he is now confident that God magnifies his son, raises him from the dead, and sends forth the "Spirit of Truth." Augustine knows about the Son at Cassiciacum, but he does not know about the Spirit. Yet even there he hears God's Spirit speaking through the Psalms, where in this as in so many other cases, the primary role of the Spirit is to call our attention to the Word of God. Augustine speaks "strongly"; and this time, he wishes that the Manichaeans could hear him (9.4.8). If they could, perhaps they would repudiate their errors and God would hear them; for he tells us that by a true death in the flesh, the one who now makes intercession for us also dies for us. Thus, even though he does not know about the Holy Spirit at Cassiciacum, the words he utters there are not about a phantom that dies, but the cry of a passionate heart, thanking God for coming into the world and for dying in his place (9.4.9).

When he writes the *Confessions*, Augustine remembers what happens at Cassiciacum; and as if to illustrate this, he reports what seems to be a trivial incident. During the long vacation, God "tortures" him with a toothache; and when the pain becomes so great that he is unable to speak, he urges all his friends who are present to pray for him. He writes this request on a tablet that he gives them to read; and when they bow their knees, the pain is gone. Yet Augustine wonders what kind of pain it is and how it flees away; he is terrified because from his earliest years, he has never experienced such pain; and when it vanishes so quickly, he rejoices in faith, praises the name of God, and is profoundly impressed with his providence (9.4.12).

The pain that Augustine feels is a later reflection of the illness that he experiences as a child. On that earlier occasion, he is at the point of death and begs his mother for baptism; but she does not call the priest because he recovers (1.11.17). Now he has a toothache that is even more painful, and it vanishes immediately when his friends pray for him. In the first case, God watches over him in silence; in the second, God responds to the prayers of his friends. Yet at a deeper level, Augustine's toothache is so painful that he cannot speak; and as a consequence, he must write his request on a tablet for his companions to read. At this moment, the pagan rhetorician is finally silenced, and he waits in silence for God to answer the petitions of his friends.

The faith that Augustine expresses does not allow him to rest from his past sins until baptism washes them away, and he begins to take the necessary steps of preparation. At the end of the long vacation, he notifies the officials in Milan that they must find another teacher; and he gives two reasons for his decision. The first is his determination to serve God, and the second is his incapacity to continue in his vocation because of difficulty in breathing and because of the pain in his chest (9.5.13). These reasons are connected, since the former calls our attention to the grace of God, and the latter is a concrete reflection of Augustine's sin. Earlier, he stakes everything on his capacity to speak; but now he is willing to accept redemption, to turn away from his profession, and to allow God to begin to speak through him.

When the time comes for him to submit his name for baptism, Augustine leaves the villa at Cassiciacum for Milan; and his friend, Alypius, follows him, having decided to receive baptism as well. The great rhetorician's description of his friend confirms his earlier account of his character; and the irony in what Augustine says about him can scarcely be disguised:

> He was now clothed with that humility which befits your sacra-
> ments. Valiantly had he brought his body into subjection, even to
> the point that, with unusual daring, he would tread the icy Italian
> ground with bare feet. (9.6.14)

This description of Alypius reflects Augustine's admiration for asceticism,[9] but it also contains an all too obvious comparison between Alypius and Socrates. In the *Symposium*, we hear that Socrates walks in the snow without any shoes;[10] and when these stories about Socrates and Alypius are taken together, the radical subordination of the body to the will points to an absence of Eros in both of them. Augustine's problem, by contrast, is how to embrace the ascetic life without the loss of the erotic fire that has begun to express itself in his love of God.

Augustine and Alypius take Adeodatus with them to Milan; and though he is the offspring of Augustine's sin, it is far more important that he is a concrete reflection of the creative power of God. Though he is barely fifteen years old, his remarkable intelligence exceeds that of many learned men; and Augustine is eager to acknowledge that nothing in the boy except his sin belongs to him, while everything else is a reflection of the redemptive grace of God. Nevertheless, Augustine's fatherly affection surfaces when he insists that in his book, *The Teacher*, all the words put into the mouth of his interlocutor belong to Adeodatus, though he is only sixteen at the time. At the age when Augustine steals pears with his adolescent companions and falls into the bottomless pit to which sin for its own sake points, his son, who is brought up with the discipline the young Augustine lacks, is able to engage in philosophical discussion with a talent that provokes the awe of his gifted father (9.6.14).

Finally, Augustine returns to the vertical dimension of experience by informing us that his son dies; but he also insists that when he remembers him, he does so with a sense of security because he fears nothing about his childhood, his youth, or his entire career (9.6.14). As created, Adeodatus lives in an unfallen spatiotemporal matrix; as the son of his father, he is born in sin; but as a Christian, he moves through a converted spatiotemporal matrix toward fulfillment. Having been converted already, Augustine, Alypius, and Adeodatus are baptized; and their anxiety about their former life passes away. Augustine has already prepared us for the death of two of his closest friends, as well as the death of his son; but baptism convinces him that neither death nor life will be able to separate them from the love of God as it expresses itself in the death and resurrection of Christ.

Augustine plunges beneath the level of consciousness to reveal his feelings rather than his thoughts; and as he mediates on the mystery of salvation, he weeps as he sings the hymns of the Church. The *voices* of others move him at a level deeper than words; they *flow* into his ears; the truth of what he hears *pours* into his heart; the tide of his emotions *overflows;* his tears *run down;* but amidst his *tears,* all is well with him. The force of these words is not confined to their content, but also incarnates Augustine's response to the redemptive grace of God; and as the words he sings flow into his heart, they begin to give him access to the happy life he has been seeking for so long (9.6.14).

The custom of singing together in the church develops in Milan in response to a crisis. A year earlier, the mother of the Emperor persecutes Ambrose because of her commitment to the Arian heresy; and in response to her threats, the parishioners keep guard at the church, willing to die with their bishop. Augustine's mother takes a leading part in defending Ambrose; and she lives in the church for an extended period, keeping watch. Augustine admits that at this earlier stage, the heat of God's Spirit had still not melted him completely; but the alarm and disturbance in the city excites him nonetheless. At this difficult moment, the custom of singing hymns and psalms begins in the Western Church; and Ambrose institutes it because it allows those who are afraid to replace their cries of lamentation with songs of redemption. Augustine knows that music reaches deeper than cognition; and on this occasion, it gives the congregation in Milan access to the Word of God that quiets their fears (9.7.15).

The music in the air leads Ambrose to a vision; and inspired by what he sees, he finds the burial place of two martyrs. Members of his congregation dig them up in time to check the fury of the queen; and as they carry them along the road, God heals several people who are possessed with unclean spirits. A well-known man in the city who is blind for many years also recovers his sight, leading us to expect that Augustine models his narrative at this point on a similar episode in the Gospel of John.[11] In both cases, the crucial message is clear: where the spirit of God is present, wholeness always comes, not only to the soul, but to the body as well. Finally standing erect, the Prodigal Son, who feeds husks to the swine, is thankful for the life of faith that opens out before him; and though he cannot breathe well enough to teach, he breathes in the power of God as he begins to return to the house of his father.

MONICA'S CHARACTER (9.8.17–9.9.22)

After his baptism, Augustine continues his narrative in a disarming way, telling us that his friend, Evodius, joins him and his other companions. Evodius is a former secret service agent of the Emperor who becomes a Christian (9.8.17); and by introducing him at this stage of his narrative,

Augustine points in two directions: he prepares us for the role Evodius will play at a later stage in Book IX, and he reminds us of the two secret service agents whose stories inspire him to become a Christian. In both directions, former servants of the emperor of the City of Man stand beside Augustine as he prepares to become a servant in the City of God.

The placid beginning of this section of the text masks a radical disruption in the pattern of Augustine's life. He and his friends decide to abandon life in the city and return to Africa; but when they get as far as Ostia, his mother dies (9.8.17). Augustine does not surround this sentence with rhetorical flourishes, but points abruptly to a pivotal fact that drives a dagger into his heart. The author of the text prepares us for the death of two of his closest friends, and he tells us that his son will die before the year is over. Yet now without any preparation, he brings his readers face to face with the death of his mother, not simply as an immanent possibility, but as a finished fact.

How does he react to the death of the person who accompanies him during every stage of his development and who moves from city to city pursuing him, concerned not only about his journey toward God, but also devoted so persistently to his worldly success? Earlier Augustine describes the devastating personal consequences of the death of his closest philosophical friend; and from his standpoint as the author of the text, he gives a detailed account of what it means to love our friends in God. Now his recollection of the death of his mother, who is both an obstacle and a catalyst in his quest for autonomy, threatens to call both his theory and his faith into question.

Augustine responds to the death of his mother by devoting the last part of his autobiography to her. First, he depicts Monica's character; then he describes a mystical experience he shares with her a few days before her death; and finally, he faces her death directly, responding with tears, with memories, and with a prayer that places the life of both of his parents within the context of the Christian community. In this context, Augustine stands beside his parents; and in doing so, he stands at a place where questions of genetic succession pale by comparison with the deeper relation between God and the soul.

Death does not have the last word in this chapter, and Augustine makes this clear immediately after he mentions the death of his mother. He says,

I omit many things, as I am making great haste. Accept my confessions and acts of thanksgiving, O my God, for countless

> things, even those I pass over in silence. But I will not pass over
> whatever my soul brings to birth concerning that handmaid of
> yours, who brought me to birth, both in her flesh, and in her
> heart, that I might be born into eternal light. (9.8.17)

Augustine is hastening beyond silence to the themes of memory, time, and the hermeneutics of creation; but by focusing in detail on the death of his mother, he is also anticipating the resurrection. Augustine is convinced that Monica has returned to God, and he is finally ready to climb the communal and reflective ladder that will lead him back to his origins.

In disrupting the continuity of his narrative by discussing the death of his mother, Augustine is moving in a Christian rather than in a Neoplatonic direction. Plotinus never mentions his family or his earthly origins, nor does he even allow a sculptor to create a bust of him.[12] By contrast, after Augustine says that he must hasten, he pauses for six paragraphs to focus on the life and death of his mother (9.8.17–9.9.22). Yet even here, Augustine knows that the most important aspect of his recollections points from death to life and by implication, calls our attention to the vertical relation between God and the soul. Thus, he does not intend to speak of the gifts of his mother in merely personal terms, but of the gifts of God *in* her, where creation *ex nihilo* rather than natural generation is the central theme.

The details of Monica's character emerge quickly. Her good training results from the diligence of an elderly maidservant, who had been a member of the family for many years and had been the nurse of Monica's father. Because he values her so much, her father commits the care of his daughters to her; and she performs her duties persistently, restraining and instructing Monica with wisdom and severity. For example, she does not allow her to drink water except at mealtimes; for she anticipates the day when Monica will have control of the wine cellar, when the habit of drinking excessively can easily establish itself (9.8.17).

Yet Monica is not a pliable pupil, and she tells Augustine how a love for wine begins to steal over her when she is still a child. When her parents send her to draw wine for the table from the cask in the cellar, she wets her lips with a taste of it. At first, she does not do this because she has a craving to drink, but from the youthful exuberance that often emerges from an affirmation of life. Yet she moves from exuberance toward addiction by adding a little wine day after day, slipping gradually into the habit of drinking the entire cup. Only when a servant girl who accompanies Monica to the wine cellar calls her "a drunkard" is she able to renounce and turn away from her habit (9.8.18).

Throughout his account of his mother's development, Augustine wants to be clear about the order of grace in relation to the order of works. Thus he insists that God subjects his mother to her parents more than they subject Monica to Him (9.9.19). When she reaches an appropriate age, her parents find a husband for her; and in the order of grace, she quickly becomes his "servant," preaching to him through her actions, and enduring his infidelities with patience. There is no dissension between them about this, not because Monica is pleased with her husband's behavior, but because she is prepared to wait for God's mercy to transform him. Her husband has a violent temper, but even here she does not criticize him, preferring to wait until he is calm to give him an explanation for her actions (9.9.19).

Their husbands beat many of Monica's friends, and the bruises on their faces point to the almost unbearable burden that some of them endure. Yet instead of focusing on the husband whose behavior she cannot control, Monica encourages her battered friends to modify their own behavior. In what she clearly takes to be a joke hurled in the face of what is by no means a joking matter, she admonishes them to regard themselves as "slaves" rather than as rivals of their "lords." These women know about the furious temper of Patricius, and they marvel that he has never beaten his wife. Yet when they ask her why this is so, Monica tells them that it is because she follows the rule she has given them (9.9.19).

In a society where the only living options are abuse and passive resistance, those who follow Monica's advice confirm the wisdom of it and rejoice, while those who do not continue to be bullied and beaten by their husbands (9.9.19). This does not mean that Monica endorses the domestic behavior of barbarians, or that she is recommending passive aggression as the only viable alternative to domestic abuse. Rather, she is suggesting that the path of grace is more powerful than the path of resistance, passive or otherwise, and that the transformation of society can come about, not by a readjustment of the relations of power, but only by redemptive acts that express the grace of God. Those with ears to hear can sometimes embrace this path; and when they do so, grace not only redeems them from destruction, but also transforms those who try to snatch their dignity away.

Even more surprisingly, Monica comes to terms with her mother-in-law, not through conquest, but submission. Meddling servants spread rumors about her to cause dissension between the two women; but because of Monica's patience, her mother-in-law orders her son to punish the servants who have tried to separate them. She also promises similar treatment to anyone who dares to malign the character of her daughter-in-law (9.9.20). Monica's victory in this case is an unusual feat in any culture, and Augustine acknowledges this by exclaiming that the entire family lives together with extraordinary harmony and goodwill.

Another dimension of Monica's character is the role she plays as a peacemaker in the community. If the poor in spirit inherit the kingdom of heaven, and if the gentle inherit the earth, the peacemakers shall be called the children of God. In calling our attention to grace that is greater than sin, Augustine says that when Monica hears bitter things on either side of a controversy, she discloses nothing to either party except what reconciles them to one another. Where grace is the central theme, it is not enough to restrain ourselves from inciting conflict, but important to extinguish it altogether with gentle words that bring the parties in the dispute back to themselves. God teaches Monica to do this in the "school of her heart," causing Augustine not to praise his mother, but to praise her willingness to allow the grace of God to express itself through her (9.9.21).

At the beginning of his remarks about Monica's capacity as a peacemaker, Augustine points to the distance between God and the soul and to the act of grace that makes a positive relation between these two radically different spheres of existence possible. In the Magnificat, Mary calls herself the handmaiden of the Lord and accepts her role as the mother of the son God begets.[13] By contrast, Monica is a different kind of handmaiden because God *creates* Augustine in her womb. Monica's womb is the place where both the distance and the positive relation between the creator and the creature express themselves. Thus, Augustine is not a soul that has fallen into the body, or a soul that God begets, but a soul and a body created *ex nihilo*; and because of the sin his mother shares with Adam, he is also an *embodied being* in need of redemption.

Finally, Augustine informs us that toward the end of his father's life, Monica brings her husband to the place of transformation. In this case, Monica turns the other cheek; and her husband moves from a position of power to the humility required to accept the grace of God (9.9.22). Monica is also the servant of the servants of God, honors her parents, guides her house in piety, and raises her children with discipline. Before her death, she also cares for her son and his friends who live together; and in a beautiful antithesis, Augustine says,

> Before she fell asleep . . . , she took care as though she had been mother of us all, and she served us as though she had been a daughter to us all. (9.9.22)

In this case, the handmaiden of the Lord becomes the servant of his children.

We know nothing about Monica's character except what Augustine tells us; but throughout his narrative, he does not disguise the tensions that define her life.[14] First, there is a tension between Monica and God. Though she devotes her life to him, she never ceases to entreat and challenge him on behalf of her son. The fullness of life that drives her to the wine cellar expresses itself in a relentless attempt to bring Augustine to God; and in the process, she exasperates a priest who tells her to leave her son alone. Nevertheless, she moves from one city to the next, never ceasing to pray that God will bring Augustine home.

There is also a tension at the horizontal level between Augustine's mother and her son. She pursues him to Carthage, to Milan, and into retirement at Cassiciacum; and she never turns loose. Like Aeneas, Augustine tries to escape on the shore at Carthage; but the more persistently he turns away from his mother, the more determined she becomes to follow him. Her will opposes his willfulness, and it is only near the end of her life that they share a mystical experience that brings them both into the presence of God. Monica finally lets Augustine go a few days before her death, but she is willing to do so even then only because she is confident that he is safe in the arms of God (9.10.26).

The tension within Monica's character also surfaces in her marriage. She suspends herself between duty to her husband and love for God; and at an early stage in Augustine's development, she wishes that God would become his father rather than Patricius. When she submits to her husband in obedience, she also brings him to the place where he submits himself to the will of God; and it is always with a measure of irony that she advises her friends to be the servants of their husbands. In the culture of the late Roman Empire, this is good advice; but Monica never disguises her superiority to her husband, and calls our attention to God's capacity to transform slavery at the human level into its radical inversion by the grace of God.

In planning Augustine's education, Monica faces a further tension between her admiration of classical culture and her commitment to the Christian Church. She wants Augustine to become a great rhetorician, and she makes elaborate plans for a marriage that will guarantee his success as a government official. She is also ruthless in demanding that he abandon his mistress because she is an impediment to his career. On the other hand, Monica wants Augustine to become a Christian and to place his life in the hands of God. In Richard Niebuhr's felicitous phrase, the opposition between Christ and culture defines Monica's character; and it often pulls her in opposing directions about the future of her son.

Monica experiences a tension between her natural capacity as a rhetorician and her awareness that silence is necessary if we are to hear the Voice of God. There can be no doubt that she possesses the gift of choosing appropriate places to speak; and this is nowhere more evident than in her choice not to defy her husband when he is angry. On the other hand, when he is calm, she patiently explains the reason for her actions that he has been unable to discern for himself (9.9.19). On her way to find Augustine in Milan, she even calms the sailors who are afraid during a storm at sea; and on this occasion, her words even calm the waters of destruction so she can join her son as he prepares to climb the mountain toward the City of God.

Monica is sensitive to the words of others; for even when she is a child, a single insult from a servant girl is enough to turn her away from drinking too much wine. On the other hand, she is silent at the most crucial moments of her life: when the priest tells her to leave her son alone, she finally does so; and when Augustine tells her that he rejects Manichaean dualism and renews his commitment as a catechumen of the Catholic Church, she holds her peace. On her deathbed, she even abandons discourse altogether, slips away into the silence of eternity, and lets Augustine go by loving him in God.

Finally, Monica expresses a tension between practical wisdom and superior intuition. The first trait allows her to deal with her husband and her friends, while the second permits her to have dreams and visions about the will of God and the destiny of her son. Monica embraces the world with the relentlessness of a Mother who wants to bring her son to God, but she can do this only because she finally turns away from the world to catch a glimpse of Augustine's ultimate destiny. When she dreams about the wooden ruler, she sees her son standing on the rule of faith; and as she works her way through the world, this intuition sustains her even when she almost despairs that her son will ever find God. In this process, her character, which is so often an obstacle to Augustine's progress, becomes a vehicle through which he reaches the place where he is able to join his mother in responding to the grace of God.

THE GARDEN IN OSTIA (9.10.23–9.10.26)

The fundamental problem of the *Confessions* is the relation between God and soul; but as the narrative develops, it also becomes the problem of the relation between a son and his mother. Monica tries to smother Augustine, planning his education, pushing him toward professional success, and insisting that he return to his origins by embracing God as his father. Though this Christian Aeneas, who is destined to found a new world, tricks his mother and sails to Rome without her, he carries a sense of guilt with him that makes him susceptible to a serious illness when he finally reaches the shore. Now these days of tension are over; for even though Augustine had not expected an existential transformation to occur in Italy, it does so in a few months, and in a sequence of three stages. First Augustine embraces Neoplatonism; then he becomes a Christian; and finally, he joins his mother in a new kind of community that reflects the redemptive power of the Christian tradition.

Shortly before her death, Augustine and Monica share a mystical experience that expresses the structure of this new community. As the day of Monica's death approaches, Augustine and his mother lean out a window and look into the garden at the center of the house they are occupying in Ostia before they sail back to Africa (9.10.23). As is the case in Cassiciacum, they are separated from the crowd, resting from the long land journey they have just completed, and preparing for the long sea journey they are about to undertake. Yet even more fundamentally, they are engaged in conversation, not about the past or the future, or about their relationship with one another, but about eternity; and standing in the present, they stretch forth to contemplate the City of God. In doing so, they begin to consider things that the eye has not seen, the ear has not heard, and that have never "entered into the heart of a man" to comprehend (9.10.23). Indeed, the mouths of their hearts open out, seeking to drink from the fountain where the most profound mystery about the nature and the destiny of man is contained.

Augustine places the death of Monica and the experience they are about to share in the hands of God, and he does so in two ways. First, he tells us that only God knows the day of his mother's death; then he says that though he and his mother happen to be alone at the window, the providence of God arranges it (9.10.23). From a horizontal point of view, death hides its face; and as they stand together at the open window, Augustine and his mother are alone at the end of one journey and at the beginning of another. Yet from a vertical perspective, God knows when Monica will die; and along the eternal axis of experience, the episode in which Augustine and his mother participate takes them on a journey that points beyond space and time and leads them to the gates of heaven. As they look out the window into the garden at the center of the house, space, time, and eternity intersect; and the providence of God manifests itself, making it possible for them to transcend the contrast between chance and necessity.

The garden that appears at this juncture is not the Garden of Eden, the orchard in which the pear-stealing episode occurs, nor the garden in Milan where Augustine's conversion to Christianity takes place. Rather, it is a place at the center of the house, and by implication, at the center of the hearts of the mother and the son who are moving into it. Indeed, the place into which they are moving is not only at the center of their souls, but also expresses the infinite richness of God. Augustine takes us from one garden to another, where we first stand beside Adam and Eve in the Garden of Eden, not only in their original innocence, but also in their original sin. From this first garden, we turn to an orchard to join Augustine and his adolescent companions in a gratuitous act of self-accentuation that separates us from God. Then we move to a garden attached to the house where Augustine lives in Milan; and when we follow him in moving as far away from the house as possible, we listen to the voice of redemption that comes from beyond the garden wall that separates him from the presence of God. Finally, we come to the garden at the center of the house where Augustine and his mother are resting, where the journey toward inwardness they undertake begins to reach its culmination, pointing beyond the center of their souls toward the shared experience of self-transcendence that will bring them into the presence of God.

The new theme to which Augustine turns in this fourth garden is the nature of eternal life, where both the garden and the eternal rest to which it points are the appropriate circumstances for a conversation about it (9.10.23). Learning to speak the language of God and the soul is the central task of the *Confessions*, but now the focus shifts to a conversation between a mother and a son who want to live in the presence of God. Augustine and Monica forget what is past, reach toward the future, and stand in the present. The present is the only place where they are alive, and as we shall discover from Augustine's analysis of the nature of time in Book XI, it is the standpoint from which they can bind the modes of time together. This is so because time and eternity converge in the present, permitting us to move away from our distension and distraction and allowing us to stretch forth toward the redemptive grace of God. The God in whose presence Augustine and Monica want to live is a dynamic center of mystery, power, and meaning; but he is also both present and absent, requiring those who seek him to forget the past, embrace the future, and allow him to put their souls in motion in the present as they begin their journey toward the City of God.

God begins to do this when Augustine and Monica discuss the eternal life of the saints. This conversation soon leads beyond them to the place where the "highest delight of fleshly sense" and "the brightest corporeal light" seem to be unworthy of comparison with the sweetness of eternity (9.10.24). Then they lift themselves toward God, passing gradually through "all bodily things" and "up to that heaven whence shine the sun and the moon and all the stars down upon the earth." By "inward thought" they soar still higher, not only musing inwardly, but also speaking and marveling at the works the voice of God has created. Finally, Augustine describes the path to transcendence by claiming that he and his mother come at last to their own minds and go beyond them to the source of wisdom from which the world is created (9.10.24). From a philosophical point of view, the object of the quest for understanding is *Sophia;* and from a Christian perspective, it is the eternal *Word.* Yet they are both united in the act of creation *ex nihilo* from which everything other than God comes into existence.

In describing this mystical experience, which unites the Neoplatonic vision of Book VII with the Christian conversion of Book VIII,[15] Augustine says,

> And while we were thus speaking and straining after her, we just barely touched her with the whole effort of our hearts. Then with a sigh, leaving the first fruits of the Spirit bound to that ecstasy, we returned to the sounds of our own tongue, where the spoken word had both beginning and end. But what is like to thy word, our Lord, who remains in himself without becoming old, and "makes all things new?" (9.10.24)

Four important considerations emerge from this passage. First, having begun a conversation about the nature of eternal life, Augustine and his mother continue to speak as they strain after Wisdom. Second, they barely touch her with the entire effort of their hearts. Third, they sigh in the presence of the eternal Word before they return to the sounds of their own voices, where the spoken word has both a beginning and an end. Finally, they express their need for a new way of speaking by beginning to look for analogies for the creative and transforming Word of God that not only brings them into existence, but that also makes all things new (9.10.24).

Augustine reports the shared mystical experience with his mother in the first-person plural, pointing first to the fact that they undergo this mystical experience together, and then to the fact that the common context in which they stand does not swallow them up. Both Augustine and Monica participate in this experience without losing their integrity, and they also participate in it without losing one another. Experiences like this are rare in mystical literature; for moments of mystical ecstasy often obliterate the individuals who engage in them, and usually involve a single individual to the exclusion of a larger community. However, in this case, Augustine describes a shared mystical experience that mirrors the structure of the Christian community, and within which individuals stand alone together in the presence and absence of God.

Augustine and Monica have simultaneous mystical experiences, but the "object" of their experiences is the same, where these two facts bind them together and hold them apart. Augustine and his mother stand before God as two centers of power, both of whom have heard God speak; and they long for the day when they will hear God speak again. Yet speaking and hearing one another also undergirds the voyage the mother and her son undertake together. Throughout the *Confessions*, speaking and hearing express the interaction between God and the soul; but in this case, they also sustain the community between two individuals as they climb the ladder of self-transcendence toward the radical otherness of God.

Many of the elements in the earlier Neoplatonic vision reappear in the mystical experience Augustine shares with his mother. In both cases, the journey begins with the return of the soul to itself, moves through the various levels of the Neoplatonic hierarchy, and culminates in an encounter with God that can only be sustained for an instant (9.10.24). However, the two experiences are also radically different. In the first, Augustine sees God with a trembling glance (7.10.16). In the second, he and his mother touch on Wisdom before they return to the sound of their own voices (9.10.24). The first experience is visual, and is a vision of *God* (7.10.16). The second is tactile, and the "object" is *Wisdom* rather than God as he is in himself (9.10.24). In the Neoplatonic experience described in Book VII, the presence of God balances the trembling glance; and in the communal experience depicted in Book IX, the substitution of Wisdom for God balances the immediacy of the sense of touch (9.10.24).

In both experiences, there is an interplay between identity and difference, but the most important difference between the two episodes is that Augustine undergoes the first experience alone and shares the second experience with his mother. In this second case, Augustine and his mother are (finite$\perp$infinite) images of one another, allowing him to take the structure of the Christian community up into the mystical experience in which they

both participate. In doing so, he is not reading his conversion to Christianity from a Neoplatonic point of view, but driving his Christian conversion
into the philosophical heart of Neoplatonism. In this case, the solitude of
Augustine's Neoplatonic vision becomes the community of the shared
mystical experience with his mother, where the conversation to which this
experience leads is part of the distinctive work of the Christian community.

This conversation moves upward and downward, but it also stabilizes
the relation between these two directions by allowing dialogic interaction
to provide a middle term between them. Though the infinite richness of
truth allows Augustine and Monica to remain in its presence for only a
moment, they are able to return to it by participating in a conversation in
which figurative language expresses what literal language about the relation between God and the soul can never say. Both Monica and Augustine have embraced the incarnation as the middle term that binds God
and the soul together; and as a consequence, the incarnated language they
speak on this occasion places them in the middle ground between God
and the soul, where they express the richness of God in the figurative
discourse appropriate to it.

Augustine emphasizes the communal nature of the experience in Ostia
without canceling the uniqueness of its participants, but the fact remains
that this experience lasts for only an instant. What Augustine and his
mother long for is an experience that will sustain itself, and Augustine is
acutely aware of the fact that they will never find it in this life (9.10.25).
Nevertheless, he tries to find a language that balances the upward and
downward movements toward God, that occupies the middle ground
between God and the soul, and that describes what standing before God
would be like by reporting the conclusion of the conversation between
himself and his mother. In doing so, Augustine says,

> What we said went something like this: If to any man the tumult
> of the flesh were silenced; and the poles were silent as well;
> indeed, if the very soul grew silent to herself, and went beyond
> herself by not thinking of herself; if fancies and imaginary revela-
> tions were silenced; if every tongue and every sign and every
> transient thing—for actually if any man could hear them, all
> these would say, 'We did not create ourselves, but were created by
> Him who abides forever'—and if having uttered this, they too
> should be silent, having stirred our ears to hear him who created
> them; and if then he alone spoke, not through them but by
> himself, that we might hear his word, . . . we then with rapid

thought might touch on that Eternal Wisdom which abides over all. And if this could be sustained, and other visions of a far different kind be taken away, and this one alone should so ravish and absorb and envelop its beholder in these inward joys that this life might be eternally like that one moment of knowledge which we now sighed after—would not *this* be the reality of the saying, Enter into the joy of your Lord,? But when shall such a thing be? Shall it be, when we shall all rise again, though we, shall not all be changed? (9.10.25)

Augustine does not report this conversation in the language that he and his mother use, and he alerts us to this fact by confessing that they do not speak in this manner and in these very words (9.10.25). However, the significance of this declaration is unclear. Do Augustine and his mother use Neoplatonic language originally, while he uses biblical language now? Or do they speak less technically in Ostia, while Augustine clothes their experience in a mixture of biblical and Neoplatonic language in the account he gives in the *Confessions?* Either interpretation raises difficulties: the first presupposes that Monica understands the language of the Neoplatonists; the second assumes that the Christian Bishop, writing thirteen years after the fact, uses Neoplatonic as wells as biblical language to report the episode.

The evidence points in both directions. On the one hand, Monica is not a philosopher; and it would be reasonable for them to speak about the experience they share in a language they both understand. However, this suggests that the original conversation uses ordinary discourse that the *Confessions* disguises. On the other hand, why would Augustine introduce Neoplatonic language into the *Confessions* after even his most severe critics admit that he has become a Christian who is saturated in the language of the Bible? Surely, it would be more reasonable for him to use the language of scripture in recasting an experience that had occurred so many years before. The most reasonable conclusion is that Augustine uses biblical language in speaking with his mother and a mixture of biblical and Neoplatonic language in giving an account of the experience some thirteen years later. At the time of the original experience, the rhetorician takes the capacities of his mother into account, subordinating philosophical to biblical language; but in his later account of the experience, he writes for a wider audience to which both Neoplatonism and Christianity are familiar. In both cases, he displays an attitude toward biblical and philosophical discourse that is appropriate to the occasion.

There is a more profound reason for Augustine's claim that he is only approximating what he and his mother say, for reference to the concept of approximation prepares us for the distance that separates God from the soul. The passage of thirteen years makes it difficult to report an earlier conversation, but the infinite distance between God and the soul makes it even harder to find a language that can express our experience of him. In Book VII, a trembling glance separates Augustine from *He Who Is*; and in Book IX, Augustine and his mother barely touch on the Wisdom of God before they turn away from it with a sigh. The crucial question becomes, "How can figurative discourse, and the language of approximation to which it leads, allow them to sustain their experience?"

Augustine proceeds to deal with this problem in three stages. First, he speaks in the language of counterfactual conditionals, saying for example, "If to any man the tumult of the flesh *were* silenced; and the phantoms of earth and waters and air *were* silenced; and the poles *were* silent as well." Language like this not only underlines the differences between himself and his mother, but also points to the distance between their present state and communion with God. Second, Augustine introduces a distinction between silence and speech and uses it repeatedly. He tells us that if we are to hear God's Voice, the flesh, the world, the soul, and the imagination must be silent so God can speak with words of his own. Third, God speaks through creation; and Augustine insists that if we could hear what every creature says, they would exclaim, "We did not create ourselves!" Indeed, language of this kind would give us access to the most important fact about the relation between God and the world, where the infinite distance between them is mediated by the fact the Word of God binds them together.

Augustine says that if we could hear God speak, all earthly language would fall away; and he tells us that if this should occur, "we then with rapid thought might touch on the Eternal Wisdom that abides." Then the great rhetorician claims that if we could sustain this vision, and if other visions like the Neoplatonic experience described in Book VII might be taken away, it would ravish, absorb, and envelop its beholder. However, he also says that in this moment, our lives would be *like* the one moment of knowledge that he and his mother had already experienced. Finally, Augustine wonders whether this kind of knowledge would not reflect the meaning of the saying, "Enter into the joy of thy Lord," where, having raised the crucial question about when this shall be, he points to the resurrection of both the soul and the body by asking, "Shall it be 'when we shall all rise again,' though we 'shall not all be changed'?"[16] (9.10.25).

Even if Augustine and his mother could have sustained their mystical experience, advancing beyond the earlier Neoplatonic vision into a vision of God that would not be merely momentary, their souls and God would still have remained in radical contrast. The separation between God and the soul is not a function of the momentary character of the mystical experience Augustine and Monica undergo, but a positive reflection of the dimension of difference creation *ex nihilo* establishes and sustains between God and the world. The language of approximation and the language of counterfactual conditionals, the contrast between speech and silence, and the fundamental distinction between the creator and the creature point to the fact that the space between God and the soul can never be obliterated, even in eternity.

If we hear God speak as we stand in his presence and absence, earthly language falls away; and this takes us into a region where we must learn to speak a new kind of language appropriate to the unity and the separation between God and the soul. In this Place of places, we touch on the Eternal Wisdom of God that abides; but to touch on wisdom is not to grasp it, or to imprison it within the confines of literal discourse that denies its infinite richness. Indeed, if we follow Augustine and Monica into their encounter with God, what we touch is not God in himself, but the Eternal Wisdom through which he creates the world; and even though the vision of the eternal Word ravishes, absorbs, and envelops us, it is the *experience* that does this rather than the Word itself.

At this crucial moment, Augustine uses the language of analogy rather than the language of identity, suggesting that when we find the wisdom we seek, our lives will be eternally like the momentary experience that has just occurred. Analogical language not only binds these experiences together, but also holds them apart; and it is this *region of similarity* he longs to enter that Augustine describes as the joy of the Lord. The philosopher also suggests that this moment will occur only in the resurrection. The resurrection does not involve the separation of the soul from the body, but issues in a new body by which we see God face to face. The (finite⊥infinite) being who has been created, the (finite⊤infinite) being who has fallen, the (finite-infinite) being who has accepted its limitations and come back to itself, finally becomes the (finite–infinite) being in whom the infinite richness of God can express itself fully. Both the soul and the body of this transformed being serve as principles of individuation; for even in eternity, Augustine and his mother will stand in contrast, not only with one another, but also with the one they have touched. As John formulates the point, "And when we see him, we shall be like him."[17] Likeness is not identity, and it always preserves the difference between God and the soul.

Once more, Augustine assures us that though their language may have been different, what they say comes to focus on the meaning of eternity. In addition, Augustine says that when their experience is over, Monica tells him that she is ready to die.

> "Son, for my own part, I now find no delight in anything in this life. What I can still do here, and why I am here, I do not know, now that all my hopes in this world have been accomplished. One thing there was, for which I desired to linger a little while in this life, that I might see you a Catholic Christian before I died. God has granted this to me in more than abundance, for I see you his servant, with even earthly happiness held in contempt. What am I doing here?" (9.10.26)

With this brief question, Augustine's mother finally lets him go. As she prepares herself to stand before the eternal Word of God that she and her son have encountered, Monica's Christian life comes to an end, while life in the world that opens out before her son is just beginning. However, in this case, life and death are two sides of the same coin, where neither death nor life are able to separate Augustine and his mother from the love of Christ. Monica loves Augustine in a variety of ways, wanting him to be the father of her grandchildren, wanting him to be a professional success, and wanting him to return to the house of his father. Yet God converts her first two desires into the third, answering her deepest desire in more abundant ways than she had ever anticipated. Because her own desires are purified before she dies, Monica is finally able to love Augustine in God; and it is love like this that gives her access to eternity.

THE DEATH OF AUGUSTINE'S MOTHER (9.11.27–9.13.37)

Augustine does not remember how he replies to his mother's suggestion that her work on earth is over (9.11.27), and there is no reason why he should. He is no doubt remembering the feeling generated by the empty space that separates him from her, and he does not try to replace this emptiness with the rationality of a verbal formulation. Instead, he says that five days later, his mother falls prostrate with fever. She faints and is unconscious for a little while, and when she awakes, she asks, "Where was

I?" (9.11.27). The place of fulfillment Monica and Augustine anticipate as they gaze out the window in Ostia draws her upward, and her question indicates that she is preparing to move from one place to another.

Monica indicates this when she says, " 'Here you put your mother.' " The author records this statement just as Monica utters it; for though it is ungrammatical in Latin, it is an authentic expression of a wish that startles the members of her immediate family (9.11.27). Augustine remains silent; but his brother speaks, claiming that he wants their mother to die in her own country rather than abroad. In suggesting that the proper place for burial is her own land, Augustine's brother reflects the traditions of the ancient family (9.11.27). In the ancient world, the dead lie beside their ancestors so the circle of the family will not be broken.[18] On an earlier occasion, Monica had attempted to bring these traditions into the church; Ambrose had forbidden her to do so, and she had obeyed without knowing the reason. Now having been transformed from an ambitious mother to a child of God, she understands the difference between pagan circularity and Christian transcendence. Thus she turns an anxious eye toward Augustine's brother and exclaims, " 'See what he says.' " Then she says to both her sons:

> "Put this body away anywhere. Don't let care about it disturb you. I ask only this of you, that you remember me at the altar of the Lord, wherever you may be." (9.11.27)

It is easy to misunderstand this passage, regarding it as evidence that Monica despises the body. If this were so, we could not distinguish her Christianity from the Neoplatonism that is often attributed to her son. Yet Monica's later reference to the resurrection makes it clear that what Monica wants is not freedom from the body, but freedom from "the body of this death." In her case as well as in the case of Augustine, fallenness rather than finitude is the fundamental problem; and in both instances, the entire person seeks deliverance from sin. Because Augustine knows this, he rejoices that his mother is no longer concerned about her burial place. She had wanted to lie beside her husband in Africa, and she had wanted others to know that they share the same gravesite "after a journey across the sea." Yet now she is preparing for a pilgrimage that reflects a new creation, where Monica is seeking "a city not made with hands, whose builder and maker is God."[19]

Later Augustine learns that his mother has expressed contempt for her life in the world and has discussed the blessings of death with some of her Christian friends. Yet in a culture that binds them to custom and tradition, they find it hard to believe that she can show such courage, and they wonder whether Monica dreads burial so far from her own city. Yet she points beyond death and the need to place the body in a particular place by responding, " 'Nothing is far from God. I need not fear that he will not know where to raise me up at the end of the world' " (9.11.28).

Finally, Augustine writes, "So, on the ninth day of her sickness, in the fifty-sixth year of her life and in the thirty-third of mine, this devout and holy soul was set loose from the body" (9.11.28). At the end of her life, Monica speaks about the resurrection; and Augustine speaks about freedom from the body. Yet the perceptive rhetorician also points to a new kind of body when he says that he is thirty-three when she dies. Perhaps it is a coincidence that Monica does not die until her son reaches this age, but it is no coincidence that he tells us about it. What more can we ask from a rhetorician who has not only learned to speak the philosophical language of Neoplatonism, but has also learned to speak the language of redemption that permits him to participate in the resurrection of Christ?

Augustine closes his mother's eyes; sadness flows into his heart; but as he is passing over into tears, his mind commands his eyes to suck "the fountain dry" (9.12.29). In the Christian symbolism that undergirds the *Confessions,* dry land is the destination that displaces the abyss of the ocean that threatens to engulf us (13.16.19). Nevertheless, sorrow shakes Augustine like a convulsion; Adeodatus bursts into tears; and Augustine must struggle to check the tears his childish feelings and youthful heart want to express. The philosopher, the Christian, and the visionary can still feel the child crying inside him; but the one who has finally come to himself by putting on a new garment does not believe that it is appropriate to mark the death of Monica with tears and groaning. As a consequence, he echoes the memorial ode of Horace by exclaiming, "She did not die in misery, nor did she meet with total death"[20] (9.12.29).

Though the child within wants to cry, the philosopher insists on analyzing his feelings; and when he does so, Augustine concludes that what hurts most is the recent wound of Monica's death and the disruption of their habit of living together (9.12.30). Yet Augustine's analysis cuts deeper than this, for he is careful to say that he is happy because his mother praises him during her final illness and that she says that she has never heard any harsh or reproachful word from his mouth spoken against her (9.12.30). Nevertheless, one side of Augustine feels that his mother has abandoned him; and as the life they had enjoyed together breaks apart, he feels both sick and destitute (9.12.30). Earlier, Augustine grieves about the loss of a philosophical friend whose soul had become one with his own; now he feels the knife of separation that cuts him off from his mother. In the first case, he does not know what it means to love his friend in God; but in this case, he has a final opportunity to learn what loving things in God involves.

Evodius takes up the Psalter and begins to sing, and many of those who are present join him in the singing. By contrast, Augustine talks in another part of the house with those who think he should not be alone (9.12.31). As he moves from one hemisphere of consciousness to the other, truth softens his anguish; and his friends who are not aware of the depth of his feelings believe that he is free from any sense of sorrow. In the ears of God, where no one else can hear, Augustine reproaches himself for the mildness of his feelings; and he restrains the flow of his grief that bows a little to his will. Yet the paroxysm of anguish seizes him again; he represses what he feels in his heart; and though he does not cry or even change expressions, he is annoyed that his natural feelings have such a power over him. Augustine's sadness focuses on both his mother and himself; and though he is sad that she is gone, he is angry that he misses her so much. Yet the most important fact about his reaction to the death of his mother is that though he hides it from his friends, he does not try to hide it from God behind a philosophical facade (9.12.31).

When Augustine carries Monica to her burial place, he goes and returns without tears, nor does he cry at the grave. Yet he is sad all day, and he begs God to heal his sorrow. When God does not respond, he tries a familiar philosophical remedy on the day of the funeral. It occurs to him that it might be helpful to go to the public baths, for he knows that the word for bath in Greek derives its name from the fact that it often washes anxiety from the mind [21] (9.12.32). On this occasion, Augustine imitates Socrates in the *Symposium*, who after a discussion of the nature of love that lasts until dawn, takes a bath and goes about his customary business.[22] Yet in Augustine's case, he feels the same after the bath as he does before, and the bitterness of his grief does not flow from his heart. Socrates' love for beauty and Augustine's love for his mother are radically different; and in the case of Augustine, there is no philosophical treatment that is adequate for dealing with his anguish.

When Augustine finally falls asleep, rest from the threat of death assuages his grief. Then verses of one of Ambrose's hymns come to mind; and they call his attention to God the creator, to the healing powers of sleep, and to the grace of God that restores both the mind and the body (9.12.32). As a consequence, Augustine begins to turn away from his grief and to remember his mother, focusing first on her devout life, and then speaking about her tenderness and attentiveness toward him. Yet even here, God and the soul stand at the center of Augustine's reflections; and in God's presence, Augustine weeps for both his mother and himself (9.12.33). In doing so, he refuses to disguise his loss with a religious or philosophical doctrine, and tells us instead,

> I gave way to the tears that I had held back, so that they poured forth as much as they wished. I spread them beneath my heart, and it rested upon them, for at my heart were placed your ears. (9.12.33)

On this occasion, loving things in God means that Augustine can bring both his mother and himself into relation to God by crying from the depths of his being; and if anyone objects, he simply asks them to weep for his sins (9.12.33).

When Augustine writes the *Confessions*, the wound of his mother's death has healed; and this allows him to pour out a different kind of tears to God. The incarnational dimension of his thinking emerges once more when he cries for every soul that dies in Adam, and when he also cries for those that Christ has made alive. Augustine does not say that his mother remains sinless after baptism, but he trusts God's mercy to transcend his justice and prays that Monica will find a place of rest in God. His confidence that this will occur does not depend on her merits, but on the work of God in her. Thus, Augustine places the sins of his mother within the context of the grace of God by praying,

> I now beseech you in behalf of my mother's sins. Hear me for the sake of him who is the medicine for our wounds, of him who hung upon the tree, of him who now sits at our right hand and makes intercessions for us. I know that she was merciful to others and that from her heart she forgave her debtors their debts. Do you also forgive her debts, if she contracted any in so many years after receiving the water of salvation. Forgive her, Lord, forgive her, I beseech you. Enter not into judgment with her. Let your mercy be exalted above your justice, for your words are true, and you have promised mercy to the merciful. Such you made them to be, for you will have mercy on whom you will have mercy, and you will show mercy to whom you will show mercy. (9.13.35)

Augustine believes that God has already done what he asks; for he reminds us that before she dies, his mother does not ask anyone to wrap her body and embalm it. She does not want a handsome monument; she does not want her children to bury her in her own country; and her only desire is that her friends will remember her at the altar of God where she served every day (9.13.36). This altar is the place where God wipes away her sins and writes her name in the Book of Life. Here God sets the punishment for eating the fruit from the tree of the Knowledge of Good and Evil aside and gives her access to the tree of life. Monica places her faith in God; nothing can separate her from the love of Christ; and if someone asks about her sins, she will not reply that she owes nothing, but "will answer that her sins have been forgiven by him to whom no one can return that price which he who owed nothing returned for us" (9.13.36).

Now Augustine returns to the language of prayer; and in doing so, he imitates the pattern of the prayer of Jesus in the seventeenth chapter of John. In that prayer, Jesus begins with his disciples and broadens his concern to everyone who will one day come to God through him. In a similar way, Augustine prays for his mother and his father, whose flesh has brought him into the world in a fashion that he does not understand;[23] and he asks all of his readers to remember them in prayer as well (9.13.37). In doing so, the Christian philosopher makes the crucial transition from bondage to his mother to the freedom of the Christian community. Augustine focuses the prayers of this community, not only on his mother, but also on his father, and on all his fellow citizens in the City of God. In this moment, both of his parents stand beside Augustine as citizens of a new kind of community, where the prayers of this larger community are richer than his prayers alone.

The son whom Augustine's mother loves so persistently finally quits thinking about himself and loves her in return; but in the final analysis, the author of the *Confessions* refers their love for one another to the Christian community, which is a concrete reflection of the love of God for the world that he wants to redeem. As a part of this community, Augustine loves all things in God, where this attitude not only emerges from the final experiential episode of the *Confessions,* but also defines the reflective standpoint from which he writes the text. At the end of Book IX, Augustine prays for his mother, his father, himself, and his readers; and as he does so, loving things in God becomes the end of his experiential journey, and the beginning of the reflective journey he is about to undertake.

Notes

PREFACE

1. References to the *Confessions* and to Augustine's other writings are given in parentheses in book, chapter, and paragraph form. The purpose of this convention is to permit readers to find the references in any Latin edition and in any translation.

2. Pierre Courcelle, *Recherches sur les Confessions de saint Augustin*, 2nd ed. (Paris: E. de Boccard, 1968), 188–202 and *Les "Confessions" de Saint Augustin dans la tradition litteraire, antecedents et posterite* (Paris: Études Augustiniennes, 1963), 91–197; Aime Solignac, "Bibliotheque Augustinienne," *Oeuvres de saint Augustin* (Paris: Desclee de Brouwer, 1962), vol. 13, 252–255 and vol. 14, 548; and F. Bolgiani, *La conversione di s. Agostino e l'VIII libro delle "Confessioni"* (Turin, 1956).

3. Two examples of what I have in mind are Courcelle and Robert J. O'Connell, both of who filter Augustine's thinking too exclusively through Neoplatonic spectacles. Courcelle's hypothesis that Augustine was not only influenced by a circle of Neoplatonists, but that Ambrose had citied Plotinus in his sermons and might even have been the person who introduced Augustine to Neoplatonic ideas suggests that the young philosopher was more a Neoplatonist than a Christian at the time of his conversion. [Courcelle, *Late Latin Writers and their Greek Sources*, trans. H. E. Wedeck (Cambridge, MA: Harvard University Press, 1969), 79–92, esp. 81]. For further discussion of this issue see Peter Brown, *Augustine of Hippo: A Biography*, new edition with an epilogue (Berkeley: University of California Press, 2000), 496–498 and James O'Donnell, *Augustine: Confessions*, vol. 2 (Oxford: Clarendon Press, 1992), 413–418.

O'Connell approaches the problem of Augustine's Neoplatonism by focusing his attention on the Neoplatonic doctrine of the fall of the soul, by which he claims that Augustine was influenced decisively. His examination of the issue begins with a series of articles: "Ennead VI, 4 and 5 in the Works of St. Augustine," *Revue des études Augustiniennes* 9 (1963): 1–39; "The Plotinian Fall of the Soul in St. Augustine," *Traditio* 19 (1963): 1–35; and "The Riddle of Augustine's 'Confessions: A Plotinian Key," *International Philosophical Quarterly* 4 (1964): 327–372) and continues in a series of later, book-length publications: *St. Augustine's*

Early Theory of Man: A.D. 386–391 (Cambridge, MA: The Belknap Press of Harvard University Press, 1968); *St. Augustine's Confessions: The Odyssey of Soul* (Cambridge, MA: The Belknap Press of Harvard University Press, 1969); *Art and the Christian Intelligence in St. Augustine* (Cambridge, MA: Harvard University Press, 1978); *St. Augustine's Platonism* (Villanova: Villanova University Press, 1984); *Imagination and Metaphysics in St. Augustine* (Milwaukee, WI: Marquette University Press, 1986) and *The Origin of the Soul in St. Augustine's Later Works* (New York, NY: Fordham Press, 1987).

4. In developing this distinctively Augustinian framework, it is not necessary to claim that Augustine is a Christian rather than a Neoplatonist, as Boyer argued in his well-known controversy with Alfaric, who claimed that the Bishop of Hippo concealed the fact that his conversion in 386 was not to Christianity but to Neoplatonism. [C. Boyer, *Christianisme et néo-platonisme dans la formation de saint Augustin* (Paris: Beauchesne, 1920) and Prosper Alfaric, *L'évolution intellectuelle de Saint Augustin: I, Du Manichéisme au Néoplatonisme (Paris: Nourry, 1918)*]. However, it *is* necessary to move beyond the mediating position of Courcelle according to which Augustine is more a Neoplatonist than a Christian. See Pierre Courcelle, *Recherches sur les Confessions de S. Augustin* (Paris: Boccard, 1968), 7–12, 138. See also A. Pincherle, "Sources platoniciennes di l'augustinisme," and the debate between them [*Augustine Magister,* vol. 3 (Paris: Etudes Augustiniennes, 1954), 71–93, 97, 100].

In this book, I develop the view that Augustine's thought *tilts* in the direction of Christianity, however Neoplatonic it may be. This tilt is expressed in four ways: first, Augustine is committed to the doctrine of creation *ex nihilo* rather than to the Neoplatonic doctrine of emanation; second, his doctrine of the fall is more radical than the fall of the soul in Neoplatonism, both because it involves the fall of the entire person [Augustine, *On the Catholic and the Manichean Ways of Life*, vol. 56, *The Fathers of the Church*, ed. R. J. Deferrari, trans. D. and I. Gallagher (Washington, D.C.: Catholic University Press,1966], 1.22.40; *The Literal Meaning of Genesis*, trans. by John H. Taylor in *Ancient Christian Writers*, vols. 41–42 (New York: Newman Press, 1982), 6.25, 9.3; and *The City of God*, trans. by R. W. Dyson in *Cambridge Texts in the History of Political Thought* (Cambridge: Cambridge University Press, 1998), 13.3, 13.23]. Third, Augustine believes that a mediator is necessary if the infinite chasm between the divine and the human realms is to be bridged, and he differs from Plotinus by denying that the soul can be transformed by efforts of its own [Plotinus, *Enneads*, trans. A. H. Armstrong, 7 vols. in *The Loeb Classical Library* (Cambridge: Harvard University Press, 1966–1984), 4.3.17]; finally, Augustine is committed to the resurrection of the body, even is his early works. [*On the Greatness of the Soul The Fathers of the Church*, vol. 2 (New York: CIMA Publishing Co., 1947), 33.76].

5. Carl G. Vaught, "Theft and Conversion: Two Augustinian Confessions," in *The Recovery of Philosophy in America: Essays in Honor of John Edwin Smith,* ed. Thomas P. Karsulis and Robert Cummings Neville (Albany, New York: State University of New York Press, 1997), 217–249.

INTRODUCTION

1. Robert O'Connell argues that the episodes in Books VII and IX are not mystical experiences, but fundamental insights that are expressed in narrative form. The mystical expression of Augustine's experience is a vexed question in Augustinian scholarship. For a detailed discussion of this issue, see O'Connell, *St. Augustine's Confessions: The Odyssey of Soul* (Cambridge, MA: The Belknap Press of Harvard University Press, 1969), 71–89; 118–119.

2. G. W. F. Hegel, *Lectures on the Philosophy of Religion*, vol. 1, trans. R. F. Brown, P. C. Hodgson, and J. M. Stewart (Los Angeles: University of California Press, 1984), 113.

3. Alfred North Whitehead, *Religion in the Making* (Cleveland: The World Publishing Company, 1963), 16.

4. Francis Petrarch, *Petrarch: The First Modern Scholar and Man of Letters*, ed. and trans., James Robinson (New York: G. P. Putnam, 1898), 316–318.

5. I use the familiar phrase from Paul Tillich, not because it is to be found in the *Confessions*, but because it expresses Augustine's fundamental intentions. It is not by accident that Tillich locates himself within the Augustinian tradition. See "Two Types of Philosophy of Religion," in *Theology of Culture*, ed. Robert C. Kimball (New York: Oxford University Press, 1959), 10–29.

6. *The Confessions of Saint Augustine*, F. J. Sheed, trans. (Indianapolis and Cambridge: Hackett Publishing Co., 1993), xxvii.

7. Ibid., xxix.

8. Pierre Courcelle, *Recherches sur les Confessions de saint Augustin*, 2nd ed. (Paris: E. de Boccard, 1968), 49, 248.

9. Augustine makes all these dimensions explicit without ever binding them together in an overarching framework. He does this with respect to time by distinguishing stages of the life cycle. He does it with respect to space by describing the various communities of which he is a part in the course of his development. And he does it with respect to eternity by pointing to the ultimate significance of many of the experiences that he undergoes. By bringing all of these dimensions together, I am pointing to ways in which they intersect at various stages of Augustine's development.

10. Peter Brown comments on the inner dimensions of his own approach in his extensive biography of Augustine. [Peter Brown, *Augustine of Hippo: A Biography*, new edition with an epilogue (Berkeley: University of California Press, 2000)], ix.

11. Brown remarks that a reciprocal relationship exits between Augustine and his surroundings, so that new settings and routines affect his inner life as his developing preoccupations affect both the meanings inherent in these circumstances and the people who surround him. [Brown, ix].

12. Augustine, *On Free Choice of the Will*, trans. Anna S. Benjamin and L. H. Hackstaff (Englewood Cliffs, NJ: Prentice Hall, 1964), (1.1.11). Augustine never uses the more familiar Anselmian phrase, *"fides quarens intellectum"* Cf.

Anselm, *Monologion and Proslogion, with the Replies of Gaunilo and Anselm,* trans. with an intro. Thomas Williams (Indianapolis and Cambridge: Hackett Co., 1995), 93. However, Augustine's motto and Anselm's formula are related closely, not only because Anselm is an Augustinian monk, but also because both thinkers insist that in religious matters faith must always precede understanding.

13. My understanding of this issue, as well as the stages of Augustine's development, have been influenced by Erik H. Erikson, *Identity and the Life Cycle* (New York: W. W. Norton & Company, 1980).

14. Ibid., 60, 66.

15. Ibid., 68–69, 78.

16. Ibid., 87.

17. Ibid., 119.

18. A. Hilary Armstrong, *Augustine and Christian Platonism* (Villanova: Villanova University Press, 1967), 3–37; Pier Franco Beatrice, "Quosdam Platonicorum Libros," *Vigiliae Christianae* 43 (1989): 248–281; Tom Finan, "Modes of Vision in 'De Genesi ad Litteram' XII," in *The Relationship between Neoplatonism and Christianity,* ed. by Tom Finan and Vincent Twomey (Dublin: Four Courts Press, 1992), 141–154; Earnest L. Fortin, "Saint Augustin et la doctrine neoplatonicienne de l'âme," *Augustinus Magister* (Paris: Études Augustiniennes, 1954), vol. 3, 371–380; Pierre Hadot, *Porphyre et Victorinus,* 2 vols. (Paris, 1968); Carol Harrison, *Beauty and Revelation in the Thought of Saint Augustine* (Oxford: Clarendon Press, 1992); Paul Henry, "The Adversus Arium of Marius Victorinus, the First Systematic Exposition of the Doctrine of the Trinity, *Journal of Theological Studies* 1 (1950): 42–55; Robert J. O'Connell, *St. Augustine's Early Theory of Man* (Cambridge: Harvard University Press, 1968); Gerard O'Daly, "Did St. Augustine Ever Believe in the Soul's Pre-Existence?" *Augustinian Studies* 5 (1974): 227–235; T. O'Loughlin, "The Libri Philosophorum and Augustine's Conversions," *The Relationship between Neoplatonism and Christianity,* 101–126; John J. O'Meara, *Porphyry's Philosophy from Oracles in Augustine* (Paris: Études Augustiniennes, 1959).

19. Mark 14.32; Luke 22.39, 22.44; John 18.1.

20. Luke 23.43; Revelation 2.7.

21. Frederic E. Van Fleteren, "Augustine's Ascent of the Soul in Book VII of the Confessions: A Reconsideration," *Augustinian Studies* 5 (1974): 29–72.

22. For a further explanation see my essay, "Participation and Imitation in Plato's Metaphysics," *Contemporary Essays on Greek Ideas: The Kilgore Festschrift,* ed. Robert M. Baird, William F. Cooper, Elmer H. Duncan, Stuart E. Rosenbaum (Waco, TX: Baylor University Press, 1987), 17–31.

23. Courcelle, *Rechercehes sur les Confessions de saint Augustin,* 136–138. See also John J. O'Meara, *The Young Augustine: The Growth of St. Augustine's Mind up to His Conversion* (New York: Longmans, Green and Co., 1954), 116–125.

24. It is important to emphasize the fact that the relationship between Neoplatonism and Christianity is complex, not only with reference to Augustine's

appropriation of them, but also when these ways of thinking are considered in themselves. For example, even though continuity dominates Neoplatonism and discontinuity dominates Augustinian Christianity, the opposite strand is also present in both contexts.

25. Again, Augustine and Plotinus are related more closely on this issue than might appear to be the case. In fact, Plotinus says that evil is a turning away from God. [Plotinus, *Enneads*, trans. A. H. Armstrong (Cambridge: Harvard University Press, 1966–1984), 6.5.12, 3.5.12. However, the position of Augustine remains more radical because he understands the absolute *nihil* as what the soul sometimes attempts to embrace (*Confessions*, 2.10.18, 7.12.18).

26. Augustine does not use these terms in formulating his account of the relation between God and the soul. However, his description of this complex relation presupposes the concepts to which these terms call our attention. Finitude points to the bounded dimension of the human situation, and infinitude points to the aspect of it that transcends itself in relation to God. I also use the (finite-infinite) distinction throughout this book in understanding the transitions from creation to the fall, from the fall to conversion, and from conversion to fulfillment. These categories are not imposed on the text, but are ways of pointing to crucial distinctions that emerge from it. For analogous uses of this distinction see the works of Søren Kierkegaard, *The Concept of Irony*, trans. and ed. by Edna H. Hong and Howard V. Hong (Princeton, NJ: Princeton University Press, 1992) and Reinhold Niebuhr, *The Nature and Destiny of Man*, vol. I (New York: Charles Scribner's Sons, 1953).

27. Martin Luther, *Bondage of the Will*, in *Luther and Erasmus: Free Will and Salvation*, trans. E. Gordon Rupp (Philadelphia: The Westminster Press, 1969).

28. Augustine develops this theme in his analysis of memory in Book X of the *Confessions* (10.9.16). I will expand this theme in detail in a later book.

29. This is the insight expressed in Augustine's claim that he becomes a Christian when he "puts on" Jesus, the Christ (8.12.29).

30. Alfred North Whitehead, *Religion in the Making*, 50.

31. For authors who move in a Neoplatonic direction see, for example, P. Alfaric. *L'évolution intellectuelle de Saint Augustine*. Vol. 1: *Du Manichéennes au Néoplatonisme* (Paris: Nourry, 1918); A. Hilary Armstrong, *The Cambridge History of Later Greek and Early Medieval Philosophy* (Cambridge: Cambridge University Press, 1967); Robert J. O'Connell, *St. Augustine's Confessions: The Odyssey of Soul* (Harvard University Press, 1969); *St. Augustine's Platonism* (Villanova: Villanova University Press, 1984); and John J. O'Meara, "Augustine and Neo-Platonism," *Recherches Augustiniennes*, 1 (1958): 91–111.

32. The tendency to tie these concepts together makes it difficult to draw an adequate distinction between Neoplatonism and Christianity, the first of which has no counterpart to the Christian concept of sin.

33. Romans 7.24.

34. *Confessions*, 4.10.15–4.11.16, 7.15.21, 11.30.40.

35. With regard to his exposure to Aristotle's *Categories*, Augustine writes:

The book seemed to me to speak clearly enough of substances . . . and the innumerable things that are found in these nine categories, of which I have set down some examples, or in the category of substance. (4.16.28)

36. Augustine traces the journey from the senses, through the power of sensation, through memory and forgetfulness, to the place beyond memory where God is encountered as Truth, and where he describes the happy life in sensory terms (10.6.8–10.27.38). David Chidester also discusses the power of sensory language about God in *Seeing, Hearing, and Religious Discourse* (Chicago: University of Illinois Press, 1992), 53–67.

37. Ibid., 55–56.

38. Pertaining to vision, Augustine says: "One object is before both of us and is viewed by both of us at the same time" (2.7.63) and of hearing he says that "whatever sound occurs is present in its entirety, to be heard by both of us" (2.7.64). He also notes that "the other senses of the body . . . do not behave exactly as do the senses of the eyes or ears, because they have contact with the object" (2.7.65). *On Free Choice of the Will*, trans. Anna S. Benjamin and L. H. Hackstaff (Englewood Cliffs, NJ: Prentice-Hall, 1964).

39. Ibid., 2.14.

40. An example of an auditory image can be found in Augustine's numerous quotations from the Bible. For example, he says on the Psalms:

"Say to my soul: I am your salvation" (Psalms 34.3). Say this, so that I may hear you. Behold, my heart's ears are turned to you, O Lord: open them, and "say to my soul: I am your salvation" (Psalms 142.7). I will run after that voice, and I will catch hold of you." (1.5.5)

Augustine not only uses auditory images when he quotes the Bible, but also when he uses his own voice, as illustrated at the beginning of Book 10:

"But with what benefit do they wish to hear me? Do they wish to share my thanksgiving, when they hear how close it is by your gift that I approach to you, and to pray for me, when they hear how I am held back by my own weight? To such men I will reveal myself." (10.4.5)

41. Leo Ferrari, *The Conversions of Saint Augustine* (Villanova: Villanova University Press, 1984), 53–55.

42. Margaret Miles, *Desire and Delight: A New Reading of Augustine's Confessions* (New York: Crossroad, 1992), 57–59.

43. Chidester, 53–67.

44. For a discussion of this issue, see Brown, 93–107.

45. Colin Starnes, *Augustine's Conversion: A Guide to the Argument of Confessions I–IX* (Waterloo: Wilfrid Laurier University Press, 1990), 252.

46. Adolf Harnack, "Die hohepunkte in Augustins Konfessionen," reprinted in his *Redens und Aufsätze*, vol. 1 (Giessen: Ricker, 1904), 51–79 and Prosper Alfaric, *L'évolution intellectuelle de saint Augusti* (Paris: Nourry, 1918). See Starnes, 5 for a summary of the evidence.

47. C. S. Lewis, *Surprised by Joy* (New York: Harcourt, Brace & World, 1955), 17–18.

48. Kenneth Burke, *The Rhetoric of Religion* (Los Angeles: University of California Press, 1970), 43–171.

CHAPTER 1

1. As I have indicated already, Robert O'Connell disputes the claim that Augustine's encounter with God involves either a vision of God or a mystical experience. Instead, he claims that what Augustine recounts at this juncture expresses insights derived from many years of reflection about the nature and existence of God. [Robert J. O'Connell, *St. Augustine's Confessions: The Odyssey of Soul* (Cambridge: Harvard University Press, 1969)], 84–89; "Faith, Reason, and Ascent to vision in Saint Augustine," *Augustinian Studies* 21 (1990): 83–125; "Where the Difference Still Lies," *Augustinian Studies* 21 (1990): 139–153. For further debate see Frederick Van Fleteren, "A Reply to Robert O'Connell," *Augustinian Studies* 21 (1990): 127–137.

Perhaps the hesitation to speak of mystical experiences expresses a wish to avoid the subject of ontologism according to which the soul merges with God. However, this is not what Augustine means by religious experience. For him, a vision of God involves a divine self in which God and the soul remain distinct.

2. James J. O'Donnell, *Augustine: Confessions*, vol. 2 (Oxford: Clarendon Press, 1992), 52–55.

3. Augustine illustrates the doctrine of the "inner teacher" in a dialogue that involves the ability of humans to acquire knowledge made possible by consultation with Christ, who is the divine teacher, or Christ. [*On the Teacher*, trans. Peter King in *Against the Academicians and The Teacher* (Indianapolis and Cambridge: Hackett Publishing Co., 1995)].

4. Only later will Augustine realize that this materialist conception of God's infinity is incompatible with his omnipresence.

5. This is the principle reason for believing that Augustine's remarks about the nature of God in Book VII derive from an encounter with God.

6. Augustine does not find the immaterial substance he seeks until he embraces Neoplatonism, where the substance in question becomes accessible to him only as the result of an experiential encounter. However, it is important to notice that the spiritual substance that Augustine encounters can only be expressed by metaphorical discourse.

7. Etienne Gilson, *The Christian Philosophy of Saint Augustine*, trans. L. E. M. Lynch (New York: Random House, 1960), 44.

8. Gareth B. Matthews, *Thought's Ego in Augustine and Descartes* (Ithaca, New York: Cornell University Press, 1992), 50–51

9. Though he develops this insight within a different context, I have found it helpful in understanding the *Confessions*. See Henry Johnstone, *The Problem of the Self* (University Park, Pennsylvania: The Pennsylvania State University Press, 1970).

10. There is considerable debate about which books of the Platonists influenced Augustine [Oliver du Roy, *L'Intelligence de la Foi en lat Trinite selon Saint Augustin* (Etudes Augustiniennes: Paris, 1966)]. James O'Donnell also notes the difficulties in identifying the texts that influenced Augustine (O'Donnell, *Augustine: Confessions*, vol. 2, 413–420). Some scholars assert that Plotinus influenced Augustine most [O'Connell, *Saint Augustine's Platonism* (Villanova: Augustinian Institute, Villanova University, 1984)], while others claim that Porphyry had the most influence [Willy Theiler, *Die chaldaischen Orakel und die Hymnen des Synesios* (Halle: Neimeyer, 1942) and John J. O'Meara, *Porphyry's Philosophy from Oracles in Augustine* (Paris: Educes Augustiniennes, 1969)]. Still other scholars stress the influence of both thinkers on Augustine [Pierre Courcelle, *Recherches sur les Confessions de S. Augustin* (Paris: Boccard, 1950)]. However this may be, it is certain that Augustine encountered Platonism through Victorinus's translations of the *Enneads* (7.9.13), Ambrose's sermons that reflected Christianized Plotinianism [Courcelle, *Recherches sur les Confessions de S. Augustin*, 124 and Pierre Hadot, *Plotinus and the Simplicity of Vision*, trans. M. Chase (Chicago: University of Chicago Press, 1993), 103], and the intellectual circles in Milan [Peter Brown, *Augustine of Hippo: A Biography*, new edition with an epilogue (Berkeley: University of California Press, 2000), 485–486 and O'Donnell, 413–418].

11. Gilson, 27–37.

12. This relation is analogous to what John Henry Newman calls "notional assent." *A Grammar of Assent* (Notre Dame: University of Notre Dame Press, 1992), 52–76.

13. Newman calls this kind of commitment "real assent." *A Grammar of Assent*, 86–92.

14. John 1.14.

15. For a discussion of the effects of the Neoplatonists on Augustine's philosophical development, see O'Donnell, *Augustine: Confessions*, vol. 2, 413–418; Colin Starnes, *Augustine's Conversion: A Guide to the Argument of Confessions I–IX* (Waterloo: Wilfrid Laurier University Press, 1990), 182–83; and Brown, 94–100.

16. John 1.1–5.

17. Gilson, 105–111.

18. John 1.8–12.

19. Philippians 2.6–11.

20. Romans 5.6; 8.32.

21. Matthew 11.25.

22. One of the clearest ways to point to the difference between the Neoplatonic and Christian dimensions of Augustine is to notice what he does and does not do with his Neoplatonic books [O'Donnell, 413]. As Colin Starnes claims, it would have been easy for Augustine to document his Neoplatonic influences, but he chooses to describe their subject matter in terms of scripture. [Starnes, *Augustine's Conversion: A Guide to the Argument of Confessions I–IX* (Waterloo: Wilfrid Laurier University Press, 1990)], 182–183.

23. Matthew 11.25–29.

24. Romans 1:21–22.

25. In a new edition of his biography of Augustine, Peter Brown notes the need to point beyond the influence of Plotinus on Augustine by calling our attention to a number of important considerations. He tells us that the " 'Milanese circle' of 'Christian Platonists' that Augustine was believed to have encountered at the time of his conversion seems less compact and less tolerant than we had once thought." In addition, Brown notes that paganism was not widespread in intellectual circles. For this reason, he concludes that "the brand of Platonism that Augustine adopted in 386 was already Platonism poised for battle" (Brown, 486–487). Nevertheless, Brown is careful to emphasize the fact that the French scholars of the 1960s have played an invaluable role in documenting the influence of Neoplatonism on Augustine's thinking (Brown, 496–497).

26. Augustine's remarks about this issue are more complex than is usually thought, and I have attempted to do justice to their complexity in what I have said about them. The usual interpretation of Augustine's intention is to claim that Neoplatonic doctrine is identical with Egyptian gold and to suggest that just as the Israelites stole Egyptian gold, so Christian theories stole the gold of the Neoplatonists and made it their own. However, Augustine also says that the children of Israel transformed Egyptian gold into statues of men, birds, beasts, and serpents that they worshiped (Exodus 11:1–2; 32:1–6). Thus, fixing his attention on Egyptian gold and on his right to find ideas in pagan texts without embracing polytheism, Augustine is careful not to worship the idols that sometimes emerge from the gold and the books in question. These idols are especially visible in the later writings of Porphyry. [J. J. O'Meara, *Porphyry's Philosophy from Oracles in Augustine* (Paris: Études augustiniennes, 1959)].

27. While the impact of Neoplatonism on Augustine cannot be underestimated, Robert O'Donnell stresses the importance of not interpreting Augustine's turn in Book 7 as a conversion to Neoplatonism:

It is a misreading to say that in Book 7 Augustine becomes a neo-Platonist. What he *says* is that in the midst of all his philosophizing—Platonic, neo-Platonic, and idiosyncratic—the specific texts put in front of him brought him new light and new frustration, and thus had the effect of driving him towards scriptural authority, where, in Book 8, the real resolution of his difficulties would be worked out. Book 7 teaches, in the end, that intellectual enlightenment, contrary to all Augustine's youthful expectations, is not sufficient. There is no suggestion, anywhere in A. or in any of the modern commentators, that he ever took his 'Platonism' so far as to indulge in theurgy. The only possible liturgy for him now was Christianity; the ascent of the mind was non-sectarian in that important, even crucial, sense. But in one significant way, the Platonic pattern may have influenced his expectations of Christianity in a way that also goes unattended. The function of theurgy is to bring about the presence of the God, visibly. [O'Donnell, 415]

28. See Bernard McGinn, *Foundations of Mysticism*, vol. 2, *The Presence of God: A History of Western Christian Mysticism* (New York: Crossroad, 1991), 228–262 for a detailed defense of the view that Augustine's experiences of Neoplatonic ecstasy were mystical. For the contrary view, see O'Connell, 71–89.

29. See Kirk for a discussion about whether Augustine participated in two mystical experiences or in one experience with two stages. [Kenneth Kirk, *The Vision of God: The Christian Doctrine of the Summum Bonum* (London: Longman, Green and Co., 1947)], 319–346.

30. Romans 1.20.

31. These are the first two references to the (finite-infinite) structure of the soul that I make in this book to express the original relation between man and God and the transition from creation to the fall. This concept is not imposed on the text, but is a way of pointing to a crucial distinction that emerges from it.

32. What I intend to convey at this juncture is that the first stage of Augustine's vision is not merely a self-reflexive activity in which Augustine turns inward to find God within his soul, but also a self-transcendent act in which he finds God beyond the confines of the human realm.

33. Plotinus, *Enneads*, vol. 7, trans. A. H. Armstrong (Cambridge: Harvard University Press, 1988), 6.9.4.

34. Romans 1.20.

35. Plato, *Republic*, trans. G. M. A. Grube, rev. C. D. C. Reeve in *Plato: Complete Works*, ed. with an intro. and notes John M. Cooper (Indianapolis and Cambridge: Hackett Publishing Co., 1997), 509b.

36. Ibid., 514a–517c.

37. Plato, *Phaedo*, trans. G. M. A. Grube in *Plato: Complete Works*, ed. with an intro. and notes John M. Cooper (Indianapolis and Cambridge: Hackett Publishing Co., 1997), 65a–67b.

38. *On Free Choice of the Will*, trans. Anna S. Benjamin and L. H. Hackstaff (Englewood Cliffs, NJ: Prentice-Hall, 1964), (2.7.65).

39. Ibid., 69.

40. Ronald H. Nash, *The Light of the Mind: St. Augustine's Theory of Knowledge* (Lexington, KY: The University Press of Kentucky, 1969), 48–51 and Margaret R. Miles, "Vision: The Eye of the Body and the Eye of the Mind in Saint Augustine's *De Trinitate* and *Confessions*," *Journal of Religion* 63 (1983): 125–142.

41. David S. Chidester, "Symbolism and the Senses in Saint Augustine," *Religion: Journal of Religion and Religions*, 14 (1984): 31–51.

42. Ibid.

43. *The City of God*, trans. R. W. Dyson in *Cambridge Texts in the History of Political Thought* (Cambridge: Cambridge University Press, 1998), (22.30).

44. *The Trinity*, trans. Edmund Hill (Brooklyn: New City Press, 1991), (15.8.51).

45. Romans 9.5.

46. John 14.6.

47. For an alternative view, see Anselm's theory of the incarnation according to which God would have become man even if we had never sinned. [Anselm, *Why God Was Made Man*, trans. John Henry and James Parker (London: Oxford, 1865)].

48. O'Donnell, *Augustine: Confessions*, vol. 2, xxxvii.

49. Pierre Courcelle, *Les confessions de saint Augustin dans la tradition littéraire* (Paris: Études Augustiniennes, 1963), 186.

50. John K. Ryan, *The Confessions of St. Augustine* (New York: Doubleday, 1960), 179.

51. Romans 7.24–25.

52. Proverbs 8.22.

53. Anselm, *Why God Became Man*, trans. Jasper Hopkins and Herbert Richardson (Lewiston, NY: The Edwin Mellen Press, 1974), (2.20). Anselm says, "What can be . . . more merciful than for God . . . to say to a sinner, condemned to eternal torments, and having no way to redeem himself: 'Receive my only begotten son and render him in place of yourself,' and for the Son to say, 'Take me and redeem yourself'?"

54. Eugene TeSelle, Eugene, *Augustine the Theologian* (New York: Herder and Herder, 1970), 168.

55. This is not to say that Christ commits sin on the cross, but that he bears our sin in virtue of which he participates in them. As Chadwick notes, "Augustine often allegorizes the 'coats of skin' of Adam and Eve to mean the morality of the human condition." [Henry Chadwick, *Saint Augustine's Confessions* (Oxford: Oxford University Press, 1991)], 14.

56. Ibid., 176.

57. Matthew 11.28.

58. Matthew 11.25.

CHAPTER 2

1. Henry Chadwick believes that Augustine is referring to the distinction between married and unmarried believers. [Chadwick, *Saint Augustine's Confessions* (Oxford: Oxford University Press, 1991)], 133. However, since Augustine speaks of many directions in which members of the church are moving, he could also be

speaking of the variety of Neoplatonisms current in Milan. [James J. O'Donnell, *Augustine: Confessions*, vol. 2 (Oxford: Clarendon Press, 1992)], 413–418.

2. I Corinthians 7.27–35.

3. Matthew 13.46.

4. James J. O'Donnell, *Augustine: Confessions*, vol. 3 (Oxford: Clarendon Press, 1992), 6–7, 13–15.

5. Colin Starnes, *Augustine's Conversion: A Guide to the Argument of Confessions I–IX* (Waterloo: Wilfrid Laurier University Press, 1990), 217.

6. Luke 15.4–32.

7. At this juncture, I am beginning to enrich my use of the distinction between the finite and the infinite. To say that person is a (finite-infinite) being is to say that limitations and self-transcendence intersect in our journey toward God. On the one hand, if we accept our limitations, we are (finite-infinite) beings; and our souls stretch out toward God without denying our created limitations. On the other hand, if we attempt to encroach on the mystery and the majesty of God, we turn away from our finitude to accentuate our infinite dimension. As a consequence, we become (finite-infinite) beings who are separated from God. Søren Kierkegaard makes a similar characterization of the condition of the self when he writes, "A human being is a synthesis of the infinite and the finite, of the temporal and the eternal, of freedom and necessity, in short, a synthesis." Søren Kierkegaard, *The Sickness Unto Death*, trans. Howard Vincent Hong and Edna H. Hong (Princeton, NJ: Princeton University Press, 1980), 13.

8. Galatians 5.17.

9. Notice how Chadwick formulates the forging of the chain: passion is the consequence of a distorted will; servitude is passion from habit; and habit to which there is no resistance becomes necessity. Chadwick, 8.5.10.

10. Romans 7:24, 25.

11. The *agentes in rebus* were an inspectorate of the imperial bureaucracy, sometimes used as intelligence gatherers and secret police, but mainly responsible to the master of the offices for the operation of the government communications system. On rare occasions, promotion in the department could lead to a provincial governorship. "Friends of the emperor," to which the two agents refer as the highest secular honor they can attain are honored individuals in high office and are not members of a branch of the civil service.

12. Homer, *The Iliad*, trans. Robert Fagles with notes by Bernard Knox (New York: Penguin Books, 1998), (16. 125).

13. Dihle, Albrecht, *The Theory of Will in Classical Antiquity* (Berkeley: University of California Press, 1982), 123–144.

14. Romans 3.23.

15. Psalms 6.4, 78.5.

16. Chadwick reminds us that the oldest manuscript says, "home of God" rather than "a nearby house." Chadwick, 152.

17. John 5.4–9.

18. Matthew 19.21.

19. Romans 13.13–14.

20. Genesis 3.6.

21. Matthew 26.36, Mark 14.32, Luke 22.39–40, and John 18.1.

22. Genesis 2.17.

23. Matthew 26. 39, Mark 14.35, and Luke 22.41.

24. Matthew 21.19.

25. John 1.48–51.

26. G. W. F. Hegel, *Science of Logic*, trans. A. V. Miller (New York: Humanities Press, 1969), 105–106.

27. Ibid.

28. A more profound expression of the crucial points can be formulated by returning to our earlier distinction among the four modes of the (finite-infinite) dimension of the person. Since this hyphenated characterization of the person remains constant from stage to stage in Augustine's development, he displays a continuity in which something is always preserved. However, since a (finite↑infinite) creation, a (finite↑infinite) fall, a (finite-infinite) conversion, and a (finite↷infinite)↗ fulfillment are so radically different, discontinuity is a crucial theme as well. In this formulation of what is at stake in Augustine's position, the (finite-infinite) matrix forms a common core in terms to express the stages of his development. Yet even though this matrix is present in all four contexts to supply the moment of identity, the irreducible differences among them reveal themselves the fact that none of them can be taken up into the others.

I have added arrows to all the modifications of Augustine's development to indicate the differences among the creation, the fall, conversion, and fulfillment in graphic terms. The arrow that goes up from the hyphen points to the relation of the self-transcendent creature to God. The arrow that points in the opposite direction expresses the fall. The arrow that curves from the infinite to the finite conveys the process of conversion; and the arrow that begins with the hyphen and curves around the infinite strives for fulfillment. With reference to this schematic formulation, it is important to emphasize the fact that though original sin is conquered in conversion, the person who has been converted continues to suffer from its stain in the fourth stage of development. In this connection, see Augustine's confession of his "present" sins in (10.28.39–10.40.65).

The relations among the creation, the fall, conversion, and fulfillment are not dialectical, but analogical, precisely because Augustine does not move from stage to stage through a series of positive negations that occur in time, philosophical or otherwise. Rather, he makes these transitions within the temporal, spatial, and eternal framework that we have presupposed and in which we can articulate the subsequent relations among the four stages of his development in analogical terms. The analogies in question presuppose that what we have called the (finite-infinite) structure of the person provides the element of identity and that the four modifications of this structure provide the elements of difference. In addition, the proper understanding of these analogies does not presuppose that analogy is a function of identity and difference, but an expression of what might be called "irreducible similarity." For an analysis of this conception, see Carl G. Vaught, "Participation and Imitation in Plato's Metaphysics," in *Contemporary*

Essays on Greek Ideas: The Kilgore Festschrift, ed. Robert M. Baird, William F. Cooper, Elmer H. Duncan, and Stuart E. Rosenbaum (Waco, Texas: Baylor University Press, 1987), 17–31; Vaught, "Hegel and the Problem of Difference: A Critique of Dialectical Reflection," in *Hegel and His Critics*, ed. William Desmond (Albany, NY: State University of New York Press, 1989), 35–48; and Vaught, "Categories and the Real Order: Sellar's Interpretation of Aristotle's Metaphysics," *The Monist*, 66 (1983): 438–449.

29. O'Donnell, *Augustine's Confessions*, vol. 3, 69.

30. Ibid., 61.

31. Matthew 26.39.

32. Ibid.

33. In this case, the (finite-infinite) being that participates in the resurrection has participated in the crucifixion.

34. Genesis 3.9.

35. Ibid. 3.21.

36. Ibid. 3.21–22.

37. I owe this phrase to one of my former graduate students, Janice M. Stabb. See her article, "Standing Alone Together: Silence, Solitude, and Radical Conversion," in *Contemporary Themes in Augustine's Confessions: Part II, Contemporary Philosophy*, ed. Carl G. Vaught, 15 (1993): 16–20.

38. Romans 14.1.

39. Plato, *Republic*, trans. G. M. A. Grube in *Plato: Complete Works*, ed. with an intro. and notes John M. Cooper (Indianapolis and Cambridge: Hackett Publishing Co., 1997), 412c–417b.

40. Thomas Hobbes, *Leviathan*, ed. by J. C. A. Gaskin (Oxford: Oxford University Press, 1998).

41. Jean Jacques Rousseau, *The Social Contract and Discourses*, trans. with an intro., G. D. H. Cole, London: Dent, 1991.

42. John Locke, "Second Treatise" in *Two Treatises of Government: A Critical Edition with Apparatus Criticus*, ed. Peter Laslett (London: Cambridge University Press, 1967).

43. In terms of our earlier distinctions, they move though four stages: the (finite-infinite) that is oriented initially toward God, the (finite-infinite) that falls away from God, the (finite-infinite) that comes back to itself, and the (finite-infinite), that moves toward fulfillment.

Chapter 3

1. Once more I am retelling Augustine's story so the reader can hear his voice and so the text will not be reduced to a cluster of abstract problems. This is not to say that what Augustine has written does not require interpretation or that theoretical problems never arise with respect to it. However, when interpretation is needed and abstract issues surface, I attempt to deal with them within the larger narrative and dialogical context that they presuppose.

2. See Colin Starnes's and James O'Donnell's explanations of the Trinitarian position expressed in Books VII–IX. [Colin Starnes, Augustine's *Conversion: A Guide to the Argument of Confessions I–IX* (Waterloo, ONT: Wilfrid Laurier University Press. 1990), 1 and James J. O'Donnell, *Augustine: Confessions,* vol. 2 (Oxford: Clarendon Press, 1992)], 391, 417.

3. The long vacation lasted from the summer of 387 to August 388. [Henry Chadwick, *Saint Augustine's Confessions* (Oxford: Oxford University Press, 1991)], 158.

4. James J. O'Donnell, *Augustine: Confessions,* vol. 3 (Oxford: Clarendon Press, 1992), 78–79.

5. O'Donnell, *Augustine: Confessions,* vol. 3, 85–91; Peter Brown, *Augustine of Hippo* (Berkeley: University of California Press, 1969), 113–126; and Bonner, Gerald, *St. Augustine of Hippo* (Norwich: The Canterbury Press, 1963), 45.

6. O'Donnell, 85–91.

7. Bonner, 45–46.

8. *Soliloquies,* trans. Thomas F. Gilligan (New York: Cima Publishing Co., 1948), 343–350.

9. Chadwick tells us that going barefoot was a typical practice in imitation of Moses at the burning bush and Isaiah's going barefoot for three years. Chadwick, 163.

10. Plato, *Symposium,* trans. Alexander Nehamas and Paul Woodruff in *Plato: Complete Works,* ed. with an intro. and notes John M. Cooper (Indianapolis and Cambridge: Hackett Publishing Co., 1997), 220b.

11. John 9.6–7.

12. Plotinus, *Enneads,* vol.1, trans. A. H. Armstrong (Cambridge: Harvard University Press, 1989), 3.

13. Luke 1.48.

14. I am pleased to refer at this juncture to an article by one of my former graduate students. Sylvia Benso, "Monica's Grin of Tension," in *Contemporary Themes in Augustine's Confessions: Part II, Contemporary Philosophy,* ed. Carl G. Vaught, 15 (1993): 5–10.

15. See Kenneth E. Kirk, *The Vision of God* (New York: Harper and Row, 1946), 323.

16. I Corinthians 15.51.

17. I John 3.2.

18. Numa Denis Fustel De Coulanges, *The Ancient City,* trans. Willard Small (Garden City, NY: Doubleday, 1956), 21–33.

19. Hebrews 11.10.

20. John K. Ryan, *The Confessions of St. Augustine* (NY: Doubleday, 1960), 224, n. 1.

21. Ibid., 226.

22. *Symposium,* 223d.

23. This claim is one more indication that Augustine does not take a definitive stand about the question of the origin of the soul and how the soul is united to the embryo, whether by heredity, the special creation of God, or because

the preexistent soul either falls or is sent into the body. It is noteworthy that he never decides which theory to embrace throughout his lengthy philosophical career. [*On Free Choice of the Will,* trans. Anna S. Benjamin and L. H. Hackstaff, (Englewood Cliffs, NJ: Prentice Hall, 1964), (3.21.59); *The Retractations,* trans. Sister Mary Inez Gogan. (Washington, DC: The Catholic University of America Press, 1968), (1.1.3); *Select Letters,* trans. James Houston Baxter in *The Loeb Classical Library,* vol. 239, Cambridge: Harvard University Press, 1980, (1.66); and *The Literal Meaning of Genesis,* trans. John H. Taylor in *Ancient Christian Writers,* vols. 41–42 (New York: Newman Press, 1982), (10.1).] As I indicate on p. 160 of *The Journey toward God in Augustine's Confessions: Books I–VI,* Augustine considers four theories about for the origin of the soul. The first theory (traducianism) presupposes that the souls of human beings evolve from the one soul that God created. The second (creationism) claims that souls are created individually at birth. The third maintains that God sends existing souls to bodies when they are born and that the soul in question then governs the individual. Finally, according to the fourth theory, souls are not sent by God, but fall into bodies of their own accord.

Bibliography

SELECTED ENGLISH TRANSLATIONS OF
AUGUSTINE'S WRITINGS, LISTED IN THE
APPROXIMATE ORDER OF THEIR COMPOSITION

Against the Academicians. Translated by Peter King in *Against the Academicians and The Teacher.* Indianapolis and Cambridge: Hacket Publishing Co., 1995.

The Happy Life. Translated by Ludwig Shopp in *The Fathers of the Church,* vol. 1. New York: CIMA Publishing Co., Inc., 1948.

Divine Providence and the Problem of Evil. Translated by Robert P. Russell in *The Fathers of the Church,* vol. 1. New York: CIMA Publishing Co., Inc, 1948.

Soliloquies. Translated with an introduction and notes by Kim Paffenroth in *The Work of Saint Augustine: Translations for the Twenty-first Century,* vol. 2. Edited by John E. Rotelle. Brooklyn: New City Press, 2000.

On the Immortality of the Soul. Translated with a preface by George G. Leckie in *Concerning the Teacher* and *On the immortality of the soul.* New York and London: D. Appleton-Century Co., 1938.

The Catholic and the Manichaean Ways of Life. Translated by Donald A. Gallagher and Idella J. Gallagher. Washington, DC: *Catholic University of America Press,* 1966.

The Greatness of the Soul. Translated and annotated by Joseh M. Colleran in *The Greatness of the Soul* and *The teacher.* Westminster, MD: Newman Press, 1950.

On Free Choice of the Will. Translated by Anna S. Benjamin and L. H. Hackstaff. Englewood Cliffs, NJ: Prentice Hall, 1964.

On Genesis: Two Books on Genesis against the Manichees. Translated by Roland J. Teske in *On Genesis: Two Books on Genesis against the Manichees and On the Literal Interpretation of Genesis, an Unfinished Book.* Washington, DC: Catholic University of America, 1990.

The Teacher. Translated by Peter King in *Against the Academicians and The Teacher.* Indianapolis and Cambridge: Hackett Publishing, 1995.

On the Profit of Believing. Translated by C. L. Cornish in *Basic Writings of Saint Augustine,* vol. 1. Edited with an introduction and notes by Whitney J. Oates. New York: Random House, 1948.

On the Literal Interpretation of Genesis, an Unfinished Book. Translated by Roland J. Teske in *On Genesis: Two Books on Genesis against the Manichees* and *On the Literal Interpretation of Genesis, an Unfinished Book.* Washington, DC: Catholic University of America, 1990.

Eighty-three Different Questions. Translated by David L. Mosher. Washington, DC: Catholic University of America Press, 1982.

Teaching Christianity. Translated by Edmund Hill in *The Works of Saint Augustine: Translations for the 21st Century.* vol. I.11. Edited by John E. Rotelle. Brooklyn: New City Press, 1996.

Confessions. Translated by Maria Boulding, in *The Works of St. Augustine: A Translation for the 21st Century.* vol. I.1. 2nd edition. Edited by John E. Rotelle. Brooklyn: New City Press, 1996; Henry Chadwick, Oxford: Oxford University Press, 1991; Albert Outler in *The Library of Christian Classics,* vol. VII. Edited by Albert Outler. Philadelphia: The Westminster Press, 1955; John K. Ryan, New York: Image Books, Doubleday, 1960; and F. J. Sheed, revised edition, introduced by Peter Brown. Indianapolis and Cambridge: Hackett Publishing Co. Inc., 1993.

The Trinity. Translated with an introduction and notes by Edmund Hill in *The Works of Saint Augustine: A Translation for the 21st Century.* Brooklyn: New City Press, 1991.

The Literal Meaning of Genesis. Translated by John H. Taylor in *Ancient Christian Writers,* vols. 41–2. New York: Newman Press, 1982.

The City of God against the Pagans. Translated by R. W. Dyson in *Cambridge Texts in the History of Political Thought.* Cambridge: Cambridge University Press, 1998.

Select Letters. Translated by James Houston Baxter in *The Loeb Classical Library,* vol. 239. Cambridge, Mass.: Harvard University Press, 1980. In addition, there are some important, recently discovered Letters numbered 1*–29*. Translated by R. Eno in *The Fathers of the Church,* vol. 81. New York: CIMA Publishing Co. Inc., 1989.

The Retractations. Translated by Sister Mary Inez Gogan. Washington, DC: The Catholic University of America Press, 1968.

SELECTED GENERAL STUDIES

Bonner, Gerald. *Augustine of Hippo: Life and Controversies.* New York and Rome: Canterbury Press, 1986.

Bourke, Vernon Joseph. *Augustine's Quest of Wisdom: Life and Philosophy of the Bishop of Hippo.* Milwaukee: The Bruce Publishing Company, 1945.

Burnaby, John. *Amor Dei: a Study of the Religion of St. Augustine.* Reissued with corrections and a new forward. New York and Rome: Canterbury Press, 1991.

Chadwick, Henry. *Augustine,* in *Past Masters Series.* Oxford: Oxford University Press, 1986.

Clark, Gillian. *Augustine: the Confessions.* Cambridge: Cambridge University Press, 1993.

Clark, Mary T. *Augustine.* Washington, DC: Georgetown University Press, 1994.

Gilson, Etienne. *The Christian Philosophy of Saint Augustine.* Translated by L. E. M. Lynch. New York: Random House, 1967.

Kirwan, Christopher. *Augustine,* in *The Arguments of the Philosophers.* New York and London: Routledge, 1989.

Meagher, Robert E. *Augustine: An Introduction.* New York: Harper Colophon Books, 1979.

Mendelson, Michael. "Augustine." *The Stanford Encyclopedia of Philosophy.* Fall 2000 ed. Edited by Edward N. Zalta.URL = http://plato.stanford.edu/archives/fall2000/entries/augustine/.

O'Donnell, James. *Augustine.* In *Twayne's World Author Series.* Boston: Twayne Publishers, 1985.

O'Meara, John J. *The Young Augustine, The Growth of St. Augustine's Mind Up to His Conversion.* New York and London: Longmans, Green and Co., 1954.

O'Meara, John Joseph. *Understanding Augustine.* Dublin, Ireland: Four Courts Press, 1997.

Portalie, Eugene. *A Guide to the Thought of Saint Augustine,* with an introduction by Vernon J. Bourke. Translated by Ralph J. Bastian. Chicago: H. Regnery Co., 1960.

Rist, John. *Augustine: Ancient Thought Baptized.* Cambridge: Cambridge University Press, 1994.

Scott, T. Kermit. *Augustine: His Thought in Context.* New York: Paulist Press, 1995.

Wills, Gary. *Saint Augustine.* New York: Viking, 1999.

SELECTED SECONDARY WORKS

Alfaric, Prosper. *L'évolution intellectuelle de Saint Augustin: I, Du Manichéisme au Néoplatonisme.* Paris: Nourry, 1918.

Anselm. *Monologion and Proslogion, with the Replies of Gaunilo and Anselm.* Translated with an Introduction by Thomas Williams. Indianapolis and Cambridge: Hackett Co., 1995.

Anselm. *Why God Became Man.* Translated by John Henry and James Parker. London: Oxford, 1865.

Arendt, Hanna. *Love and Saint Augustine.* Edited by Joanna Scott and Judith Stark. Chicago: University of Chicago Press, 1996.

Aristotle, *The Complete Works of Aristotle,* 2 vols. Revised Oxford translation. Edited by Jonathan Barnes. Princeton, NJ: Princeton University Press, 1984.

Aristotle, *Poetics*. Translated by I. Bywater in *The Complete Works of Aristotle*, vol. 2. Revised Oxford translation. Edited by Jonathan Barnes. Princeton, NJ: Princeton University Press, 1984.

Armstrong, A. Hilary. "St. Augustine and Christian Platonism," in *Collectanea Augustiniana*. Villanova, PA: Villanova University Press, 1967.

Armstrong, A. Hilary. *The Cambridge History of Later Greek and Early Medieval Philosophy* (Cambridge: Cambridge University Press, 1967).

Augustine: A Collection of Critical Essays. Edited by Markus, R. A. Garden City, NY: Anchor Books, 1972.

Augustine, Saint, Bishop of Hippo: The Confessions of Augustine. Edited by John Gibb and William Montgomery. Cambridge: Cambridge University Press, 1908.

Augustine Through the Ages: An Encyclopedia. Edited by Allen D. Fitzgerald. Grand Rapids, MI: Eerdmans Publishing Company, 1999.

Augustinian Studies. Villanova, PA: Villanova University Press.

The Augustinian Tradition. Edited by Gareth B. Matthews. Berkeley: University of California Press, 1999.

Babcock, William S. "Augustine's Interpretation of Romans (A.D. 394–396)." *Augustinian Studies* 10 (1979): 55–74.

Bearsley, Patrick. "Augustine and Wittgenstein on Language." *Philosophy* 58 (1983): 229–236.

Beatrice, P. F. "*Quosdam platonicorum libros*, The Platonic Readings of Augustine in Milan." *Vigiliae Christianae* 43 (1989): 248–281.

Bennett, C. "The Conversion of Virgil: The *Aeneid*, in Augustine's *Confessions*." *Revue des études Augustiniennes* 34 (1988): 47–69.

Benso, Sylvia, "Monica's Grin of Tension," in *Contemporary Themes in Augustine's Confessions: Part II*. Edited by Carl G. Vaught. *Contemporary Philosophy* 15 (1993): 5–10.

Bolgiani, F. *La conversione di s. Agostino e l'VIII libro delle "Confessioni*. Turino, 1956.

Borresen, K. E. *Subordination and Equivalence: The Nature and Role of Woman in Augustine and Thomas Aquinas*. Translated by Charles H. Talbot. Lanham, MD: University Press of America, 1981.

Bourke, Vernon J. *Augustine's View of Reality*. Villanova, PA: Villanova University Press, 1963.

Bourke, Vernon J. *Augustine's Love of Wisdom: An Introspective Philosophy*. West Lafayette, IN: Purdue University Press, 1992.

Boyer, C. *Christianisme et néo-platonisme dans la formation de saint Augustin*. Paris: Beauchesne, 1920.

Brown, Peter. *Augustine of Hippo: A Biography*. New edition with an epilogue. Berkeley University of California Press, 2000.

Bubacz, Bruce. *St. Augustine's Theory of Knowledge: A Contemporary Analysis*. New York: E. Mellen Press, 1981.

Burke, Kenneth. *The Rhetoric of Religion: Studies in Logology.* Berkeley: University of California Press, 1970.

Burkitt, F. C. *The Religion of the Manichees.* Cambridge: Cambridge University Press, 1925.

Burnaby, John. *Amor Dei: A Study of the Religion of St. Augustine.* Reissued with corrections and a new foreword. New York and Rome: Canterbury Press, 1991.

Burnyeat, M. F. *The Skeptical Tradition.* Berkeley: University of California Press, 1983.

Bussanich, John. "Plotinus' Metaphysics of the One," in *The Cambridge Companion to Plotinus.* Edited by Lloyd P. Gerson. Cambridge: Cambridge University Press, 1996, 38–65.

The Cambridge Companion to Plotinus, Edited by Lloyd P. Gerson. Cambridge: Cambridge University Press, 1996.

The Cambridge History of Later Greek and Early Medieval Philosophy. Edited by A. H. Armstrong. Cambridge: Cambridge University Press, 1967.

Chidester, David S. "Symbolism and the Senses in Saint Augustine." *Religion: Journal of Religion and Religions* 14 (1984).

Chidester, David S. *Word and Light: Seeing, Hearing, and Religious Discourse.* Urbana: University of Illinois Press, 1992.

Colish, M. *The Mirror of Language: A Study in the Medieval Theory of Knowledge.* New Haven and London: Yale University Press, 1968.

Contemporary Themes in Augustine's Confessions: Part I. Edited by Carl G. Vaught. *Contemporary Philosophy* 15 (1993).

Contemporary Themes in Augustine's Confessions: Part II. Edited by Carl G. Vaught. *Contemporary Philosophy* 15 (1993).

Courcelle, Pierre. *Late Latin Writers and Their Greek Sources.* Translated by H. E Wedeck. Cambridge, MA: Harvard University Press, 1969.

Courcelle, Pierre. *Le Confessions de Saint Augustin dans la tradition littéraire, antecedents et posterite.* Paris: Études Augustiniennes, 1963.

Courcelle, Pierre. *Recherches sur les Confessions de saint Augustin,* 2nd ed. Paris: E. de Boccard, 1968.

Curley, Augustine J. *Augustine's Critique of Skepticism: A Study of Contra Academicos.* New York: Peter Lang, 1996.

Daly, L. "Psychohistory and St. Augustine's Conversion Process," in *Collectanea Augustiniana,* Edited by Joseph Schnaublet and Frederick Van Fleteren. Villanova, PA: Villanova University Press, 1978.

Dante. *Hell: The Comedy of Dante Alighieri.* Translated by Dorothy L. Sayers. London and New York: Penguin Books, 1949; *Purgatory.* Translated by Sayers, 1955; and *Paradise.* Translated by Sayers and Barbara Reynolds, 1962.

Dawson, D. "Transcendence as Embodiment: Augustine's Domestication of Gnosis." *Modern Theology* 1 (1994): 1–26.

De Coulanges, Numa Denis Fustel. *The Ancient City.* Translated by Willard Small. Garden City, NY: Doubleday, 1956.

Descartes, René. *Meditations on First Philosophy*, in *The Philosophical Writings of Descartes*, vol. 2. Translated by John Cottingham, Robert Stoothoff, and Dugald Murdoch. Cambridge: Cambridge University Press, 1984.

Diehl, Albrecht. *The Theory of Will in Classical Antiquity*. Berkeley: University of California Press, 1982.

Djuth, Marianne. "Will" in Fitzgerald, 881–885.

Dudden, F. Homes. *The Life and Times of St. Ambrose*, vol. 1. Oxford, The Clarendon Press, 1935.

Dyson, R. W. "St. Augustine's Remarks on Time." *The Downside Review* (1982): 221–230.

Erikson, Erik H. *Identity and the Life Cycle*. New York: W. W. Norton and Company, 1980.

Evans, G. R. *Augustine On Evil*. Cambridge: Cambridge University Press, 1982.

Ferrari, Leo C. *The Conversions of Saint Augustine*. Villanova, PA: Villanova University, 1984.

Finan, Tom. "Modes of Vision in 'De Genesi ad Litteram' XII," in *The Relationship between Neoplatonism and Christianity*. Edited by Tom Finan and Vincent Twomey. Dublin: Four Courts Press, 1992.

Findlay, J. N. *The Discipline of the Cave: Gifford Lectures Given at the University of St. Andrews*. New York: Humanities Press, 1966.

Flores, Ralph. "Reading and Speech in St. Augustine's Confessions," *Augustinian Studies*, 6 (1975): 1–13.

Fortin, Earnest L. "Saint Augustin et la doctrine neoplatonicienne de l'âme." *Augustinus Magister*. Paris: Études Augustiniennes, 1954, vol. 3, 371–380.

Gilson, Etienne. *The Christian Philosophy of Saint Augustine*. Translated by L. E. M. Lynch. New York: Random House, 1960.

Hadot, Pierre. *Porphyre et Victorinus*, 2 vols. Paris, 1968.

Hadot, Pierre. *Plotinus and the Simplicity of Vision*. Translated by M. Chase. Chicago: University of Chicago Press, 1993.

Harnack, Adolf. *"Die Hohepunkte in Augustins Konfessionen."* Reprinted in his *Redens und Aufsätze*, vol. 1. Giessen: Ricker, 1904.

Harrison, Carol. *Beauty and Revelation in the Thought of Saint Augustine*. Oxford: Clarendon Press, 1992.

Hartle, Ann. *Death and the Disinterested Spectator: An Inquiry into the Nature of Philosophy*. Albany, NY: State University of New York Press, 1986.

Hegel, G. W. F. *Hegel's Phenomenology of Spirit*. Translated by A. V. Miller. Oxford: Oxford University Press, 1977.

Hegel, G. W. F. *Science of Logic*. Translated by A. V. Miller. New York: Humanities Press, 1969.

Hegel, G. W. F. Hegel. *Lectures on the Philosophy of Religion*, vol. 1. Translated by R. F. Brown, P. C. Hodgson, and J. M Stewart. Los Angeles: University of California Press, 1984.

Heidegger, Martin. *Being and Time*. Translated by John Macquarrie and Edward Robinson. San Francisco: Harper Collins, 1962.

Henry, Paul. "The Adversus Arium of Marius Victorinus, the First Systematic Exposition of the Doctrine of the Trinity." *Journal of Theological Studies* 1 (1950): 42–55.

Hobbes, Thomas. *Leviathan.* Edited by J. C. A. Gaskin. Oxford: Oxford University Press, 1998.

Holscher, Ludger. *The Reality of the Mind: Augustine's Philosophical Arguments for the Human Soul as a Spiritual Substance.* New York and London: Routledge and Kegan Paul, 1986.

Homer. *The Iliad,* Translated by Robert Fagles with notes by Bernard Knox. New York: Penguin Books, 1998.

Johnstone, Henry. *The Problem of the Self.* University Park, PA: Pennsylvania State University, 1970.

Søren Kierkegaard. *The Concept of Irony.* Translated and edited by Edna H. Hong and Howard V. Hong. Princeton, NJ: Princeton University Press, 1992.

Kierkegaard, Søren. *The Sickness Unto Death.* Translated by Howard Vincent Hong and Edna H. Hong. Princeton, NJ: Princeton University Press, 1980.

Kirk, Kenneth E. *The Vision of God: The Christian Doctrine of the Summum Bonum.* New York and London: New York and London: Longmans and Green, 1946.

Lewis, C. S. *Surprised by Joy.* New York: Harcourt, Brace & World, 1955.

Locke, John. "Second Treatise," in *Two Treatises of Government: A Critical Edition with Apparatus Criticus.* Edited by Peter Laslett. London: Cambridge University Press, 1967.

Luther, Martin. *Bondage of the Will,* in *Luther and Erasmus: Free Will and Salvation.* Translated by E. Gordon Rupp. Philadelphia: The Westminster Press, 1969.

Mallard, William. *Language and Love: Introducing Augustine's Religious Thought through the Confessions Story.* University Park, PA: Pennsylvania State University Press, 1994.

Markus, R. A. "Marius Victorinus and Augustine," in Armstrong, 331–419.

Matthews, Gareth B. "The Inner Man." In *Augustine: A Collection of Critical Essays,* 176–190.

Matthews, Gareth B. *Thought's Ego in Augustine and Descartes.* Ithaca, NY: Cornell University Press, 1992.

Matthews, Gareth B. "Augustine and Descartes on Minds and Bodies," in *The Augustinian Tradition,* 222–232.

McGinn, Bernard. *Foundations of Mysticism,* vol. 2. *The Presence of God: A History of Western Christian Mysticism* (New York: Crossroad, 1991).

McMahon, Robert. *Augustine's Prayerful Ascent: An Essay on the Literary Form of the Confessions.* Athens, GA: University of Georgia Press, 1989.

Mendelson, Michael. "The Dangling Thread: Augustine's Three Hypotheses of the Soul's Origin in the *De Genesi ad Litteram.*" *British Journal of the History of Philosophy* 3 (1995): 219–247.

Mendelson, Michael. "The Business of Those Absent, The Origin of the Soul in Augustine's *De Genesi ad Litteram* 10.6–26." *Augustinian Studies* 29 (1998): 25–81.

Mendelson, Michael. "Augustine." *The Stanford Encyclopaedia of Philosophy*. Edited by Edward N. Zalta. Fall 2000 Edition. URL = http//plaato/stanford.edu/archives/fall2000/entries/augustine/.

Miles, Margaret R. "Vision: The Eye of the Body and the Eye of the Mind in Saint Augustine's De Trinitate and Confessions." *Journal of Religion* 63.2 (1983): 125–142.

Miles, Margaret R. *Desire and Delight: A New Reading of Augustine's Confessions*. New York: Crossroad, 1992.

Murphy, James J. *Rhetoric in the Middle Ages*. Berkeley: University of California Press, 1974.

Nash, Ronald H. *The Light of the Mind: St. Augustine's Theory of Knowledge*. Lexington, KY: The University Press of Kentucky, 1969.

Newman, John Henry. *A Grammar of Assent*. South Bend, IN: University of Notre Dame Press, 1992.

Niebuhr, Reinhold. *The Nature and Destiny of Man*, vol. 1, New York: Charles Scribner's Sons, 1953.

Nygren, Anders. "The Structure of Saint Augustine's Confessions." *The Lutheran Church Quarterly* 21 (1948): 214–230.

O'Connell, Robert J. "The Plotinian Fall of the Soul in St. Augustine." *Traditio* 19 (1963): 1–35.

O'Connell, Robert J., "The Riddle of Augustine's 'Confessions: A Plotinian Key." *International Philosophical Quarterly* 4 (1964): 327–372.

O'Connell, Robert J. *St. Augustine's Early Theory of Man*. Cambridge: Harvard University Press, 1968.

O'Connell, Robert J. *St. Augustine's Confessions: The Odyssey of Soul*. Cambridge: Harvard University Press, 1969.

O'Connell, Robert J. "Action and Contemplation," in Markus, 38–58.

O'Connell, Robert J. "Augustine's Rejection of the Fall of the Soul." *Augustinian Studies* 4 (1973): 1–32.

O'Connell, Robert J. *Art and the Christian Intelligence in St. Augustine*. Cambridge, MA: Harvard University Press, 1978.

O'Connell, Robert J. *Saint Augustine's Platonism*. Villanova, PA: Augustinian Institute, Villanova University, 1984.

O'Connell, Robert J. *Imagination and Metaphysics in St. Augustine*. Milwaukee, WI: Marquette University Press, 1986.

O'Connell, Robert J. *The Origin of the Soul in St. Augustine's Later Works*. New York: Fordham University Press, 1987.

O'Connell, Robert J. "Faith, Reason, and Ascent to vision in Saint Augustine." *Augustinian Studies* 21 (1990)

O'Connell, Robert J. "Where the Difference Still Lies." *Augustinian Studies* 21 (1990): 139–153.

O'Connell, Robert J. *Images of Conversion in St. Augustine's Confessions*. New York: Fordham University Press, 1996.

O'Daly, Gerard. *Augustine's Philosophy of Mind.* London: Gerald Duckworth & Co., Ltd., 1987.

O'Donnell, James J. *Augustine, Confessions. Text and Commentary,* in 3 vols. Oxford: Oxford University Press, 1992.

O'Loughlin, T. "The Libri Philosophorum and Augustine's Conversions." *The Relationship between Neoplatonism and Christianity,* 101–126.

O'Meara, Dominic J. "The Hierarchical Ordering of Reality in Plotinus," in Gerson, 66–81.

O'Meara, John J. "Augustine and Neo-Platonism," *Recherches Augustiniennes,* 1 (1958): 91–111.

O'Meara, John J. *Porphyry's Philosophy from Oracles in Augustine* (Paris: Étude Augustiniennes, 1959).

Pagels, Elaine. *Adam, Eve, and the Serpent.* New York: Random House, 1988.

Pepin, J. "Saint Augustin et la fonction protreptique de l'allegori," *Recherches Augustiniennes* 1 (1958): 243–286.

Petrarch, Francis. *The First Modern Scholar and Man of Letters.* Edited and translated by James Robinson. New York: G. P. Putnam, 1898.

Pincherle, A. "Sources platoniciennes di l'augustinisme," and the debate with Courcelle *Augustine Magister,* vol. 3. Paris: Etudes Augustiniennes, 1954.

Plantinga, Alvin. "Augustinian Christian Philosophy." *Monist* 75 (1992): 291–320. Reprinted in Mathews, 1–26.

Plato. *Meno.* Translated by G. M. A. Grube in *Plato: Complete Works.* Edited with an introduction and notes by John M. Cooper. Indianapolis and Cambridge: Hackett Publishing Co., 1997.

Plato, *Phaedo.* Translated by G. M. A. Grube in *Plato: Complete Works.* Edited with an introduction and notes by John M. Cooper. Indianapolis and Cambridge: Hackett Publishing Co., 1997.

Plato. *Republic.* Translated by G. M. A. Grube in *Plato: Complete Works.* Edited with an introduction and notes by John M. Cooper. Indianapolis and Cambridge: Hackett Publishing Co., 1997.

Plato, *Symposium.* Translated by Alexander Nehamas and Paul Woodruff in *Plato: Complete Works.* Edited with an introduction and notes by John M. Cooper. Indianapolis and Cambridge: Hackett Publishing Co., 1997.

Plotinus, *Enneads.* Translated by A. H. Armstrong, 7 vols., in *The Loeb Classical Library.* Cambridge: Harvard University Press, 1966–1984.

Poland, L. M. "Augustine, Allegory, and Conversion." *Journal of Literature and Theology* 1 (1988): 37–48.

Power, Kim. *Veiled Desire: Augustine's Writing on Women.* London: Darton, Longman, Todd, 1995.

Rigby, Paul. *Original Sin in Augustine's Confessions.* Ottawa: University of Ottawa Press, 1987.

Rist, John. *Augustine: Ancient Thought Baptized.* Cambridge: Cambridge University Press, 1994.

Robbins, Jill. *Prodigal Son/Elder Brother: Interpretation and Alterity in Augustine, Petrarch, Kafka, Levinas*. Chicago: University of Chicago Press, 1991.

Rousseau, Jean Jacques. *The Social Contract and Discourses*. Translated with an introduction by G. D. H. Cole. London: Dent, 1991.

Roy, Oliver du. *L'Intelligence de la Foi en lat Trinite selon Saint Augustin*. Etudes Augustiniennes: Paris, 1966.

Schroeder, Frekeric M. "Plotinus and Language," in Gerson, 336–355.

Solignac, Aime. "Bibliotheque Augustinienne." *Oeuvres de saint Augustin*. Paris: Desclee de Brouwer, 1962.

Spence, Sarah. *Rhetorics of Reason and Desire: Virgil, Augustine, and the Troubadours*. Ithaca, New York: Cornell University Press, 1988.

Spinoza, Benedict. *The Ethics*. Translated by R. H. M. Elwes. New York: Dover Publications, 1955.

Stabb, Janice M. "Standing Alone Together: Silence, Solitude, and Radical Conversion, in *Contemporary Themes in Augustine's Confessions: Part II*. Edited by Carl G. Vaught. *Contemporary Philosophy* 15 (1993): 16–20.

Starnes, Colin. *Augustine's Conversion: A Guide to the Argument of Confessions I–IX*. Waterloo, ONT: Wilfrid Laurier University Press, 1990.

Stock, Brian. *Augustine the Reader: Meditation, Self-knowledge, and the Ethics of Interpretation*. Cambridge: Harvard University Press, 1996.

TeSelle, Eugene. *Augustine, the Theologian*. New York: Herder and Herder, 1970.

TeSelle, Eugene. "Pelagius, Pelagianism," in Fitzgerald, 633–640.

Teske, Roland J. "St. Augustine's View of the Original Human Condition in *De Genesi contra Manichaeos*." *Augustinian Studies* 22 (1991): 141–155.

Teske, Roland J. "Soul," in Fitzgerald, 807–812.

Theiler, Willy. *Die chaldaischen Orakel und die Hymnen des Synesios*. Halle: Neimeyer, 1942.

Tillich, Paul. "Two Types of Philosophy of Religion," in *Theology of Culture*. Edited by Robert C. Kindall. Oxford: Oxford University Press, 1959.

Van Fleteren, Frederick. "Augustine's Ascent of the Soul in Book VII of the Confessions: A Reconsideration." *Augustinian Studies* 5 (1974): 29–72.

Van Fleteren, Frederick. "A Reply to Robert O'Connell." *Augustinian Studies* 21 (1990): 127–137.

Vaught, Carl G. *The Quest for Wholeness*. Albany, New York: State University of New York Press, 1982.

Vaught, Carl G. "Signs, Categories, and the Problem of Analogy," in *Semiotics*, 1985. Edited by John Deely. Lanham, MD: The University Press of America, 1986, pp. 64–82.

Vaught, Carl G. "Metaphor, Analogy, and the Nature of Truth," in *New Essays in Metaphysics*. Edited by Robert C. Neville. Albany, New York: State University of New York Press, 1986: 217–236.

Vaught, Carl G. "Participation and Imitation in Plato's Metaphysics," in *Contemporary Essays on Greek Ideas: The Kilgore Festschrift*. Edited by Robert M. Baird, William F. Cooper, Elmer H. Duncan, and Stuart E. Rosenbaum. Waco, Texas: Baylor University Press, 1987, 17–31.

Vaught, Carl G. "Hegel and the Problem of Difference: A Critique of Dialectical Reflection," in *Hegel and His Critics*. Edited by William Desmond. Albany, NY: State University of New York Press, 1989: 35–48.

Vaught, Carl G. "Categories and the Real Order: Sellar's Interpretation of Aristotle's Metaphysics." *The Monist* 66 (1983): 438–449.

Vaught, Carl G. "The Quest for Wholeness and Its Crucial Metaphor and Analogy: The Place of Places." *Ultimate Reality and Meaning* 7 (1984): 156–165.

Vaught, Carl G. "Metaphor, Analogy, and System: A Reply to Burbidge." *Man and World* 18 (1984): 55–63.

Vaught, Carl G. "Semiotics and the Problem of Analogy: A Critique of Peirce's Theory of Categories." *Transactions of the Charles S. Peirce Society* 22 (1986): 311–326.

Vaught, Carl G. "Subject, Object, and Representation: A Critique of Hegel's Dialectic of Perception." *International Philosophical Quarterly* 22 (1986): 117–135.

Virgil, *The Aeneid of Virgil*. Translated by Robert Fitzgerald. New York: Random House, 1990.

Wetzel, James. *Augustine and the Limits of Virtue*. Cambridge: Cambridge University Press, 1992.

Whitehead, Alfred North. *Religion in the Making*. Cleveland: The World Publishing Company, 1963.

Zepf, Max Virgil, "Augustine's *Confessions*." *The Lutheran Church Quarterly* 21 (1948).

Index

Academic Skepticism, 29, 57

Adam, 49–50, 58, 59, 87, 122, 137

Adam and Eve, 1, 93, 97, 98, 126, 149n

addiction, 8, 13, 68, 70, 75, 78–79, 82, 84, 99, 120

Adeodatus, 117, 134

adolescence, 8, 26, 61, 70, 98, 102–103, 105, 117, 126

Aeneas, 123, 125

aesthetic, 17, 69, 81–84, 91

Alypius, 60, 65, 79–80, 84–85, 90, 92–93, 99–103, 114, 116–117

Ambrose, 34, 37, 57, 70, 72, 80, 93, 118, 134, 136, 139n, 146n

analogy or analogical discourse, 2, 10, 12, 18, 28, 30, 44, 54, 98, 102, 106, 127, 132, 151

angels, 47, 93

anima and *animus*, 59, 109

Anselm, 32, 62, 141n, 142n, 149n

Cur Deus Homo, 62

Anthony, 80–81, 83, 91–93

Apollinarian heresy, 60

Aquinas, Thomas, 3, 10

arche, 52

Aristotle, 10

   Categories, 144n

astrology, 93

attitude, 19, 37–38, 54, 68, 115, 130, 138

auditory images and metaphors, x, 16–18, 44, 54–57, 90, 111, 113, 144n

autobiography, ix–x, 20–21, 119

axis, 5–8, 11, 14, 43, 50, 78, 106, 108–109, 125

anxiety, 79, 84, 117, 136

baptism, 10–11, 34, 73, 96, 105, 107, 109–110, 113–114, 116–118, 137

beauty, 49–50, 136

Being, 13, 43

being, 10–12, 15, 17–18, 28, 44–49, 51–52, 59, 61, 122, 132, 150n
   as composite entities, 7, 12, 14, 17–18, 20, 30, 57, 74, 82, 85, 107, 109
   center of one's, 3, 6–7, 16–17, 43, 68, 137
   of God, 25, 27–28, 34, 46, 51, 61, 64, 84

belief, 28, 31, 50, 110

Bishop of Hippo, 108, 140n

body, 13, 17, 26–27, 30, 37, 49, 51, 58–60, 63–64, 68, 74, 76–77, 84, 86, 95–96, 107, 109–111, 116–118, 122, 131–132, 134–136, 140n, 144n, 154n

body of this death, 15, 62, 77, 134

bondage of the will, *See* will

Burke, Kenneth, 24

caritas, 60

Cartesian subjectivity, 52

Carthage, 29, 123

Cassiciacum 110–116, 123, 125
   dialogues, 20–21

catechumen, 34–36, 114, 124